DATE DUE

OCT 3 1 2007	

DEMCO, INC. 38-2931

Terrorism and the UN

Terrorism and the UN

Before and After September 11

Edited by Jane Boulden and Thomas G. Weiss

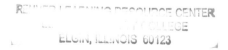
Indiana University Press

Bloomington and Indianapolis

345.02
T328

This book is a publication of
Indiana University Press
601 North Morton Street
Bloomington, Indiana 47404-3797 USA

http://iupress.indiana.edu

Telephone orders   800-842-6796
Fax orders   812-855-7931
Orders by e-mail   iuporder@indiana.edu

The paper used in this publication meets the minimum requirements
of American National Standard for Information Sciences—Permanence
of Paper for Printed Library Materials, ANSI Z39.48-1984.

Manufactured in the United States of America

Library of Congress Cataloging-in-Publication Data
Terrorism and the UN : before and after September 11 /
edited by Jane Boulden and Thomas G. Weiss.
        p. cm.
Includes index.
  ISBN 0-253-34384-4 (cloth : alk. paper) — ISBN 0-253-
21662-1 (pbk. : alk. paper)
   1. Terrorism—Prevention—International cooperation.
2. United Nations. 3. War on Terrorism, 2001– 4. World
politics—1995–2005. I. Boulden, Jane, date II. Weiss, Thomas George.
  HV6431.T4635 2004
  345'.02—dc22

                        2003020232

1 2 3 4 5 09 08 07 06 05 04

In memory of those
who gave their lives
working for peace at
United Nations Headquarters
Baghdad, Iraq
August 19, 2003

Contents

August 19, 2003

Having been prompted by the terrorist attacks of September 11, 2001, and then completed in the midst of the Security Council debate on Iraq, this book goes to press only a few days after the tragic bombing of the UN headquarters in Baghdad on August 19, 2003.

The perils of unilateralism and multilateralism have been starkly presented in the events following the declared "end" of the War in Iraq on May 1, 2003. The aftermath of this war has demonstrated that while U.S. power may be an order of magnitude greater than that of any other state at present, that power has limits. It also demonstrates that these concepts are not as mutually exclusive as they may seem. Global security problems require global solutions. It is beyond the capability of any actor, even the remaining superpower, to tackle problems by going it alone. Transnational security problems require multilateralism.

In our introduction, we suggest that the events surrounding Iraq are "quite separate" from the UN's role in dealing with terrorism. The bombing in Baghdad has effectively eliminated most of that separateness. The fact that the division of labor between the non-UN-authorized "coalition" forces and the United Nations was clear (by both UN choice and U.S. design), and that the UN's presence was oriented toward helping the Iraqi people meant little to the forces that determined that terrorist tactics would help achieve their ends. Indeed, it may be the very constructive and humanitarian nature of the world organization's activities that made it such a target. There is a bitter irony in this fact, but it is an irony that is precisely indicative of the inherent complexity and pernicious nature of terrorism.

The Baghdad bombing presents the United Nations with an extraordinarily difficult dilemma with implications that extend well beyond its role in Iraq. A retreat behind fortified walls and a failure to confront the source of the threat is a *de facto* victory for terrorists. Plowing ahead without taking protective measures may result in more attacks. Either option contains within it the likelihood that the accessibility and efficacy of the world organization will be limited and, perhaps, even undermined. One of our starting points in undertaking this book was the assumption that as the institution mandated to deal with issues of international peace and security, the United Nations *should* be at the forefront of the debate on how to deal with terrorism. Whatever else we might conclude about the attack, it is now the case that the UN *must* be at the forefront of that debate.

It remains too soon to develop firm conclusions, but it may yet be that the August 19th attack will be a turning point that marks a fundamental change in the UN itself. In any case, we dedicate this book to our dead and seriously injured colleagues.

J.B. and T.G.W.
August 25, 2003

Acknowledgments

The chapters of this volume are the product of a workshop held in late September 2002, jointly sponsored by the Ralph Bunche Institute for International Studies at The City University of New York and the Centre for International Studies, University of Oxford. We decided that New York City was a most appropriate place to convene such a discussion. The dust had settled, but only barely, from the tragic events of September 11 of 2001 that put the issue of terrorism so squarely back on the international agenda.

The Centre for International Studies, University of Oxford, funded the workshop in pursuit of its project titled "International Organisation and Security Issues of the Post–Cold War Era." Generous funding support for this project comes from the Ford Foundation and the John D. and Catherine T. MacArthur Foundation and the governments of Norway and Sweden. The Graduate Center provided host costs and a most congenial and productive setting.

In pulling together this volume, we are most grateful to the contributors for providing thoughtful and provocative analyses of a difficult and ever-changing subject. Their profiles are found at the back of the volume. We would be remiss if we did not mention the participants in the workshop at which the draft chapters were presented. Contributors benefited from the comments and suggestions from our key participants: José Alvarez, Zehra Arat, Mark Bowden, Margaret Crahan, Carlos Diaz, Shepard Forman, John Goering, John Hirsch, James O. C. Jonah, Bruce Jones, Angela Kane, Charlotte Ku, Jeffrey Laurenti, David M. Malone, José Luís Renique, Andres Salazar, James Sutterlin, José Thompson, John Wallach, Susan Woodward, and Sarah Zaidi.

We would also like to express our appreciation to Jason File of New College, University of Oxford, for acting as rapporteur for the workshop and to Nancy Okada at the Ralph Bunche Institute for International Studies for her able administrative support for the workshop. Most important, we are truly grateful to Danielle Zach for her editorial assistance during the production of the book; quite simply, this volume would not have appeared in such a timely fashion without her able helping hands.

Jane Boulden and Thomas G. Weiss
Oxford and New York
May 2003

Abbreviations

ACC	Administrative Committee on Coordination
AIDS	Auto-Immune Deficiency Syndrome
ANC	African National Congress
ASEAN	Association of Southeast Asian Nations
ASEM	Asia-Europe Meeting
AWB	Afrikaner Weerstandsbeweging
BSEC	Black Sea Economic Cooperation
CACO	Central Asian Cooperation Organization
CAT	Committee Against Torture
CBSS	Council of the Baltic Sea States
CEI	Central European Initiative
CFE	Conventional Forces in Europe
CFSP	Common Foreign and Security Policy
CHR	Commission on Human Rights
CIA	Central Intelligence Agency
CICP	Centre for International Crime Prevention
CIS	Commonwealth of Independent States
COE	Council of Europe
CONGO	Conference on Non-Governmental Organizations in Consultative Status with ECOSOC
CSCE	Conference on Security and Cooperation in Europe
CTC	Counter-Terrorism Committee
DfID	Department of International Development (UK)
DHA	Department of Humanitarian Affairs

DPA	Department of Political Affairs
DPKO	Department of Peace-keeping Operations
EADRCC	Euro-Atlantic Disaster Response Coordination Centre (NATO)
EAPC	Euro-Atlantic Partnership Council
ECOMOG	Military Observer Group of the Economic Community of West African States
ECOSOC	Economic and Social Council
ECOWAS	Economic Community of West African States
ESDP	European Security and Defense Policy
ETA	Euskadi ta Askatasuna (Basque Fatherland and Liberty)
EU	European Union
EUROJUST	European Justice
EUROPOL	European Police
FARC	Fuerzas Armadas Revolucionarias de Colombia
FATF	Financial Action Task Force [on Money Laundering]
FBI	Federal Bureau of Investigation
FMLN	Frente Farabundo Martí para la Liberación Nacional (Farabundo Martí National Liberation Front)
G-7/G-8	Group of Seven/Group of Eight
HRC	Human Rights Commission
IAEA	International Atomic Energy Agency
ICAO	International Civil Aviation Organization
ICC	International Criminal Court
ICG	International Crisis Group
ICJ	International Court of Justice
ICRC	International Committee of the Red Cross
ICTR	International Criminal Tribunal for Rwanda
ICTY	International Criminal Tribunal for the Former Yugoslavia
IFOR	Implementation Force [for the former Yugoslavia]
ILO	International Labour Organization

IMF	International Monetary Fund
IMO	International Maritime Organization
INTERPOL	International Police
IO	International organization
IOM	International Organization for Migration
IRA	Irish Republican Army
ISAF	International Security Assistance Force
KLA	Kosovo Liberation Army
LRA	Lord's Resistance Army
LTTE	Liberation Tigers of Tamil Eelam
MNF	Multinational Force
MPLA	Movimento Popular para a Libertação de Angola
NAM	Non-Aligned Movement
NATO	North Atlantic Treaty Organization
NGO	Nongovernmental Organization
NIEO	New International Economic Order
NSC	National Security Council
OAS	Organization of American States
OAU	Organization of African Unity
OCHA	Office for the Coordination of Humanitarian Affairs
ODCCP	Office for Drug Control and Crime Prevention
OECD	Organisation for Economic Co-operation and Development
ONUC	United Nations Operation in Congo
OPCW	Organisation for the Prohibition of Chemical Weapons
OSCE	Organization for Security and Co-operation in Europe
P-5	Permanent Five members of the Security Council
PIRA	Provisional Irish Republican Army
PKK	Kurdistan Workers Party
PLO	Palestine Liberation Organization
RUF	Revolutionary United Front

SADC	Southern African Development Community
SECI	Southeast European Cooperative Initiative
SFOR	Stabilization Force [for the former Yugoslavia]
TPB	Terrorism Prevention Branch
TREVI	Terrorism, Radicalism, Extremism, and International Violence group
UNDP	United Nations Development Programme
UNEP	United Nations Environment Programme
UNESCO	United Nations Educational, Social and Cultural Organization
UNHCHR	United Nations High Commissioner for Human Rights
UNHCR	United Nations High Commissioner for Refugees
UNICEF	United Nations Children's Fund
UNIS	United Nations Information Service
UNITA	Union for the Total Independence of Angola
UNMOVIC	United Nations Monitoring, Verification and Inspection Commission
UN ODC	Office on Drugs and Crime
UN ODCCP	Office for Drug Control and Crime Prevention (renamed ODC as of October 1, 2002)
UPU	Universal Postal Union
USSR	Union of Soviet Socialist Republics
UTA	Union des Transports Aériens
WHO	World Health Organization
WMD	Weapons of mass destruction

Part I

Framing the Debate

1

Whither Terrorism and the United Nations?

Jane Boulden and Thomas G. Weiss

> Terrorism is a global menace. It calls for a united, global response. To defeat it, all nations must take counsel together, and act in unison. That is why we have the United Nations.
>
> —Kofi A. Annan, September 2001[1]

> The fight against terrorism cannot be used as an excuse for slackening efforts to put an end to conflicts and defeat poverty and disease. Nor can it be an excuse for undermining the bases of the rule of law—good governance, respect for human rights and fundamental freedoms. The long-term war on terrorism requires us to fight on all these fronts. Indeed, the best defense against these despicable acts is the establishment of a global society based on common values of solidarity, social justice and respect for human rights.
>
> —Kofi A. Annan, October 2001[2]

This volume explores the situation of the United Nations in the wake of the events of September 11, 2001, and international responses to them. On that basis, it looks ahead to possible problems and issues for the world organization in its continuing attempts to counter terrorism. To this end, two interrelated analytical frameworks are used. The first addresses the issue of whether or not the UN now finds itself in a new international environment. In the immediate aftermath of September 11, it was commonplace to hear that the world had changed irrevocably, that a paradigm shift had occurred. Is that the case? If so, why and how is this manifested? If not, why not?

The second analytical framework looks directly at the specific role of the UN as both an arena where governments make decisions and as an independent operational actor in its own right. How has the UN dealt with the question of terrorism, both before and after September 11? Two different approaches are used within this framework. One examines the specifics of various measures debated and taken by the two main organs, the Security Council and the General Assembly. The other is issue-oriented, detailing the world organization's efforts to deal with terrorism through its perceived sources and resources. This second analytical framework thus complements the first by highlighting the extent to which international thinking on terrorism at the United Nations is as much a product of past experience as it is a product of September 2001.

Two points of clarification are necessary. First, the attacks of September 11 may be characterized as acts of terrorism and evidence of trends in terrorism, but they are considered separately from the concept of terrorism itself. From the vantage point of the UN, the events of September 11 and terrorism as an international phenomenon have different sets of implications and impacts, so they are treated accordingly. Second, this is a book that is primarily about the United Nations. It is not an analysis of terrorism per se. The starting point for the analysis is the question of how the world organization has sought to deal with terrorism.

The fact that the UN has taken action against terrorism, even while not being able to agree on how to define the phenomenon, is an important part of the story. The lack of consensus—many observers point to the aphorism that "my freedom fighter is your terrorist"—exposes the depth of the problem terrorism poses for the world organization. The conclusion of one group of practitioners about this lacuna is noteworthy: "Action in the absence of an agreed-upon definition exposes the United Nations to the charge of double standards, thus undermining the very legitimacy and universality that are among its most precious assets."[3] In recognition of the extent to which efforts to define terrorism are part and parcel of the analysis, this volume does not put forward its own definition of terrorism, even though the absence of such a definition is a persistent theme in this book specifically and in international relations more generally. The essays in this collection explore how the United Nations and the community of states generally have sought to deal with terrorism (including the struggle to define it), how the dramatic events of September 2001 have affected those efforts, and what all of that says about how we deal with international security in the twenty-first century.

The purpose of this first chapter is to outline the framework and substance of the volume as a whole and to draw conclusions based on the information and analysis in the chapters that follow. The first section situates the contents of the book in relationship to existing literature. The next two sections of the chapter focus on the two analytical frameworks that form the basis of the book—the shape of the so-called new international arena and how the UN responds to terrorism—drawing on the main issues and themes raised by the contributors to discuss what they tell us about the nature of the international environment and the future role of the world organization on this issue.

This first chapter, therefore, acts as both a conclusion as well as an introduction to the volume. We conclude with a short summary of the individual chapters so that readers can then pursue the individual chapters with an over-view in mind.

The Literature

Academic literature about the world organization and terrorism has been at best sporadic and at worst simply nonexistent. This state of affairs is due, in part, to the fact that activities at the UN on this issue were few and far between and because specialized analyses in the literature on terrorism generally ignored the role of the world body. Indeed, for all intents and purposes, the issue was largely peripheral to mainstream analyses of either UN affairs or U.S. foreign policy until the events of September 2001.[4] The present volume seeks to contribute to filling the significant void in the existing literature.

The academic literature on terrorism most relevant to this discussion includes cross-cutting work that derives from the disciplines of international law and political science. Each has its own particular focus, but they are joined by the most consistent element found in all of the terrorism literature—the need to define and conceptualize the phenomenon.

A great deal of terrorism-related work has been done with reference to specific historical examples. For example, over the years a large body of work has developed on the Irish Republican Army (IRA) and other groups in Ireland,[5] on the Shining Path in Peru,[6] and on a number of Middle Eastern examples.[7] Perhaps the largest body of such writing relates to the ethics and politics of self-determination struggles, which led to the widespread debate about what to call a freedom fighter.[8] Indeed, commentators often overlook the fact that human rights, and especially the right of self-determination, can serve as a justification for terror. Much of the anti-colonial struggle—in India, Algeria, and Vietnam, to cite the most obvious examples—justified terror as a means. The Tamil Tigers of Sri Lanka and the Palestinians are the most recent manifestations of this phenomenon. Much of this literature remains in the realm of case studies.

Moreover, much of this debate is simplistic. Framing terrorism in terms of self-determination confuses human rights justifications, in which the loss of civilian life cannot be condoned, and the laws of war, in which attacks on civilians are strictly regulated. It also ignores that time and again civilian deaths are not a last but a first option for much terrorist violence—for example, by Basques and Irish nationalists. Rather than good-faith efforts to pursue political action, violence is a shortcut. Killing civilians gets the world to take notice and provides the other side with the option of retaliation. A downward spiral of repression then ensues, resulting in increased delegitimacy for the authorities that retaliate.[9]

Attempts have been made to conceptualize terrorism by looking at the motives and methods of terrorist groups in order to identify common themes and practices and to generalize about the phenomenon,[10] but these are relatively few in number. In contrast to this bottom-up approach, more theoretically driven groups exist who try to conceptualize terrorism by determining where it fits within the study of politics[11] or how it relates to the evolution of warfare in the international system.[12] A related area of scholarship looks at terrorism historically with a view to exploring whether or not it is its own phenomenon rather than one that is necessarily political or has developed within the last century.[13] After the end of the Cold War, the conceptualization of terrorism was the subject of a spirited debate in relation to the possible development of a "new" terrorism. This debate was the product of a number of concurrent changes during the 1990s: the upsurge in terrorist incidents directed against the United States; fears associated with the dissolution of the Soviet Union (USSR) and the possibility that nuclear, chemical, and biological weapons were no longer under strict control; and the appearance of Osama bin Laden and his transnational network. The newness of this "new" terrorism was said to relate to the fact that some terrorist groups were religiously (rather than politically) motivated and that they were intent on inflicting harm on a massive scale.[14]

One analyst points out that religion, certainly one of the factors motivating the terrorist attacks of September 11, was largely ignored by international relations scholars. This is perhaps the most glaring of shortcomings in previous scholarship; Al Qaeda's political theology challenges "the Westphalian synthesis, the fundamental authority structure of the international order."[15]

Much of the international law literature on terrorism deals with the question of the legality or legal implications of the spectrum of responses to terrorism, especially in relation to the use of force and the laws of war. As with the rest of the terrorism literature, an increase in analytical attention follows closely on well-publicized and dramatic events. Thus, for example, there was an upsurge in attention to the issue in the aftermath of the 1983 attacks on the U.S. Marine barracks and the U.S. embassy in Beirut; the downing of Pan Am and UTA flights in the late 1980s; the first attack on the World Trade Center in 1993; the attempted assassinations of Egyptian president Hosni Mubarak and former president George H. W. Bush; the bombings of a pharmaceutical factory in the Sudan and of terrorist compounds in Afghanistan by the U.S. in response to the bombings outside American embassies in East Africa in 1998; and the attack on the USS *Cole* in Aden in 2000. In particular, there is a large body of work dealing with the Lockerbie bombing and the eventual successful prosecution of the two Libyan suspects in The Hague. To the extent that there is anything to be found on the United Nations and terrorism, it is most often within the international law literature because many of the existing international conventions on terrorism have been negotiated within the General Assembly's Sixth Committee (Legal). Even so, the discussion tends to be about the implications of the resulting conventions rather than on the UN's role as such—either as a norm-setter or an operational actor.

Overall, the literature is limited, indeed, when considered in the context of academic research and writing on international relations generally. In the scheme of things, terrorism was a relatively lower-level concern when measured against the security issues generated by the Cold War and subsequently by the security concerns resulting from the breakup of the Soviet Union. Academic fashions, along with governmental and foundation research funding, inevitably reflect such perceived priorities.

Perceptions and priorities underwent an instantaneous and fundamental change after September 2001. Since then, the issue of terrorism has dominated the academic and policy literatures. The question of how to define terrorism is on the back burner, while studies of the Al Qaeda movement and Osama bin Laden, who are accepted as the epitome of terrorism, have taken center stage.

Considerable attention has been given to the question of how best to respond to September 11 from national and international perspectives. For instance, intelligence-gathering and the tracking of human rights (national and international), along with the related question of the status of detainees at Guantanamo Bay, have generated heated debates about both human rights and the laws of war,[16] raising the question of where terrorism fits in a state-based system. Also new are examinations of actors other than the traditional ones fighting terrorism (that is, military strategists, police, intelligence analysts, and political leaders). As William O'Neill points out, "New allies in the struggle include financial analysts, bankers, arms control experts, educators, communications specialists, development planners and religious leaders."[17] This theme is a prominent one in this volume as well.

The UN featured briefly in the initial debate about the nature of the international response to September 11. The Security Council took note of Washington's reaction of self-defense, thereby effectively opting out of subsequent decision-making and leaving the military response to the United States. Article 51 of the UN Charter authorizes self-defense only until the Security Council takes action; this provision is made moot, however, when the council does not take such action or blesses self-defense. As a consequence, the studies and discussions produced in the immediate aftermath of September 11 focus on issues associated with the war on Afghanistan, U.S. policy, and whether or not this kind of response is appropriate to confront terrorism. The role of the United Nations, in either decision-making or in operational terms, is rarely visible.

The academic literature, therefore, has given little attention to the UN and terrorism, both before and after September 2001. This book is intended to fill that gap. Why is it important to do so? As the organization with the primary responsibility for the maintenance of international peace and security, the UN should be at the forefront of the international response to terrorism. The fact that it has not been deserves attention and explanation. To what extent is terrorism, and particularly the attacks of September 11, an indication of a fundamental change in the international environment in which the UN operates? What, exactly, was the world organization doing about terrorism before and after September 2001? Together, what does all of this tell us about what form future UN efforts should take and whether it can and should be at the forefront of international efforts—normative and operational—to deal with terrorism in the future?

As this volume goes to press, the war in Iraq and its immediate aftermath are dominating the international agenda. Deliberations among the permanent members of the Security Council about the text of a resolution authorizing force against Iraq were front-page news on an ongoing basis until Washington and London's decision to withdraw their draft resolution and go to war without a Security Council authorization.

For us the question of how the United Nations deals with Iraq is only loosely connected with terrorism and more particularly with the American "war on terrorism." The events surrounding Iraq are quite separate from an examination of the UN's role in fighting terrorism. Nonetheless, politics intrudes into this analytical reality because of President George W. Bush's linkage of Iraq and terrorism. Although the editors and contributors see only tenuous linkages between Iraq and terrorism, Washington's framing of the debate in this way necessarily intrudes into our discussion about the nature of the international arena and the role of the United Nations. The struggle over resolutions in the Security Council, the use of force without its authorization, and the achievement of the declared goal of "regime change" in Iraq are all important aspects of the debate about the extent to which world politics have changed in the aftermath of September 11.

One direct implication arises from unease on both sides of the Atlantic regarding tactics and goals. Robert Kagan's caricature that "Americans are from Mars and Europeans are from Venus"[18] can be dismissed as simplistic pop punditry. But clearly, the politics of the "coalition" response to Iraq, like the politics of the war on terrorism, have opened fissures in trans-Atlantic relationships. On the one hand, the North Atlantic Treaty Organization (NATO) appears more publicly divided than it has since the administration of Ronald Reagan. On the other hand, the alliance and U.S.-European relations have weathered similar strains—disagreements over Vietnam, de Gaulle's withdrawal from the integrated command, and the basing of Pershing missiles on the continent, for example. As in the earlier disagreements, part of an explanation for the charged debate is a fundamental imbalance in power and argument about whether Europeans should be expected to follow Washington's leadership—which can also be translated into several European languages as "merely accede to American policy."

Washington's unmatched power has implications for the UN's fight against terrorism, as it does for any UN efforts to manage international peace and security. At the onset of the post–Cold War era, bipolarity gave way to what was supposed to be American primacy.[19] But the technical and military prowess in the war in Iraq made crystal clear that "primacy" was a vast understatement. Whatever nuances surround academic debates about the economic and cultural leverage of American "soft power,"[20] there is no question that the United States is unrivaled in military terms. Even before the appropriations for the Iraq war, Washington spent more on its military than the next fifteen to twenty-five (depending on who was counting) countries. With an additional opening bid of $87 billion for the campaign in Iraq, the U.S. now spends more than the rest of the world's militaries combined.[21]

The debate surrounding the withdrawn resolution before the war was, according to interviews at the UN by a prominent journalist, "a referendum not on the means of disarming Iraq but on the American use of power."[22] The UK-U.S. decision to act outside the United Nations after having expended so much energy to generate Security Council approval for a war against Iraq drove home, in a way no other action could, the scale of the American power differential and its impact when wielded by an administration willing to pursue its own international agenda without the authority of the Security Council. Speaking before the UN General Assembly on September 12, 2002, President George W. Bush stated:

> All the world now faces a test, and the United Nations a difficult and defining moment. Are Security Council resolutions to be honored and enforced, or cast aside without consequence? Will the United Nations serve the purpose of its founding, or will it be irrelevant? . . . We cannot stand by and do nothing while dangers gather. We must stand up for our security, and for the permanent rights and the hopes of mankind. By heritage and by choice, the United States of America will make that stand. And, delegates to the United Nations, you have the power to make that stand, as well.[23]

His point is not that the United Nations was in danger of obsolescence but that the U.S. was in a position to make it so. Bush's remarks were not so much a call to action as they were a statement of intent. The world organization could work with the United States on Iraq, and in the process hope to preserve some elements of authority and legitimacy for the future, or it could allow itself to be sidelined while the United States independently enforced Security Council resolutions.

Hence, the second way in which the events surrounding Iraq affect the discussions in this book is in their implications for the role of the United Nations as both a stage and an operational actor. The extent to which its future effectiveness has been compromised by the U.S. and UK decision to go to war without a Security Council imprimatur is not yet clear. There is no doubt that the council's authority and legitimacy have been undermined by these events. Whether or not this translates into a diminished role for the world organization over the longer run will depend a great deal on how the permanent members choose to react to these major shifts in the nature of the international arena.

There seem to be two world organizations: the United Nations, which is global in membership, and the United States, which is global in reach and power. This emerging reality has implications for interpreting the analyses and proposals in the pages that follow. The idea that the remaining superpower would continue to participate, politically or financially, in an institution with the ability to limit its power is anathema to many in the current Bush administration. The Security Council's authority and legitimacy depends on compliance with the provisions of the Charter that created it. U.S. participation is, therefore, a sine qua non. Consequently, the negative outcome of the Security Council negotiations on Iraq has implications not just for international efforts to deal with terrorism but for international peace and security broadly defined.

The United Nations Responds to Terrorism: The Past and the Way Ahead

Until the 1990s, terrorism was dealt with almost entirely by the General Assembly, which approached the issue as a general international problem rather than one relating to specific events or conflicts. In doing so, the assembly worked to develop a normative framework on terrorism and to encourage cooperation among states on the development of an international legal framework. The struggle over how to define terrorism in a way that still allowed for "legitimate" actions on the part of oppressed peoples generated a series of international legal conventions and resolutions. While avoiding judgment on motives, these texts establish a significant set of limits even in situations where violence might be used legitimately.

As mentioned earlier, the Security Council began to take on the question of terrorism in the 1990s in response to specific events. In particular, three cases (the downing of Pan Am and UTA flights, the attempted assassination of Mubarak, and the bombings of American embassies) led to sanctions: against Libya and the Sudan for refusing to extradite the suspects and against the Taliban regime in Afghanistan for supporting terrorist groups and refusing to extradite bin Laden.

In the aftermath of September 11, the Security Council acted immediately and authorized measures ranging from the use of force in self-defense to requiring member states to undertake wide-ranging and comprehensive measures against terrorism. Previously an event-driven, lower-order issue for both the General Assembly and the Security Council, terrorism quickly became a key agenda item everywhere.

The nature and scope of the council's responses are notable. Resolution 1368, passed the day after the attacks on U.S. territory, recognized "the inherent right of individual or collective self-defense" as a legitimate response. This was the first time that self-defense was formally recognized as a legitimate response to terrorism. A few weeks later, the Security Council passed a comprehensive resolution, which outlined a series of wide-ranging measures to be undertaken by states to "prevent and suppress" terrorist acts. By recognizing the self-defense option, the Security Council refrained from taking further measures with respect to the use of force. As a result, the Security Council effectively removed itself from further decision-making about the legitimacy of self-defense and the continued use of military force in Afghanistan.

In contrast to this distancing, the various measures outlined in Security Council resolution 1373 (2001) have detailed requirements that necessitate significant actions by member states, including changes to national legislation, and are binding under Chapter VII of the UN Charter. Instead of the twelve international treaties that bind only those states that accede to them, this landmark resolution for the first time creates uniform obligations for the organization's 191 member states.

In addition, the resolution establishes the Counter-Terrorism Committee (CTC) to monitor member state implementation of these measures. Therefore, the council is inserting itself into domestic affairs in a significant way. This poses a remarkable dichotomy. The Security Council chooses to exercise no control or oversight on the use of military force in response to terrorism but is vigilant and arguably intrusive when it comes to dealing with terrorism through national mechanisms and controls.

Absent from both elements of the Security Council response is any attempt to define terrorism. Indeed, there is not even the sense that an attempt need be made. Both resolutions 1368 and 1373 refer simply to terrorism and terrorist acts as if they were self-explanatory, as if none of the drafters was aware of the problems associated with decades of frustrated efforts to establish definitions. In the context of the use of force and the provisions in resolution 1373, this generosity allows wide latitude for interpretation. In conjunction with the Security Council's acceptance and authorization of self-defense, it compounds the expansiveness of the mandate. Both the response (self-defense) and the subject of the response (terrorism) remain undefined and, by extension, unlimited.

The Security Council's abdication of responsibility on this issue leaves critical questions unanswered. At what point does self-defense end? How specific to the original act does self-defense need to be? For example, the resolution affirming the right to self-defense makes no specific mention of Afghanistan. With respect to the use of military force, the open-ended character of the self-defense authorization is worrisome, especially if the U.S. pursuit of the preemption doctrine against rogue states continues.[24] And the National Security Strategy of September 2002 could not be clearer about the role of multilateral processes: "[W]e will be prepared to act apart when our interests and unique responsibilities require."[25] In this context, has the council handed the United States a carte blanche?

Questions are also raised by the Security Council's efforts to control the sources of terrorism through the provisions of resolution 1373, which focus on international financing and cross-border movements by terrorists. Although comprehensive on paper, these provisions are likely to be very unevenly implemented in practice. Some states simply do not have the resources or the capabilities to carry out the requirements, while others are reluctant or slow to carry out the measures for a variety of reasons. These are the very states likely to attract terrorist organizations. The Counter-Terrorism Committee does not have the resources or capabilities to undertake the kind of comprehensive monitoring and follow-up that would be required to ensure that measures are implemented across the board. To what extent can it be said that this approach will in fact punish and stop the perpetrators of September 11 or hinder and prevent other terrorist groups and acts?

By virtue of their reactive and punitive nature, both sets of responses lead to questions about the root causes of terrorism. Rather than simply reacting militarily to terrorist acts, would it not be preferable to develop other responses that dealt with the motivation and issues that prompted those acts? Analogous to the emphasis on economic development and democracy as ways to prevent armed conflict, the desire to deal with root causes is based on the assumption that if specific parts of the world were better places, then terrorism would not take root. The goal is to make less likely the appearance of "bad neighborhoods," to use Michael Ignatieff's phrase.[26] Terrorism is a complex phenomenon, and there is no simple link between it and poverty and economic underdevelopment. The attractiveness of this approach is that it offers some prospect of a response that might be preventive in ways other than the application of military force. And for some, there is an added attractiveness because this approach implicitly recognizes that some situations may be dire enough that terrorism is a legitimate response. This last point brings us back to a question that the General Assembly has been unable to resolve. Are there, in fact, situations in which motives matter more than the method used, situations where terrorism can be considered by some to be legitimate?

In the post–September 11 environment, these issues have an added sensitivity. For Washington, loose talk of "root causes" has been interpreted as verging on treason by virtue of its implication that in some way the United States deserved or provoked the attacks of September 2001. While the U.S. has been the central player in the international response, its vigorous and knee-jerk rejection of responsibility is likely to be shared by any state that is the target of terrorist attacks. The root-causes route, then, has the double problem of being so broadly based as to be amorphous and so deeply connected to the political fault lines inherent in the concept of terrorism that it deters action.

What is the way ahead for the United Nations? In the initial aftermath of September 11, the Security Council has been at the forefront of the response, which has taken shape primarily as a reaction to the specifics of events. As discussed, the council's response is framed in terms of terrorism generally, not just in terms of the events of September 11. This is an implicit recognition that the UN's efforts must extend beyond a reaction to the tragedy of that September—a strategy should be developed that is preventive and comprehensive rather than merely punitive and reactive.

A number of options are already available for moving toward a more comprehensive approach by building on existing mechanisms. The CTC has the potential to be an ongoing forum for monitoring both the measures undertaken by states and general developments relating to terrorism that might require a change or addition to Security Council efforts. In order to enhance the committee's capabilities, one possibility is to consider providing a larger staff to collect information and monitor developments. This staff would be independent of the Security Council, which would allow it to protect sources of information and encourage long-term and independent analysis that could contribute to Security Council decision-making.[27]

The General Assembly's work in developing international conventions on terrorism, while now overshadowed and in some ways overstepped by the Security Council, remains important. Here the codification of emerging norms can take place in a forum that is able to take a comprehensive, politically informed, and longer-term view. The most significant advantage of the assembly is that it involves all 191 (and counting) member states. This provides a counterbalance to concerns about the potential for Western-centric emphases in the Security Council. The General Assembly is also the place where decisions about the allocation of organizational resources are made, thus giving it a direct impact on the capability of the world organization to deal with terrorism.

The UN secretary-general and the Secretariat also have a role to play, which is often overlooked. Like the General Assembly, the secretary-general has the ability to take less reactive, more comprehensive approaches than the Security Council. After September 11, Kofi Annan established a Policy Working Group on terrorism to examine how the UN should deal with terrorism. Its proposed strategy has three elements: "(a) **Dissuade** disaffected groups from embracing terrorism; (b) **Deny** groups or individuals the means to carry out acts of terrorism; (c) Sustain broad-based international **cooperation** in the struggle against terrorism."[28] At the same time, the secretary-general plays an important role in dealing with specific situations and responding to events through the use of his good offices. For example, prior to September 11, the secretary-general's special representative, Lakhdar Brahimi, was the main UN agent working in Afghanistan.[29] The secretary-general, in other words, contributes to progress at both the strategic and operational levels.

The idea of a coordinating committee or joint mechanism deserves greater consideration than it has had to date. Such a committee should involve the General Assembly, the Security Council, and the secretary-general. It would facilitate the full implementation of the council's decisions by maximizing the information available to all, contributing toward ensuring that the necessary resources are available and guarding against unnecessary overlap. In addition to basic coordination, such a mechanism could facilitate the development of a common conceptualization, if not a definition, of terrorism. In so doing, it could contribute to responses and policies with a greater potential for success. Involvement in a coordinating process, in other words, would encourage each group to think strategically in the context of its own role and would encourage them to do so together for the world organization as a whole.

One of the reasons terrorism is so challenging is that it touches on every aspect of international security. It reaches across the spectrum of actors from individuals, groups, states, and groups of states to the international system itself. In turn, it touches on every aspect of individual security, economic and social development, and root causes to the traditional national security concerns of territorial integrity and raw military power. Thinking and acting strategically is a tall order for the United Nations, and it is even taller in the aftermath of the war in Iraq. But if the world body is ever to effectively take on the question of terrorism within the broader context of international peace and security rather than in response to specific events, such a strategic approach will be necessary.

What's New, What's Not?

Inherent in the decision to examine the international environment in which the United Nations now operates is an assumption that terrorism and the attacks of September 2001 represent a significant change in international relations. But have we really witnessed a sea change in world politics? As the opening sentence of most textbooks points out, the United Nations is fundamentally state based (by and for its members). Do the increased capabilities and prominence of non-state actors,[30] as evidenced in the events of September 11 and the rise in terrorism generally, require a reexamination of that ordering principle? This book suggests that the answer is "No."

If anything, the tragic events of September 2001 have brought about a new emphasis on and reaffirmation of the importance of states. Although it is state based, the UN Charter provides a wide latitude for non-state concerns and actions, and it gives the Security Council the plenipotentiary power to determine what constitutes a threat to international peace and security. Through most of the 1990s, the council interpreted threats to international peace and security broadly. It expanded its mandate considerably by routinely putting increased emphasis on individual security and human rights. Because it includes not only humanitarian tragedies but also the AIDS pandemic under the rubric of "a threat to international peace and security," there is little that may not fall under its jurisdiction. Moreover, these stretched definitions routinely penetrate the traditional barrier of state sovereignty.

At the same time, the invoking of self-defense in response to September 11, the military campaign in Afghanistan, and the focus on weapons of mass destruction in Iraq are all indications of a return to more traditional concerns of state security. This is not a total shift to the status quo ante. The return to the state as the focus for security is not necessarily occurring at the cost of the gains made in recognizing and acting to support individual security and human rights. Rather, what is occurring is part of the ongoing evolution of international society and the associated concept of international security.

Scrambling to react to changes in the evolving international system is nothing new for the United Nations. Almost immediately after its creation, the

onset of the Cold War largely stalemated the organization's security apparatus. The waning of East-West tensions brought about a new phase, with new
opportunities, for UN action along with significant challenges, especially those
challenges dealing with the humanitarian, military, and political debris of civil
wars. Indeed, the UN's failed attempts to deal with many of them nearly
brought about its demise. To what extent the events of September 11 are a
product of ongoing long-term changes in the system or an indication of a
new and different phase in its evolution cannot be determined today. What
can be said is that in posing a challenge to the state-based nature of the system, terrorism and September 11 have brought about a reaffirmation of the
centrality of the state. The calls to replace it have been few and far between.

The challenges posed by non-state actors through terrorism and the events
of September 2001, however, reveal and accentuate the implications of the
post–Cold War trend toward a system based on a sole superpower. As discussed above, the preponderance of the United States—militarily, economically, and culturally—is ever more striking. This reality represents a serious
threat to the health of the United Nations—explaining European Union External Relations Commissioner Chris Patten's characterization of Washington's
current gear as "unilateralist overdrive."[31]

The credibility and legitimacy of the world organization were the subject
of considerable debate well before September 2001. The perception of selec-
tivity and double standards in the Security Council's decision-making about
which conflict situations warranted a response, for example, contributed to a
sense that it was simply a conduit for Western security interests. Why persist
in Bosnia and withdraw from Rwanda? Why commit so fully to Kosovo and
not to the Sudan or any number of African or other cases? The decision on
the part of the United States and several allies, supported by NATO, to use
force in Kosovo without a Security Council mandate raised a host of questions. Notwithstanding the opinion of an independent commission of human rights specialists that it was "legitimate" even if "illegal" and of another
commission about "the responsibility to protect,"[32] Kosovo confirmed for many
the sense that the world's most powerful state can break the rules of the Charter regime with impunity. The acceptance of self-defense as a response to September 11 and the blanket authorization for war on Afghanistan, in conjunction
with the Bush administration's announced determination to take on Iraq with
or without Security Council approval, contributed to the further consolida-
tion of this impression.

Many countries, some in Europe but especially in the Third World, are
unwilling to accept any use of military force that is not approved by the Security Council, even for humanitarian or human rights purposes.[33] However

flawed its composition may be, the council's decision-making process is at least subject to international oversight. The authority of the international political process, however flawed, is at least regulated. Setting aside this procedure, as NATO did in Kosovo and especially as the U.S. and UK did in Iraq, is dangerous because it threatens to break down the few agreed rules for international society.[34]

The debate within the United Nations over the war in Iraq has been at least as much about American power and its role in the world as about the risks posed by Iraq's weapons. Many political scientists examine the present unparalleled power of the U.S. and use the term "hegemony." If one examines a dictionary definition, however, hegemony is not necessarily negative—although the connotations have become so. It essentially means that the strongest member exerts natural leadership within a confederation. Indeed, many Americans and non-Americans have often regretted the lack of U.S. leadership.

Washington's multilateral record in the twentieth century conveys "mixed messages," as Edward Luck reminds us. The United States sometimes has been the prime mover for new international institutions and norms, but just as often it has kept a distance.[35] Clearly, this historical pattern is not about to change in combating terrorism. Style is of consequence. In the past, Washington was often careful and even somewhat reluctant to thumb its nose openly. The argument was that American "exceptionalism" was, well, exceptional—that is, to be saved for an unusual set of events when international cooperation was simply out of the question. The Bush administration appears to be committed to exceptionalism as a policy, the normal bill of fare whether the context be terrorism, the environment, land mines, or the International Criminal Court (ICC).

At the same time, the current administration provides an anomalous contrast to the image of the previous administration's "assertive multilateralism." The Clinton administration's missile strikes against Afghanistan and the Sudan in 1998 were launched without recourse to the United Nations, but the Bush administration went immediately to the world organization in the aftermath of September 11 for authorization of self-defense. The Bush administration also persisted with protracted and difficult negotiations in the Security Council on a resolution about how to deal with Iraq in spite of its stated intention to proceed without the council's imprimatur if necessary. These actions suggest that the United Nations still matters. Washington's military predominance exists side by side with a growing presumption in favor of more inclusive decision-making in multilateral forums. Although the results may be more conditional and constraining than the administration might desire, such an outcome is preferable to circumventing the process altogether. International legitimacy counts, even for the United States.

The benefits and requirements of multilateral cooperation, as well as the accompanying obstacles and politics, feature prominently in every chapter in this volume. The European experience, in particular, indicates the extent to which even multilateralism on a regional scale can prove problematic. In examining the issues associated with the UN and terrorism, two key factors are the symbolic and catalytic effects of the events of September 11 and the predominance of U.S. power. Both are products of long-term trends within the international system. Together, they pose a significant challenge to the form of multilateralism that is represented by the United Nations at the beginning of the twenty-first century.

For the UN, the present situation suggests an organization whose centrality to international decision-making about peace and security is fragile. What is the utility in having five permanent members of the Security Council if one state wields so much power that it is able to generate decisions favorable to its interests or abandon the process altogether if the outcome does not suit it? The phenomenon of U.S. power, which is of an order of magnitude greater than that of any other major state, has the potential to undo the world body altogether.

The larger question is not how the UN deals with terrorism but the extent to which it remains relevant. The Bush administration's approach to September 11 and to Iraq indicates a preference for using the United Nations. Its legitimacy and authority are still important enough to draw even the most powerful state in the system at a time when its leadership is actively seeking to minimize international legal and political constraints on its national security decisions. Some aspects of the UN's process may be in question, but the idea of the process itself as a value still holds. As David Malone tells us, the key question for the Security Council "is whether it can engage the United States, modulate its exercise of power, and discipline its impulses."[36] The answer has implications beyond fighting terrorism.

An Outline of the Book

Relevant for analyses of both the so-called new international arena and UN activities is Chapter 2 by S. Neil MacFarlane, the Lester B. Pearson Professor of International Relations at the University of Oxford, which, in tandem with the present chapter, forms an integral part of the "Framing the Debate" section of the book. "Charter Values and the Response to Terrorism" reminds readers that traditionally one of the UN's most significant roles is the promotion of core standards and values. He points to the gradual increase in the significance of individual as opposed to states' rights, especially during the

1990s, but he argues that September 11 threatens to reverse this trend. As he examines the impact of the terrorist attacks, MacFarlane teases out its effect on UN values. Washington's diplomacy under the Bush administration has tended to be more unilateral than its predecessors, which has a potential impact on other areas of international cooperation. The notion of self-defense is becoming increasingly open ended; and the notion of preemptive defense, while not contained in the Charter, may be justified in more and more circumstances. The goal of regime change has been revived for Iraq by the U.S. and may increasingly be justified as a legitimate objective for and by other states. Human rights are likely to experience both positive (for example, greater attention to issues of distributive justice) and negative (for example, effects on civil liberties) results after September 11 because the health of the human rights regime depends on the commitment of major states to its principles. In short, MacFarlane sees a shift back to the values tied to order—"a reemphasis on power, unilateralism, and geostrategy," in his words—and away from the individual. If this is the case, the present distinctly resembles the "old" international arena. MacFarlane, however, asserts that it is "unlikely that the international system can return to the pre-1990s version of international society."

The four essays in the second part of the book examine the "newness" of the international arena. The first year of the new millennium witnessed the traumatic terrorist attacks on the most powerful country in the international system. Had a ragtag group of non-state, transnational terrorists fundamentally changed the world order? Was there a new paradigm in the making? Did Al Qaeda—without a specific political agenda that could be negotiated and satisfied short of Western capitulation—mark the demise of international politics as studied until September 2001? Was the international arena new because the powerful became the vulnerable, because time-tested political processes (dialogue, discussion, debate, protest, legal recourse, and negotiations) by which the international system exerts some control over violence were replaced by sheer violence alone?

The first of many answers is found in Chapter 3, "September 11 and Challenges to International Law," by Nico Schrijver, Professor of International Law at Amsterdam's Vrije Universiteit. He contends that the central UN Charter concepts are not well suited to responding to September 11. Previous attempts to deal with international terrorism mainly involved prosecuting criminals in domestic law and attempting to apply an international law designed for terrorism sponsored by states or by non-state actors against a specific government. But September 11 transformed terrorist acts into threats to international peace. To date, there have been few challenges to the contention that a response to these attacks fits within both the framework of the UN Charter and the collective defense of NATO. Clearly, new interpretations and practices are required to counter the new menace, and the potential of international law and prevention is perhaps greater than many nonspecialists think. Schrijver examines four phases of UN legal responses: early responses to September 11, general anti-terrorism, support for a new regime in Afghanistan, and a broadening of the struggle. He also discusses seven challenges and dilemmas. Perhaps the most important involves the "change of *opinio juris* with respect to the parameters of the use of force norms and self-defense," a result of the clear decision by both the Security Council and the General Assembly that the response by the U.S. to "'armed attacks' by such non-state actors as international terrorists" constituted self-defense.

Relations among the major Western allies and their approaches to multilateral measures in the war on terrorism are explored in some depth in Chapters 4, 5, and 6. The analysis begins with Edward C. Luck's "The U.S., Counterterrorism, and the Prospects for a Multilateral Alternative." The author, who directs Columbia University's Center on International Organization, is a specialist on Washington's long-standing love-hate relationship toward international organization in this century. In this chapter, Luck points to the irony that in spite of the Bush administration's allergy to the UN, it actually has pursued a multilateral approach to terrorism. He reveals, moreover, that other prominent international actors, such as Japan and Western Europe, have not forsaken unilateral responses or "turned to the UN as the principal source of assistance in their hours of need following terrorist attacks." Luck argues that most of the Bush administration's image problems have been self-inflicted because it has created a perception of unilateralism and sent mixed and inconsistent messages to domestic and international audiences alike. He points to the difference between acting in a "unilateral" (or alone) or "exceptional" (that is, on the basis of unusual vital interests) manner. In contrast to the critiques in wide circulation, he finds that the U.S. approach to terrorism is "more calibrated and nuanced." Luck urges the U.S. and its allies to try to understand the relative weight given, respectively, to "results" versus "process."

Karin von Hippel, Senior Research Fellow at the Centre for Defence Studies at King's College London, continues with "Improving the International Response to the Transnational Terrorist Threat." Chapter 5 draws on the author's ongoing research about North American–European relations. She distinguishes between the solid coalition (some sixty-eight countries) for the military campaign in Afghanistan and the campaign against Iraq, which is straining relations among traditional friends in the Western Alliance. Von Hippel points to the long experience within the European Union (EU) in dealing with terrorism. While this experience is with the "old" terrorists who had political and discrete demands, it nonetheless remains pertinent. The essential demand for enhanced cooperation to fight the menace of terrorism—in intelligence especially—should point the way toward more cooperation rather than toward tensions. Von Hippel clearly views Al Qaeda as a preeminent threat whose elimination is "probable" but which "will continue to cause immense damage and undue suffering until [it is] decisively defeated." The successful eradication of terrorist cells, she contends, will require European states and the U.S. to closely align and to develop a common analytical framework and strategy. In her view, however, neither is guaranteed, or even likely, if we extrapolate from recent events.

The last chapter in the second part of the volume is Thierry Tardy's "The Inherent Difficulties of Interinstitutional Cooperation in Fighting Terrorism." The author is a faculty member at the Geneva Centre for Security Policy whose edited volume *Peace Operations and World Politics after September 11th* provides much grist for the mill in Chapter 6. This essay is designed to probe the nature of interinstitutional cooperation in general and the peculiarities of such cooperation in the contemporary fight against terrorism in particular. His analysis concentrates on the UN, the EU, the Organization for Security and Co-operation in Europe (OSCE), and NATO. Tardy argues that states remain skeptical about the potential payoffs of collaboration against terrorism and that interinstitutional cooperation represents "more a rhetorical than a practical achievement." One of the limiting factors is that intergovernmental institutions are not very aware of each other's activities; thus, a fundamental challenge is to ensure intraorganizational coordination. Perhaps the biggest problem is that intelligence is so sensitive, hence sharing by states with international institutions is viewed as a danger to national security. Ultimately, the costs and benefits of not cooperating are difficult to identify. Moreover, blurred costs and benefits and the preponderant role of the United States are characteristic of what he calls the "peculiarity of the environment."

The four essays in the third part of the book examine the UN's responses, past and future, to terrorism. Chapter 7, "The Role of the Security Council," deals with the organ that has primary responsibility for international peace and security. Chantal de Jonge Oudraat, an international security specialist from Georgetown University, brings to bear her long-standing interests and her current research on allied cooperation in the war on terror. She begins by pointing out that terrorism has been "a concern of UN member states since the late 1960s" but has been an essential item on the Security Council's agenda throughout the 1990s. The United States, increasingly a target, has been the "driving force behind the council's increasingly activist stance." One tactic has been the use of sanctions regimes on both states and non-state actors, which have been more effective than is usually thought. Historically, the use of unilateral force by states against terrorism has been exceptional, but this may be reversed in the twenty-first century. According to de Jonge Oudraat, this is "not in their long-term interests." The use of a military campaign against the Taliban government in Afghanistan may have opened the floodgates, especially since it was pursued with the blessing of the Security Council. Finally, she argues persuasively that the council's decisions in September 2001 set a precedent by making the main provisions of the anti-terrorism conventions obligations for all states. De Jonge Oudraat sees that the United Nations can make more of a contribution, but "whether it does will depend to a large degree on the United States."

Chapter 8, "Using the General Assembly," is written by M. J. Peterson, Professor of Political Science at the University of Massachusetts, Amherst. Peterson builds on her encyclopedic knowledge and past writings about the General Assembly. She outlines the two basic functions for the assembly with regard to terrorism: developing normative conceptions of the problem and encouraging cooperative actions among states. She notes advances in conventions, but she also suggests that their actual impact on state behavior is considerably less clear. Peterson traces the evolution in the language of resolutions regarding what she calls the "three streams": "measures to prevent terrorism," "human rights and terrorism," and "measures to eliminate terrorism." She writes: "The one constant feature in the General Assembly's discussion of terrorism as a general problem has been the member states' inability to agree on common definitions of the terms 'terrorism,' 'terrorist acts,' and 'international terrorism.'" The main bone of contention has, as in everything at the United Nations, been based on subjective political judgments—especially regarding the rights and interpretations of "national liberation movements," an issue that remains a controversy in today's Arab-Israeli conflict. The General Assembly, like all deliberative institutions, is reactive rather than proactive. Hence, the increase in terrorist incidents in the 1980s had already led governments to place terrorism on their collective agenda. And so, contrary to conventional wisdom, Peterson's data show that "the pace of ratification had picked up *before* September 11."

"The Political Economy of Terrorism" is written by Mónica Serrano, Research Associate at the Centre for International Studies at the University of Oxford and Professor of Politics at the Colegio de México. In Chapter 9, she does not pursue the path chosen by most international analysts and politicians, which focuses on the necessity of gaining greater control of the resources being channeled to terrorists through illegal financial transfers. Instead, she concentrates on legal channels, including workers' remittances and especially

Islamic philanthropy. According to Serrano, the "war" metaphor used against drugs is inappropriately applied to terrorists because they are not "profit maximizers," so "no war against them will be won by seizing their assets." Moreover, the actual amounts of illegal resources involved are quite insignificant. Successful efforts to control donations and transfers would provide greater leverage than efforts to halt money-laundering. Serrano writes, "Far from pulling the plug on terrorism as such, recent UN conventions may have merely ended a debate that failed to deliver what the post–September 11 climate demanded—a right answer." She sees the confrontation with Al Qaeda as an "ideological war [that] is surely winnable by the West." Rather than military and financial measures, Serrano concludes that "the war on global terror may well turn on the capacity of industrialized countries to live up to ideals of equal justice under the rule of law that have long been a source of inspiration for others elsewhere in the world."

The final chapter deals with the controversial topic of attacking "The Root Causes of Terrorism and Conflict Prevention." Rama Mani, a Cambridge-trained scholar who has just founded her own non-governmental organization (Justice Unlimited) and has worked for several others as a researcher and advocate, applies both analytical and practical insights from previous development and humanitarian assignments to the thorny question of whether it is possible to prevent terrorism. She points out in Chapter 10 that the UN General Assembly's work has moved away from its earlier focus on state-sponsored terrorism and its explicit goal of protecting claims for self-determination. While the end of the Cold War led to a shift in tone and language from prevention to suppression, the new war on terrorism, she notes, has reintroduced prevention as a legitimate objective. However, since September 11, attempts to identify the ostensible root causes have focused only on a particular strain of terrorism, namely, "amphibolous terrorism." The conflation of different varieties of terrorism, she contends, results in conceptual confusion and risks making international efforts to understand root causes ineffective. Mani examines and sets aside three of the most conventional explanations—"poverty and despair," "failed states," and "the clash of civilizations, or Islamic extremism." For her, these provide only partial insights. The true causes of terrorism, she asserts, lie in a form of globalization that "impoverishes a vast majority of humanity." Mani argues that the real goal of development assistance should be "social justice and a decent, sustainable livelihood for all" and that aid should not be used merely as a dubious weapon in the war against terrorism.

Notes

1. UN Press Release, SG/SM/7962/Rev.1, September 18, 2001.

2. UN Press Release, SG/SM/7999 AFR/344, October 22, 2001.

3. William G. O'Neill, "Conference Report," in International Peace Academy, *Responding to Terrorism: What Role for the United Nations?* (New York: International Peace Academy, 2003), 4.

4. One of the authors has a UN textbook whose third edition makes no mention of the topic. See Thomas G. Weiss, David P. Forsythe, and Roger A. Coate, *The United Nations and Changing World Politics* (Boulder: Westview, 2001). A well-known anthology about American priorities also ignored the topic; see Michael E. Brown, ed., *America's Strategic Choices* (Cambridge: MIT Press, 2000).

5. See, for example, Alan O'Day, *Terrorism's Laboratory: The Case of Northern Ireland* (Aldershot, Hants, England; Brookfield, Vt.: Dartmouth Publishers Co., 1995); and Alan O'Day, ed., *Dimensions of Irish Terrorism* (Aldershot, U.K.: Dartmouth, 1993).

6. See, for example, Simon Strong, "Shining Path: A Case Study in Ideological Terrorism," *Conflict Studies* 260 (1993): 1–28; and David Scott Palmer, "The Revolutionary Terrorism of Peru's Shining Path," in Martha Crenshaw, ed., *Terrorism in Context* (University Park, Pa.: Pennsylvania State University Press, 1995), 249–310.

7. Gal Luft, "The Palestinian H-Bomb: Terror's Winning Strategy," *Foreign Affairs* 81, no. 4 (July/August 2002): 2–7; Elizabeth Picard, "The Lebanese Shiʿa and Political Violence in Lebanon," in David E. Apter, ed., *The Legitimization of Violence* (New York: New York University Press, 1997); Bard E. O'Neill, "Towards a Typology of Political Terrorism: The Palestinian Resistance Movement," *Journal of International Affairs* 32, no. 1 (Spring/Summer 1978): 17–42.

8. See, for example, Tony Honore, "The Right to Rebel," *Oxford Journal of Legal Studies* 8, no. 1 (1988): 34–54; and David Miller, "The Use and Abuse of Political Violence," *Political Studies* XXXII, no. 3 (1984): 401–419.

9. Michael Ignatieff, "Human Rights, the Laws of War and Terrorism," Dankwart A. Rustow Memorial Lecture, The CUNY Graduate Center, October 10, 2002.

10. See, for example, Bruce Hoffman, *Inside Terrorism* (London: Victor Gollancz, 1998); C. J. M. Drake, *Terrorists' Target Selection* (London: Macmillan, 1998).

11. For an overview, see Martha Crenshaw, ed., *Terrorism, Legitimacy, and Power: The Consequences of Political Violence* (Middleton, Conn.: Wesleyan University Press, 1983). Also see Rachel Wieviorka, "Terrorism in the Context of Academic Research," in Crenshaw, ed., *Terrorism in Context*, 597–606.

12. On this see, for example, Martin van Creveld, *The Transformation of War* (New York: The Free Press, 1991).

13. A good example is David C. Rappoport, "Fear and Trembling: Terrorism in Three Religious Traditions," *The American Political Science Review* 78, no. 3 (September 1984): 658–677.

14. See, for example, Steven Simon and Daniel Benjamin, "America and the New Terrorism," *Survival* 42, no. 1 (Spring 2000): 59–75; and "America and the New Terror-

ism: An Exchange," *Survival* 42, no. 2 (Summer 2000): 156–172. Also see David C. Rappoport, "Terrorism and Weapons of the Apocalypse," *National Security Studies Quarterly* (Summer 1999): 49–67. Also see Council on Foreign Relations, *The New Terrorism: Threat and Response* (New York: Council on Foreign Relations, 2002).

15. Daniel Philpott, "The Challenge of September 11 to Secularism in International Relations," *World Politics* 55, no. 1 (October 2002): 92. Philpott analyzed four prominent journals from 1980 to 1999 (*International Security, International Organization, International Studies Quarterly*, and *World Politics*) and found that only six or so of about 1,600 articles featured religion as an important influence in international relations. See Daniel Philpott, *Revolutions in Sovereignty: How Ideas Shaped Modern International Relations* (Princeton: Princeton University Press, 2001), 9.

16. See Thomas G. Weiss, Margaret E. Crahan, and John Goering, eds., *Wars on Terrorism and Iraq: Human Rights, Unilateralism, and U.S. Foreign Policy* (London: Routledge, 2004).

17. William G. O'Neill, "Beyond Slogans: How Can the UN Respond to Terrorism?" in International Peace Academy, *Responding to Terrorism*, 5.

18. Robert Kagan, *Of Paradise and Power: America and Europe in the New World Order* (New York: Knopf, 2003).

19. This argument is developed in Thomas G. Weiss, "Whither the Security Council and Its Reform?" *The Washington Quarterly* 26, no. 4 (2003), 147–161.

20. Joseph E. Nye, Jr., *The Paradox of American Power: Why the World's Only Superpower Can't Go It Alone* (Oxford: Oxford University Press, 2002).

21. See "Last of the Big Time Spenders: U.S. Military Budget Still the World's Largest, and Growing," Center for Defense Information Table on "Fiscal Year 2004 Budget." Available online at http://www.cdi.org/budget/2004/world-military-spending.cfm. This information is based on data from the U.S. Department of Defense and the International Institute for Strategic Studies.

22. James Traub, "The *Next* Resolution," *New York Times Magazine,* April 13, 2003, 51.

23. "President's Remarks at the United Nations General Assembly," September 12, 2002. Available online at http://www.whitehouse.gov/news/releases/2002/09/20020912-1.html.

24. For an informative essay by Anthony F. Lang, Jr., Chris Brown, Michael Byers, Richard K. Betts, Thomas M. Nichols, and Neta C. Crawford, see "Roundtable: Evaluating the Preemptive Use of Force," *Ethics & International Affairs* 17, no. 1 (2003): 1–36.

25. The White House, "The National Security Strategy of the United States of America," available at http://www.whitehouse.gov/nsc/nss.pdf, p. 31.

26. Michael Ignatieff, "Intervention and State Failure," *Dissent* (Winter 2002): 115–123.

27. The United Nations Special Commission is the model for this. See Jean E. Krasno and James S. Sutterlin, *The United Nations and Iraq: Defanging the Viper* (Westport, Conn.: Praeger, 2002).

28. *Report of the Policy Working Group on the United Nations and Terrorism* (A/57/273/S/2002/875), August 6, 2002, p. 1, emphasis in original.

29. Ambassador Lakhdar Brahimi was appointed special representative for Afghanistan on October 3, 2001. From July 1997 until October 1999, he served as the secretary-general's special envoy for Afghanistan. Between his Afghanistan responsibilities, he

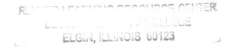

served as under-secretary-general for special assignments in support of the secretary-general's preventive and peacemaking efforts. See UN Press Release bio3397, AFG/160, November 5, 2001.

30. It is worth noting in this context that a leading analyst of terrorism argues that "the distinction between 'international' and 'domestic' terrorism is artificial and has been so for some time." Martha Crenshaw, "The Global Phenomenon of Terrorism," in International Peace Academy, *Responding to Terrorism*, 31.

31. Chris Patten, "Jaw-Jaw, Not War-War," *Financial Times*, February 15, 2002, 16.

32. See Independent International Commission on Kosovo, *Kosovo Report: Conflict, International Response, Lessons Learned* (Oxford: Oxford University Press, 2000), 4; and International Commission on Intervention and State Sovereignty, *The Responsibility to Protect* (Ottawa: ICISS, 2001).

33. See, for example, Mohammed Ayoob, "Humanitarian Intervention and State Sovereignty," *The International Journal of Human Rights* 6, no. 1 (Spring 2002): 81–102.

34. Hedley Bull, *The Anarchical Society: A Study of Order in World Politics*, 3rd ed. (New York: Columbia University Press, 2002). For a contemporary argument related to Bull's original 1977 book, see Robert Jackson, *The Global Covenant: Human Conduct in a World of States* (Oxford: Oxford University Press, 2000); and Mohammed Ayoob, "Humanitarian Intervention and International Society," *Global Governance* 7, no. 3 (July–Sept. 2001): 225–230.

35. Edward C. Luck, *Mixed Messages: American Politics and International Organization, 1919–1999* (Washington, D.C.: Brookings, 1999).

36. David M. Malone, "Conclusions," in David M. Malone, ed., *The UN Security Council: From the Cold War to the 21st Century* (Boulder: Lynne Rienner, forthcoming).

2

Charter Values and the Response to Terrorism

S. Neil MacFarlane

> I am glad that the Charter of the United Nations does not deal only with Governments and States or with politics and war but with the simple elemental needs of human beings whatever be their race, their colour or their creed. In the Charter, we reaffirm our faith in fundamental human rights. We see the freedom of the individual in the State as an essential complement to the freedom of the State in the world community of nations. We stress too that social justice and the best possible standards of life for all are essential factors in promoting the peace of the world.
>
> —Zuleta Angel, 1946[1]

This chapter is a preliminary attempt to evaluate the implications of the terrorist attacks on the United States in September 2001 for the promotion of the values articulated in the UN Charter, which are held to be universal in international society.[2] The premise of the chapter is the proposition that one of the most important roles of the world organization is to promote certain values and set "the terms" of international debates.[3] I begin with an effort to lay out just what these values are and how they evolved in the Cold War and post–Cold War eras. I then assess the impact of unilateral and multilateral actions in the "war on terror" on the promotion of these values.

I argue that the struggle against terror may have important effects on the fundamental values of peace, nonaggression, sovereignty, and nonintervention that are embedded in the Charter. Moreover, if we agree with Zuleta Angel that the Charter involves a dual pursuit of, or balance between, individual and state rights, then we may be encountering a rebalancing of that relationship through the reassertion (often unilateral) of the prerogatives of state power after a period of rapid normative development that has focused on multilateral processes and on human beings. Finally, and more positively, to the extent that September 11 is seen as a reflection of social injustice, then the response to it may over time conduce to a strengthening of this component of the UN's normative agenda by highlighting the connection between justice and great-power interest that was such a frequently encountered theme at the time the Charter was negotiated.[4]

Given the nature of the topic, it is useful to lay out my own assumptions on several issues. First, the topic implies a belief that ideas matter and that institutions matter as purveyors of ideas. I agree with neoliberal institutionalists that international institutions have a significant, although not dominant, role to play in the structuring of international cooperation. The experience of co-operation does affect state calculations, not so much by altering their preferences but by shaping the way in which they seek to attain them.[5] With regard to the role of ideas, I accept the soft constructivist view that state behavior is affected by how states and their leaders perceive their environment and that their cognitive processes are shaped by shared understandings of what international politics is about.[6] These understandings are themselves to some extent rooted in values. For these reasons, consideration of the role of the UN (and other institutions) in promoting particular normative agendas has significance in the analysis of world politics. The UN's role in this respect is particularly important, since near universality of membership conveys a degree of legitimacy that is not enjoyed by regional institutions or coalitions of like-minded states.

This is not to deny the relevance of what are claimed to be structural constants (the primacy of the state as an actor and anarchy as a condition)[7] and variables (the distribution of power) in the explanation of international politics.[8] Indeed, one way to interpret the transition in international politics after September 2001 is as a reassertion of traditional realist concerns over power and security after a bucolic (at least for the established great powers) interlude in which a permissive threat environment allowed states and non-state actors to focus on the promotion of an array of norms loosely associated with the UN system, to the extent that they were not preoccupied with internal concerns. Arguably, although the threat occasioning the reversion is hardly traditional, it has produced a reemphasis on power, unilateralism, and geostrategy that is quite familiar to students of traditional security studies. It remains to be seen to what extent the evolution of the normative framework since the end of the Cold War poses meaningful constraints on the exercise of raw power.

Third, the title assumes that one can speak meaningfully of the United Nations as an entity that possesses values. As Adam Roberts once wrote: "The UN is not an institution to which people should look if they want logic, consistency, clarity, and simplicity."[9] Anyone familiar with the relationships between the Department of Peace-keeping Operations (DPKO), the Department of Political Affairs (DPA), and the Office for the Coordination of Humanitarian Affairs (OCHA) within the Secretariat or between OCHA and the specialized agencies or among specialized agencies with overlapping mandates (e.g., in the humanitarian sphere) is aware that the United Nations encompass a wide array of often-conflicting institutional and individual perspectives. When one considers the member states, the perspectives are often more diverse still. As recent discussions of humanitarian intervention and the international responsibility to protect civilians in war suggest, there is among the membership, not least among the Permanent Five, a great disparity of views on fundamental normative issues.[10]

In a related vein, it is worth acknowledging that much of the discourse on values at the United Nations has a distinctly rhetorical and often disingenuous flavor. The fervent commitment to democracy and nonintervention by Soviet representatives during the Cold War sat uncomfortably with their oppression of their own populations and suppression by force of the peoples of Eastern Europe. American criticism of human rights in the Soviet bloc and of Soviet intervention in Afghanistan, likewise, was difficult to square with U.S. support of abusive dictatorships in Africa, Latin America, and Asia and with American interventions in Vietnam, the Dominican Republic, and Nicaragua, leaving aside Washington's role in deposing Chile's democratically elected government of Salvador Allende. The General Assembly, meanwhile, continued to accept the credentials of the Khmer Rouge authorities who had slaughtered large portions of their own population and refused to seat the Vietnamese-backed regime that had halted the slaughter.

Nonetheless, the United Nations has played a significant role in setting or strengthening standards based on the values of maintaining the system (international security), survival of the units of the system (sovereignty, territorial integrity, and nonintervention), peace, and justice (decolonization, human rights, and a more equitable redistribution of resources within the system). It has done so in at least three ways. In the first place, the organization serves as a forum in which values can be and are espoused and in which opinion can coalesce around particular understandings. The role the General Assembly played on the issues of decolonization and apartheid is illustrative. Second, the secretary-general and the specialized agencies can and do act as "norm entrepreneurs"[11] in the effort to persuade states of the need to embed certain values in world politics. The role of various agencies associated with the United Nations in the promotion of justice concerns and in clarifying the relationship between human rights, development, and security is illustrative, as is the advocacy role of the current secretary-general in the evolution of international society's understanding of sovereignty. Third, many of the UN's agencies have responsibilities to implement the normative commitments of the organization and its members; for example, the role of the UN High Commissioner for Refugees (UNHCR) in administering the international refugee regime. Particularly in the post–Cold War era, and perhaps more controversially, the UN cluster of organizations has adopted, or has been granted, a stronger role in the implementation of changing values, particularly in the humanitarian and human rights arenas.

Next, one should acknowledge in a study of this type an important methodological difficulty. The United States has dominated international response to the attack on September 11, 2001. Many of the observations made in the penultimate section below concern the impact of American actions and perspectives on the UN and on world politics. However, September 11 is not the only causal factor in play. The attacks were preceded nine months earlier by the arrival of an administration that had perspectives on the UN and on world politics that were rather distinct from those of its predecessor.[12] It is, consequently, difficult to tell to what extent U.S. actions and perspectives after September 2001 reflect the specific experience or the predispositions of a new and apparently considerably more unilateralist leadership team. In this regard, one can legitimately ask whether the campaign against Iraq is part of the global struggle against terror or whether it is an element of a broader and preexisting agenda, with the attacks of September 2001 playing a permissive rather than a proactive causal role.

Likewise, it is possible to argue that September 11 appears to undermine norms regarding collective security, in that it has fostered greater American unilateralism. On the other hand, if one believes that an approximate balance of military power (in which no single power is preponderant) is necessary for the effective functioning of collective security, then the erosion of collective security may be more a consequence of the growing relative power of the United States in military affairs than it is of discrete events.

One final clarification is necessary. Many of the UN values discussed below are embodied in texts recognized to have the status of international law (e.g., Charter principles on the use of force, sovereignty, and nonintervention).[13] Others, however, do not have this formal status (e.g., the stipulation of state duties regarding self-determination in General Assembly resolution 2734 (1970), "Declaration on the Strengthening of International Security"). This paper thus focuses on principles and norms that appear in the UN Charter and have been widely shared by UN organizations rather than on international law per se.[14]

The Values

When one considers the values promoted by the United Nations, one is tempted to jump immediately to substantive issues such as national self-determination, economic redistribution and development, and human rights and humanitarian protection. However, it is worthwhile to begin with an overarching procedural norm, multilateralism, before discussing five more substantive values (the use of force, sovereignty and nonintervention, self-determination, redistributive justice, and human rights).

The UN and its Charter are based on the idea that it is preferable that contentious issues in world politics be considered, and resolved if possible, cooperatively rather than on the basis of the unilateral exercise of power. Article 1 provides an eloquent demonstration, calling for "effective collective measures for the prevention and removal of threats to the peace." Paragraph 3 identifies the achievement of "co-operation in solving international problems of an economic, social, cultural and humanitarian character, and in promoting and encouraging respect for human rights and for fundamental freedoms" as a purpose of the organization. Paragraph 4 states the UN's intention of becoming a "centre for harmonizing the actions of nations." In this respect, multilateralism can be seen as a goal[15] that is both embodied in and promoted by the UN.

This procedural preference is clear in sections of the Charter addressing the first cluster of substantive values to be considered here, those relating to peace and security. A stable order (the maintenance of international peace and security) has been privileged as a value; multilateralism is privileged as an approach.[16] The use of force is ruled out except in two cases: member action (individually or collectively) in self-defense until the Security Council acts[17] and collective response by the Security Council when it determines that a threat to, or breach of, international peace and security exists (Chapter VII, Articles 39 and 42).

Later General Assembly resolutions strengthened the prohibition on the aggressive use of force. The "Definition of Aggression," which the assembly adopted in resolution 3314 (1974) after a debate that spanned decades, stated that "no consideration of whatever nature, whether political, economic, military or otherwise, may serve as the justification for aggression." On the other hand, the assembly was responsible for a certain dilution in the proscription of the use of force in instances related to national self-determination, apartheid, foreign occupation, or foreign domination.

The second major cluster of substantive values promoted by the United Nations is that surrounding sovereignty/territorial integrity and nonintervention. Article 2.1 states that the UN is founded on the basis of the sovereign equality of states. Article 2.4 can be interpreted to cover intervention as well as the direct aggressive use of force in its proscription of the threat or use of force against the territorial integrity or political independence of any state or in any other manner against the purposes of the United Nations. Article 2.7 extends the principle of nonintervention in domestic jurisdiction to the actions of the UN itself. The International Court of Justice (ICJ) clarified the illegality of forceful intervention in the Corfu Channel case in 1949:

> [The Court] can only regard the alleged right of intervention as the manifestation of a policy of force which cannot find a place in international law . . . [B]etween independent states, the respect for sovereignty is an essential foundation for international relations.[18]

Again, subsequent actions of the assembly stiffened the UN's commitment to these propositions. The "Declaration on Intervention" averred that no state had the "right to intervene, directly or indirectly, for any reason whatever, in the internal or external affairs of any other State."[19] Both this declaration and its successor on aggression specified that intervention was a form of aggression.[20]

The discussion of sovereignty leads naturally to that of national self-determination. However, the relevance of September 11 to this subject is limited. It is plausible that in a limited number of instances (e.g., Chechnya, Xinjiang, Mindanao, and Aceh), terrorist attacks have affected prospects for self-determination by minority communities in multinational states. With regard to Chechnya and Xinjiang, for example, Russian and Chinese officials have attempted to dismiss minority struggles for self-determination as Islamic terrorism. Before September 2001, this line was not widely accepted in the West. The apparent links between some members of the Chechen and Uighur resistance movements and Al Qaeda enhanced Western receptivity to the characterization of these conflicts as counterterrorist operations. Moreover, the desire for Russian and Chinese cooperation in the struggle against terrorism has led to a diminution of international criticism of Russian and Chinese conduct in these cases.

However, the UN's promotion of self-determination focused almost exclusively on the territorial self-determination of colonies rather than on the self-determination of defined peoples. General Assembly resolution 1514 (1961) explicitly rejects the possibility that self-determination might legitimately be applied to minorities within sovereign states. In this respect, whatever one might think of the merits of these minorities' claims, there is no obvious relationship between the UN understanding of self-determination and the consequences of September 2001 for certain minority peoples within recognized sovereign states.

The third major cluster of issues to be considered here concerns economic and social development. The discussions leading up to the Charter reflected a strong interest in economic and social development.[21] As Edward Stettinius noted in his June 1945 report on the San Francisco conference:

> The battle of peace has to be fought on two fronts. The first is the security front where victory spells freedom from fear. The second is the economic and social front where victory means freedom from want. Only victory on both fronts can assure the world of an enduring peace. . . . No provisions that can be written into the Charter will enable the Security Council to make the world secure from war if men and women have no security in their homes and their jobs.[22]

This view distinguished the UN to some degree from its predecessor, the League of Nations. The interest in economic and social issues reflected the experience of the Depression and the widely held opinion that the economic difficulties of the 1930s had contributed to the descent into World War II. It was also consistent with the growing influence of Keynesian theory during the New Deal in the United States. As indicated in the above quote, the economic and social provisions of the Charter had an instrumental logic related to peace and security. Article 55 of Chapter IX, in justifying UN efforts to promote "higher standards of living, full employment, and conditions of economic and social progress and development," noted that "conditions of stability and well being [were] necessary for peaceful and friendly relations among nations." Distributive justice was a necessary condition of peace and security.[23]

A similar consequentialist logic informed the UN Charter's treatment of human rights.[24] As was the case with development, peace and security were seen to rest to an extent on respect for fundamental human rights. As Leland Goodrich and his collaborators observed, the authors of Article 1.3 considered international economic and social problems and the promotion of respect for human rights "with a view to creation of conditions of stability and wellbeing."[25] Although the Charter commitment to human rights was rather general, it was elaborated considerably in subsequent General Assembly activities, such as the 1948 Universal Declaration of Human Rights and the 1966 international covenants on economic, social, and cultural rights and on civil and political rights.[26] In this context, the instrumental, security-related logic was quickly supplemented by an essentialist rationale. With little by way of reference to international security, the preamble to the Universal Declaration begins by referring to "recognition of the inherent dignity and of the equal and inalienable rights of all members of the human family." The Covenant on Economic, Social, and Cultural Rights and the Covenant on Political and Civil

Rights likewise asserted that the rights discussed therein "derive from the inherent dignity of the human person." The emphasis here was on the value of humanity.[27] In time, the logic of instrumentalist security for the defense of human rights weakened. For example, the notion that refugee movements and forced migration more generally are threats to security was largely absent from the foundational documents of the international refugee regime.[28]

Two Security Council actions under Chapter VII during the Cold War intruded into matters of domestic jurisdiction where human rights were at issue: sanctions against Rhodesia and South Africa. In the first instance, however, the Security Council deemed itself to be acting in support of a sovereign government responding to an act of rebellion, the "continuance" of which constituted a threat to international peace and security. Human rights were not cited as a major reason for acting in resolution 217 (1965).[29] In the second, regarding apartheid, the council condemned South Africa in 1976 for its policies of repression against the black majority in resolution 392. But in resolution 417 (1977), which invoked Chapter VII and mandated an arms embargo, the council emphasized the threat to international security that emanated from South Africa's policies, in particular its arms buildup and pressure on neighboring states. These evocations of threats to international peace and security point to an important constitutional limitation on the council's promotion of values beyond those of order and peace. It has no mandate to pursue, say, human rights or redistributive justice per se. These issues were generally left to other organs—namely the General Assembly, the Economic and Social Council (ECOSOC), and a range of specialized agencies.

At the beginning of this section, I suggested that the UN's normative agenda has five components: peace and security (the stability of international society), sovereignty and nonintervention, self-determination, redistributive justice, and human rights. As in most other arenas, all good things do not necessarily go together. As Hedley Bull has pointed out, the effort to sustain order may require breaches of the peace. Maintaining international peace and security may be seen to require overriding the sovereign rights of states. Security, peace, and sovereignty concerns may require the contravention of widely accepted standards of justice.[30] In its first forty-five years, system maintenance proceeded to a large extent outside the United Nations; the Security Council itself was largely blocked by bipolar competition. And the General Assembly (the "Uniting for Peace" resolution notwithstanding) had no obvious purchase on the choices of the superpowers in this area.

While the great powers went their own way on core security issues, the General Assembly made considerable progress, for better or worse, in establishing the primacy of norms of sovereignty and nonintervention. In general, human rights issues took a clear back seat to the norms of sovereignty and nonintervention during the Cold War. This said, the normative basis for the consideration of individual human beings as subjects of international concern expanded gradually, but substantially. In the meantime, the General Assembly made an effort to advance the redistributive agenda at the level of the state through the New International Economic Order (NIEO) but with little effect, since those states at the heights of the international economy saw no obvious advantage in accepting this agenda.

The Post–Cold War Era and Normative Development at the United Nations

The end of the Cold War considerably expanded the space available for the multilateral management of peace and security, illustrated by the radical increase in the number of Security Council resolutions in the area, the equally dramatic reduction in the use of the veto, the increasing numbers (until 1994) of UN operations or operations mandated by the Security Council in the realm of security, and the expansion in the concept of peace operations to include peacebuilding. For some, the U.S.-led operation against Iraq in 1990–1991 suggested that an era of real collective security was in the making. Although the mid-1990s experienced a retreat from the ambitions of the beginning of the decade, the Implementation Force (IFOR) and the Stabilization Force (SFOR) in Bosnia and Operation Allied Force in Kosovo (which proceeded without an explicit Security Council mandate but was launched by a multilateral organization, NATO) all suggested that multilateralism of a sort had come to be taken as a basic condition of response to threats to international peace and security.[31]

At the beginning of Secretary-General Boutros Boutros-Ghali's term, council members asked him for a report on international peace and security in the new conditions brought by the end of the Cold War. He came back with a report that reemphasized the core values of the organization and called for a new and more activist role not only in the area of peace and security but also in the realms of rights and distributive justice. As he put it: "In these past months a conviction has grown, among nations large and small, that an opportunity has been regained to achieve the great objectives of the Charter—a United Nations capable of maintaining justice and human rights and of promoting, in the words of the Charter, 'social progress and better standards of life in larger freedom.'"[32]

The sequence of interventions in northern Iraq, Somalia, the former Yugoslavia, Haiti, Liberia, Sierra Leone, Kosovo, and East Timor also had implications for the balance between the rights of the society of states and the rights of sovereign states. The relevant resolutions took advantage of the caveat of Article 2.7 that the sovereign jurisdiction of states could be overridden where events within state borders threatened international peace and security.[33] In using this facility, the Security Council broadened the definition of "threat" to include forced displacement of populations, humanitarian crises, and indeed, in the case of Haiti, in Security Council resolution 940 (1994), the continued denial of democratic rights. Although the resolutions generally made clear the unique and unprecedented character of the situations and actions in question, together they suggested an attenuation of sovereignty and a corresponding expansion of the rights of the United Nations and international society more broadly with respect to the domestic jurisdiction of states.[34] As the secretary-general put it in 1998: "The Charter protects the sovereignty of peoples. It was never meant as a license for governments to trample on human rights and human dignity. Sovereignty means responsibility, not just power."[35] The trend toward the challenge to unconditional domestic jurisdiction extended to the effort to deny impunity through the prosecution of alleged war criminals using international criminal tribunals for Rwanda (ICTR) and the former Yugoslavia (ICTY), and now using the International Criminal Court (ICC).

The increasing preoccupation of UN organs, especially the Security Council, with the issue of intervention on ostensibly humanitarian grounds suggested that the rights of individual human beings had risen in the hierarchy of values embraced by the organization. This was also evident in the shifting discourse on security in the UN's specialized agencies,[36] which increasingly privileged the individual protection and welfare concerns of human beings at the expense of the traditional security and sovereignty preoccupations of states. As was evident in the 1994 United Nations Development Programme (UNDP) *Human Development Report,* the focus on the security of the individual had developmental aspects as well, linking the security discourse of the UN to the redistributive welfare goals discussed above. In other words, one could argue that the balance among the core values promoted by the UN system had shifted and that the UN's concern to defend norms of sovereignty had diminished to a degree in the face of peace and security concerns on the one hand, and rights concerns on the other, and that the link between peace and security and rights and welfare was more strongly integrated into the organization's discourse and practice. Recalling the balance between individual and state rights discussed earlier, the 1990s appear to have been characterized by a shift in the balance between state and individual rights toward the latter. This occurred in the context of a growing multilateralization of governance in the areas of security and rights.

September 11 and UN Values

The fundamental question posed by the events of September 11 and the responses to them is whether they are tilting this balance back toward unilateralism as process and toward the rights of states at the expense of those of individuals. In Europe and much of the rest of the world, the standard image one received in the post–September 11 context was of an increasingly hegemonic military superpower that showed little interest in the broad agenda of UN values (except perhaps to undermine them), that was indifferent or hostile to multilateral approaches to the problems that it faced, that increasingly regarded its own interests and was wedded to the unilateral use of force, that stretched the boundaries of legitimate self-defense, and that had returned to intervention as an instrument of policy, even when such intervention was not mandated by the Security Council.[37] This image was enhanced by the marginalization of international organizations in the response to Al Qaeda, the Taliban, and, until September 2002, the "axis of evil," notably Iraq. It was encouraged by the bellicosity and dismissiveness toward multilateral approaches to resolving problems of global governance of many prominent members of the Bush administration. This dismissiveness appeared to extend beyond the UN to include NATO, the Organization for Security and Co-operation in Europe (OSCE), and certain multilateral arms control instruments (e.g., the withdrawal from the effort to strengthen the biological weapons convention). It went beyond the frame of security to include the environment (e.g., the withdrawal from the Kyoto process) and to some extent trade (e.g., the expansion of U.S. farm subsidies).

Yet it would be inaccurate to suggest that Washington had given up on multilateralism. In the first place, the Security Council played a role in the legitimation of the U.S. military response to the terrorist attacks.[38] Sixteen days later, the Security Council laid the groundwork for a substantial enhancement of international cooperation in the response to terrorism, notably in targeting the financial assets of terrorist groups and sympathizers; it called on all states to report within ninety days on their efforts to implement the resolution and established a committee to monitor progress in the implementation of the program laid out in the resolution. Resolution 1373 reflected the important point that many aspects of this new threat were not effectively manageable without strengthening functional multilateral cooperation in certain areas (intelligence, police, financial monitoring). To the extent this is so, one would expect a strengthening of Washington's commitment to multilateralism in these areas.

It should also be noted that although the rhetoric of the military campaign had a distinctly unilateral flavor, its implementation in Afghanistan involved close operational cooperation with a number of allies. Moreover, the United States made clear its preference for multilateral approaches to post-conflict peacebuilding and reconstruction in Afghanistan, not least because it apparently did not wish its forces to be distracted from purely military matters.

As attention turned to Iraq, the possibility of a unilateral and unmandated use of force raised serious concerns within the UN system, typified by Secretary-General Kofi Annan's opening statement to the 57th General Assembly. He stressed the necessity of multilateral cooperation in the struggle against terrorism and went on to assert that "choosing to follow or reject the multilateral path must not be a matter of simple political convenience." Acknowledging the threat that unilateral use of force would pose to the Charter-based system of norms, he observed that it would have "consequences far beyond the immediate context" and reminded his listeners that in the decision to use force to deal with threats to international peace and security, "there is no substitute for the unique legitimacy provided by the United Nations."[39]

In the period immediately prior to the General Assembly's opening in 2002, the UK and U.S. apparently agreed on the merits of exhausting the Security Council alternative prior to any attack on Iraq. President Bush reflected this conclusion in his address in New York where he called on the Security Council to enforce the many unfulfilled resolutions dealing with Iraq while reserving the right to act alone should the multilateral option fail.[40] In November 2002, Washington settled for Security Council resolution 1441, which fell short of mandating the use of force in the event of Iraqi noncompliance. In short, the U.S. did not abandon multilateralism outright for the simple reason that American policymakers appeared to believe that multilateral cooperation served their interests in the campaign in certain respects.[41]

Matters become more complex when one moves toward substantive values regarding the use of force. The United Nations has played an important role in the effort to entrench collective approaches to international peace and security and in embedding the illegality of the use of force by states except in self-defense.[42] The immediate response to the attack on the U.S. was not particularly problematic in this regard. The United States was a victim of aggression and acted in self-defense in a situation recognized by the council to be a threat to international peace and security in resolution 1368.

However, as attention shifted to Iraq, the justification of force became more problematic. There is reason to question the direct linkage between U.S. policy in the war on terror and its position on Iraq. However, as noted above, September 11 played an important permissive role in the evolution of U.S. policy. Moreover, U.S. arguments regarding preventive defense relied directly on the alleged link between "rogue states" and terrorist groups.

One approach to dealing with the Security Council's reluctance to adopt a resolution explicitly authorizing force was to argue that in view of prior actions of the council, such a resolution was unnecessary. The post–September 11 resolutions were not promising in this regard. It is difficult to see how the coverage of resolution 1368 could be extended to states that had not attacked the United States and could not be proven to be harboring terrorists. Prior resolutions on Iraq provided more fertile ground. Iraqi failure to comply with other resolutions of the Security Council (for example, resolution 687 [1991]) could plausibly serve as a justification for military action. The last paragraph in resolution 687 stated that the council "decides to remain seized of the matter and to take such further steps as may be required for the implementation of the present resolution and to secure peace and security in the region." However, the Security Council reserved to itself the right of decision on this matter, leaving little space for unilateral state action to implement the resolution.

Resolution 678 (1990) provided an indirect justification for the use of force without a supplementary resolution, since it authorized member states to "use all necessary means" not only to "uphold and implement Resolution 660 (1990) and all subsequent relevant resolutions" but also to "restore international peace and security in the area." Elsewhere, resolution 686 (1991) affirmed that until Iraq complied with the cease-fire conditions listed in paragraphs 2 and 3 of the resolution,[43] the just-mentioned provisions of resolutions 678 remained in effect. This appeared to suggest that to the extent that Iraq had not complied with these conditions, member states were authorized to act without a further mandate.[44] However, the extent to which Iraq had complied with these resolutions was a matter of debate, particularly given the imprecise quality of much of the language. It was not clear that Iraq, even with the best of intentions, would have been able to comply with some of the conditions (e.g., those pertaining to the return of remains of prisoners and missing persons), given the fog of war. The phrase "to restore international peace and security in the area" was a weak reed, given that the war in Kuwait, which presumably was the principal manifestation of instability at the time resolution 678 was adopted, has been over for eleven years.

One might take comfort in the fact that this tortuous process of justification on the basis of Security Council resolutions suggested an underlying acceptance by the United States of the normative framework constraining the use of force. However, whether or not a legal pretext existed[45] and was valid, military action vis-à-vis Iraq in the face of substantial disagreement over its legality and in the absence of a further resolution that would settle the legal question weakened restrictive norms concerning the unilateral use of force by states.

A second, and more troubling, line of argument justifying force against Iraq, and one linked far more directly to terrorism, was based on reinterpretation of the right of self-defense. It was suggested that the possession of weapons of mass destruction by Iraq ipso facto constituted a threat to the United States, either because Iraq might use these things itself or because it might leak them to terrorists.[46] Therefore, the United States argued that the preemptive or preventive use of force to remove them could be considered self-defense. In the National Security Strategy of the United States adopted in September 2002, President Bush warned that "as a matter of common sense and self-defense, America will act against such emerging threats before they are fully formed."[47] It would be difficult to square preemption or prevention with Article 51 of the Charter, which specifies that states have a right to self-defense "if an armed attack has occurred."[48]

On the other hand, the strategy rightly noted that "international law recognized that nations need not suffer an attack before they can lawfully take action to defend themselves against forces that present an imminent danger of attack."[49] In an age of weapons of mass destruction, strict adherence to Article 51 might constitute participation in a suicide pact. Practically speaking, no state could be expected to sacrifice its survival on the altar of legal principle. The key question here concerns imminence, or the slide between preemption and prevention.[50] If, as the Bush administration believed, the criterion of imminence should be relaxed in the face of the new strategic challenge posed by the marriage of radicalism and technology, then it is not clear how one would draw the boundary between legitimate acts of self-defense and illegitimate use of force.

Accepting a broad right to preemptive and preventive self-defense would tear a large hole in the normative fabric of the UN regarding the non-use of force. If it works for Iraq, why not elsewhere? If it works for the United States, why not for other states? Arguments put forward by the Russian Federation with respect to Georgia display clear parallels. Elsewhere, Indian policymakers welcomed "the administration's new emphasis on the legitimacy of pre-emption."[51] In this context, French President Jacques Chirac termed the notion "extraordinarily dangerous," for "as soon as one nation claims the right to take preventive action, other countries will naturally do the same."[52] Or, as Condoleezza Rice noted in another context: "The overly broad definition of America's national interest is bound to backfire as others arrogate the same authority to themselves."[53]

Moreover, such an action would raise disturbing questions about the relationship between power and the universality of the principles promoted by the United Nations. If the action were not seen to constitute a precedent for action by other states, it would seem to take on a distinctly Thucydidean flavor: "[T]he standard of justice depends on the equality of power to compel and . . . in fact the strong do what they have the power to do and the weak accept what they have to accept."[54]

This argument for the use of force against Iraq was linked to the issue of intervention in the American embrace of "regime change" as a policy goal. It is not immediately obvious how this objective could be squared with Article 2.4's prohibition of intervention. For reasons discussed above, one could act against Saddam's regime on the basis of Articles 2.7 and 42. But this again would require the Security Council to identify the regime as a threat to international peace and security and authorize military action to remove it.[55] The prospects for a resolution embracing the objective of regime change were low in the days immediately preceding the withdrawal of the draft resolution by the U.S. and UK. While the fallout of the war in Iraq is yet to be seen, there is a risk that states will increasingly revert to unilateral intervention, thus derailing much of the progress in prohibiting intervention for political reasons in international society. To the extent that nonintervention is seen as one basis for international order, undermining the principle carries risks for the larger edifice of stability in international politics.

Another area of concern is human rights. The promotion of civil and political rights within the international system has always depended strongly on the commitment of major states to the cause. During the 1990s, much progress was made in holding oppressive regimes accountable for the violation of the rights of their citizens. Faced with the tradeoff between short-term stability and the longer-term objectives of democratization and the rule of law, the United States and other major Western players pushed authoritarian regimes toward empowering their own people and toward the protection of their citizens' rights. In extremis, as seen above, international society (or at least the Security Council on occasion) accepted that intrusion into the domestic jurisdictions of states that would not, or could not, protect the basic rights of their citizens might be legitimate.

The evidence thus far would suggest that one consequence of September 11 is the danger of a reversal of these priorities. The key issue in relations with authoritarian regimes appears now to be whether they are capable of controlling their jurisdictions in such a way as to limit the prospects that their countries may give comfort to terrorists and whether their territory and infrastructure are useful in the wider struggle against terrorism. The countries of Central Asia are good illustrations. In Uzbekistan, despite the country's abysmal human rights record, the United States expanded military and development assistance in return for President Karimov's cooperation in the struggle

against Al Qaeda and the remnants of the Taliban. Elsewhere, Russia had attempted to convince the international community of states that the war in
Chechnya has been a counterterrorist operation since the renewal of hostili-
ties in 1999. Prior to September 2001, this characterization was resisted by key
Western states. Subsequently, the level of criticism of Russia's conduct of the
war diminished radically, and Russia appeared to have been granted carte
blanche to bring the operation to term, which to date has involved massive
violation of the rights of many of its Chechen citizens and Russia's failure to
honor numerous international legal and political obligations in the contexts
of the Geneva, OSCE, Council of Europe (COE), and Conventional Forces in
Europe (CFE) treaties.[56]

To judge from the evolution of U.S. defense and military relations with Indonesia, moreover, where a state's capacity to participate effectively in the war
on terrorism is doubted, Washington appears to have resumed relations with
military and security establishments that previously had been pariahs because
of their human rights records. To the extent that major states place military and
strategic priorities of this type ahead of the promotion of human rights, the
UN's capacity to foster a culture of rights is correspondingly reduced.

September 11 also has had an impact on states' perspectives on civil and
political rights within their own borders.[57] It was followed by significant
changes in security legislation in numerous states—including the U.S., Britain, Canada, Australia, Italy, the Netherlands, India, and New Zealand. In general, these changes involved an expansion in the right of the state to freeze or
seize assets and to hold individuals without charging them with a crime. They
also reduced individuals' right to privacy. In some instances, law enforcement
authorities were granted access to special courts outside normal judicial process to try cases related to terrorism. Finally, in North America and Europe,
the capacity for rapid extradition with minimal or no judicial review was expanded or is likely to expand.[58] Former UN High Commissioner for Human
Rights Mary Robinson registered her concern for the place of human rights
in the normative framework of international society: "The United States could
be a leader in combating terrorism while upholding human rights. Instead it
has sought to put all the emphasis on combating terrorism and has not been
fully upholding human rights standards. And that's having a ripple effect on
other less democratic countries."[59]

These legal changes have differential impacts on different categories of
people. The most obvious effect of September 11 has been the bending of, if
not challenge to, international humanitarian law implicit in the detention of
combatants at Guantanamo Bay and elsewhere. The treatment of detainees
also raises questions about the states' compliance with their obligations un-

der the Convention against Torture.[60] It is reported, for example, that sleep deprivation and light deprivation are used against terrorist suspects held by the United States and that "they are held in awkward, painful positions." Detainees who do not cooperate are allegedly turned over to foreign intelligence services with records of torture documented by human rights organizations and by the U.S. government itself. As one official is reported to have put it: "[I]f you don't violate someone's human rights, you aren't doing your job." The head of the CIA's Counterterrorist Center said in September 2002 at a House and Senate committee hearing: "There was a before 9/11, and there was an after 9/11. After 9/11 the gloves come off."[61] Such perspectives raise important questions about the strength and sustainability of the international regime against torture.

It is important to note, however, that such actions do not proceed in a political vacuum. As the experience of September 11 recedes, one may expect a growth in domestic pressure to mitigate these departures from accepted principles of human rights. The press report just cited, for example, provoked a serious challenge to the administration from Amnesty International, The Lawyers Committee for Human Rights, The Carter Center, Physicians for Human Rights, Human Rights Watch, and others, reminding the administration of its obligations under the Convention against Torture.[62] Moreover, U.S. government behavior with respect to detainees is subject to judicial review. It may be that as cases reach the Supreme Court, these trends may be reversed or attenuated. In short, the early retreat from or qualification of human rights principles evident in the response to September 11 was inconsistent with the Charter and the UN's embrace of these values; how durable this trend is remains to be seen.

Generally, post–September 11 challenges to the human rights of individuals have affected noncitizens more substantially than citizens. This leads to brief consideration of state responses to the attacks on refugees and asylum-seekers. The international refugee regime was already in trouble prior to the attacks on the United States.[63] Its difficulties had much to do with the rising numbers of refugees, the domestic political reaction to this "flood" in Western Europe in particular, and the perceived connection between asylum-seeking and economic migration and between asylum-seekers and organized crime. September 11 strengthened the security rationale for restraint on movement. This has resulted in substantial constraint on asylum rights in a number of developed countries, among them the U.S., the UK, and Canada.

Specifically, among other measures, the United States temporarily suspended its refugee resettlement program, affecting some 20,000 cleared persons. New legislation permitted the holding of aliens suspected of terrorist

activity without charge for seven days. The possibility of deportation or of prohibition on entry without judicial review was expanded. In the UK, new legislation permits the home secretary to deny asylum to those deemed a threat to
national security while broadening the right to detain those suspected of terrorism and to intern foreigners without trial[64] and curtail the right of appeal for
some asylum-seekers. In Canada, screening has been expanded to ensure that
those suspected of terrorist activities do not enter the asylum system, more resources have been allocated to the deportation process, and detention facilities
for suspect aliens have been expanded. As Matthew Gibney put it:

> A shiver ran down the spine of many people in the West on 11
> September. The world they looked out upon now seemed a much
> less secure and more uncertain place. This changed world provided
> the rationale for new measures of exclusion and control on refugees,
> asylum seekers and, in some cases, foreign residents generally. . . . At
> times of high anxiety, political communities tend to become less tol-
> erant, more insular places."[65]

Again, UN efforts to develop and strengthen norms in this area depend on
the willingness of states to implement them. September 11 has had a significant chilling effect, to the detriment of many thousands of people in refugee
processing and asylum systems. To the extent that the great powers defect
from, or qualify their support for, the regime, it becomes more difficult to
persuade other states in the system to abide by their obligations under the
convention.

The final issue for consideration is the effect of September 11 on the redistributive values promoted by the United Nations. The early focus of American
commentary on September 11 was retributive justice—effective punishment of
the perpetrators of crime—"root 'em out, get 'em running, and hunt 'em down,
wanted dead or alive." Those who suggested that the terrorist acts might in
some sense be a result of an unjust distribution of resources in the international system and the consequent hopelessness, despair, and resentment felt
by large numbers of people, particularly in the developing world, were pillo-
ried for justifying terrorism.

In time, discussion has become more reasoned. It is now acceptable to suggest that one necessary element of coping with the problem of terrorism is
coping with the problem of inequity both between and within societies through
serious efforts at development. This is hardly a dominant theme in policy
circles in the United States or beyond it. However, the Bush administration's
initiatives to expand development assistance (e.g., President Bush's speech to
the Inter-American Development Bank in March 2002 and the follow-up at

the Monterrey Conference on Financing International Development, which led to the $5 billion Millennium Challenge Account) suggest some renewed recognition that stability and peace are linked to development. The link is made far more directly in the statements and policy papers of allies in the fight against terrorism. This general point is linked to a widely held belief that failed states cannot simply be left to their own devices after a crisis has ended. There may exist among the major states a growing realization that development and redistributive justice are not merely ethical propositions but security interests in an increasingly transnationalized world where it is difficult for the wealthy to insulate themselves from the consequences of widespread poverty and disempowerment. Flows of official development assistance declined in the 1990s in part because the strategic rationale for them had disappeared with the end of the Cold War. The renewal of a strategic rationale for such assistance may reverse the decline.

Conclusion

This chapter has explored the impact of September 11 on the pursuit of the values espoused in the United Nations Charter. The analysis suggests that the attacks on the U.S. and international responses to them place pressure on reasonably well-embedded norms regarding the use of force. The notion of "regime change" that was practiced in Afghanistan and further articulated with regard to Iraq draws into question Charter-based norms concerning sovereignty and nonintervention. The effort to uncover terrorist networks has had a negative influence on state compliance with international humanitarian law and with broader principles of human rights. It has also negatively affected the already troubled international refugee regime. More positively, consideration of the roots of terrorism may draw greater attention to the inequalities of globalization and to broader issues of distributive justice.

In short, the record shows a degree of shift away from the liberal and cosmopolitan element of the UN's agenda of values and back toward a statist, power-based, and security-oriented focus in international society. That is hardly surprising, given the dimensions and political and psychological significance of the events themselves. However, to suggest that the balance is tilting back toward unilateralism and the prerogatives of states at the expense of the rights of individuals is not to say that the major power in the system has abandoned the multilateral enterprise or that the progress in embedding justice concerns in international society will be undone.

Despite the temptations of going it alone, the United States government appears to have recognized that there is value in multilateralism in security.

The cooperation of other states remains necessary in the war on terror. Multi-lateral regimes provide a degree of control over the behavior of other states in the system. The costs of defection are difficult to measure but possibly substantial across a broad range of issues. Moreover, although the implications of the international response to terror for the human rights agenda of the UN Charter are disturbing, there are substantial domestic (e.g., within judicial systems and public opinion) and transnational (e.g., regarding the role of international human rights NGOs and international judicial institutions) impediments to the abandonment of the human rights regime. In short, there is evidence of a return to more traditional modes of state practice, but it is unlikely that the international system can return to the pre-1990s version of international society. Although the normative constraints that deepened in the post–Cold War era may be weaker, they will remain a significant constraint on state behavior.

Notes

1. Zuleta Angel, "Chairman's Statement" at the opening of the first part of the first session of the General Assembly, January 10, 1946, 41. Available online at http://www.un.org/Depts/dhl/landmark/pdf/a-pv1.pdf.

2. The emphasis here is on "preliminary." It will be years before the long-term impact of these events becomes clear. The author is grateful to discussants at the September 2002 seminar at the Ralph Bunche Institute for International Studies and to the editors for their comments on earlier drafts; he also benefited from discussions with officials of Canada's Department of Foreign Affairs and International Trade in the preparation of this chapter.

3. Adam Roberts and Benedict Kingsbury, "The UN's Roles in International Society," in Adam Roberts and Benedict Kingsbury, eds., *United Nations, Divided World: The UN's Roles in International Relations,* 2nd ed. (Oxford: Oxford University Press, 1993), 19.

4. As Zuleta Angel went on to say: "Without social justice and security there is no real foundation for peace, for it is among the socially disinherited and those who have nothing to lose that the gangster and the aggressor recruit their supporters." "Chairman's Statement," 43.

5. See, for example, Robert Keohane, *After Hegemony: Cooperation and Discord in the World Political Economy* (Princeton, N.J.: Princeton University Press, 1984).

6. Judith Goldstein and Robert Keohane, eds., *Ideas and Foreign Policy: Beliefs, Institutions, and Political Change* (Ithaca: Cornell University Press, 1993); and Alexander E. Wendt, "Anarchy Is What States Make of It: The Social Construction of Power Politics," *International Organization* 46, no. 2 (Spring 1992): 391–426.

7. In view of the expansion of international institutions of governance and the increasing number and weight of non-state actors, one might question whether anarchy and the preeminence of the state are constants, but that is beyond the scope of this paper.

8. Kenneth Waltz, *Theory of International Politics* (New York: McGraw Hill, 1979).

9. Adam Roberts, "Order/Justice Issues at the UN," in Rosemary Foot, John Gaddis, and Andrew Hurrell, eds., *Order and Justice in International Politics* (Oxford: Oxford University Press, 2003), 51.

10. On this point, see S. Neil MacFarlane, *Intervention in Contemporary World Politics* (London: Oxford University Press for the International Institute for Strategic Studies, 2002).

11. The term comes from Martha Finnemore and Kathryn Sikkink, "International Norm Dynamics and Political Change," *International Organization* 52, no. 4 (Autumn 1998): 887–917.

12. On this point, see "Introduction," in Rosemary Foot, S. Neil MacFarlane, and Michael Mastanduno, eds., *U.S. Hegemony in an Organized World: The United States and Multilateral Institutions* (Oxford: Oxford University Press, 2003).

13. Some General Assembly resolutions and declarations, such as the "Declaration of Principles of International Law Governing the Friendly Relations among States in Accordance with the Charter of the United Nations" (General Assembly resolution 2625, October 24, 1970), are seen by many as having the status of law. For a summary of relevant literature, see Gene Lyons and Michael Mastanduno, "State Sovereignty and International Intervention," in Gene Lyons and Michael Mastanduno, eds., *Beyond Westphalia? State Sovereignty and International Intervention: Reflections on the Present and Prospects for the Future* (Baltimore: Johns Hopkins University Press, 1995), 250–265.

14. For this reason, although the International Court of Justice is one of the six principal organs established by the Charter and although certain of its judgments (e.g., the Corfu Channel and Nicaragua cases) bear significantly on issues dealt with here, I have chosen not to include it in the discussion.

15. Arnold Wolfers, *Discord and Collaboration: Essays on International Politics* (Baltimore: Johns Hopkins University Press, 1965).

16. The first purpose of the organization, mentioned in Article 1.1: "To maintain international peace and security, and to that end: to take collective measures for the prevention and removal of threats to the peace, and to bring about by peaceful means and in conformity with the principles of justice and international law, adjustment or settlement of international disputes or situations which might lead to a breach of the peace." See also Article 1.2 on friendly relations and the peaceful settlement of disputes and the strengthening of international peace.

17. Article 51 reserves the "inherent right of individual or collective self-defence if an armed attack occurs against a Member of the United Nations, until the Security Council has taken steps necessary to maintain international peace and security." The article also requires immediate report to the Security Council of any exercise of this right. Roberts rightly points out that the role of the UN has been far stronger in *jus ad bellum* than in *jus in bello*, the latter being left largely to other organizations (e.g., the ICRC) and processes. Roberts, "Order/Justice Issues at the UN," 67. For this reason, although there are interesting things to say about the effect of September 11 on various legal principles (e.g., discrimination and the treatment of prisoners) associated with *jus*

in bello, I do not consider this question here. For further comment, see Samuel
Makinda, "Global Governance and Terrorism," *Global Change, Peace and Security* XV,
no. 1 (February 2003): 43–58.

18. International Court of Justice, "Corfu Channel Case (Merits): Judgment of 9
April 1949." Available online at http://www.icj-cij.org/icjwww/idecisions/isummaries/
iccsummary490409.htm.

19. "Declaration on the Inadmissibility of Intervention in the Domestic Affairs of
States and the Protection of Their Independence and Sovereignty," annex to General
Assembly resolution 2131, December 21, 1965, 11–12. See also the "Declaration on Principles
of International Law concerning Friendly Relations and Co-operation among States in
Accordance with the Charter of the United Nations," annex to General Assembly
resolution 2625, 24 October 1970, 121–124. Roberts points out that this declaration went
farther in extending the prohibition from single states to "groups of states."

20. It is worth acknowledging that while the evolution of this norm was clear, its
effect on practice was limited, given superpower and proxy interventions in support of
one side or another in many of the internal conflicts of the Cold War period. See
MacFarlane, *Intervention in Contemporary World Politics,* 38–40.

21. Preamble, Article 1.3, Article 7.1, Article 13.1, and Chapter IX.

22. Cited in UNDP, *Human Development Report 1994* (New York: UNDP, 1994), 3.

23. In time, and again with the General Assembly playing a significant role,
retributive justice arguments gained influence in the UN system. The "Declaration on a
New International Economic Order" and the "Charter of Economic Rights and Duties
of States" both appear to rest on the argument that since the North was responsible for
underdevelopment in the first place, it was also responsible for righting this historical
wrong through restitutive redistribution.

24. Preamble and Articles 13, 55, 56, 62, 68, 76.

25. Elsewhere they note the distinction between the Charter and the League
Covenant in this regard, suggesting that the founders recognized that human rights and
associated economic and social problems needed to be addressed "if the world was to
be spared another catastrophe." Leland Goodrich, Edvard Hambro, and Anne Patricia
Simons, *Charter of the United Nations: Commentary and Documents* (New York:
Columbia University Press, 1969), 10, 34.

26. The latter was accompanied by an optional protocol. Several other more specific
documents are worthy of mention in this context, notably the Convention on the
Prevention and Punishment of the Crime of Genocide (1948), the Convention Relating
to the Status of Refugees (1951), the Declaration of the Rights of the Child (1959), the
Convention on the Rights of the Child (1989), the United Nations Declaration on the
Elimination of All Forms of Racial Discrimination (1963), the International Convention
on the Elimination of All Forms of Racial Discrimination (1965), the Declaration on the
Elimination of Discrimination against Women (1967), the Convention on the Elimination of All Forms of Discrimination against Women (1979), and the Convention against
Torture, and Other Cruel, Inhuman or Degrading Treatment or Punishment (1984). All
these documents applied universally, except the refugee convention, in which the rights

established pertained essentially to Europeans displaced across borders prior to 1951 (Article 1.2). The 1967 Protocol Relating to the Status of Refugees recognized the desirability of equality of status for post-1951 refugees and universalized the status established in the convention.

27. See also later General Assembly considerations of the underpinnings of humanitarian assistance in war: "Human suffering should be addressed wherever it is found. The dignity and rights of all victims must be respected and protected." General Assembly resolution 46/182 (1992), as summarized in "Draft Guidelines on the Use of Military and Civil Defence Assets to Support United Nations Humanitarian Activities in Complex Emergencies" (Geneva, May 2002, Version 4.1), 6.

28. On this point, see David M. Malone, "US-UN Relations in the UN Security Council in the Post–Cold War Era," in Foot, MacFarlane, and Mastanduno, eds., *U.S. Hegemony and International Organizations,* 81.

29. The resolution did, however, refer to General Assembly resolution 1514 and called upon the UK to reestablish conditions whereby the people of Southern Rhodesia could exercise their right to self-determination.

30. Hedley Bull, *The Anarchical Society* (New York: Columbia University Press, 1977).

31. For an elaboration of this argument, see MacFarlane, *Intervention in Contemporary World Politics.*

32. Boutros Boutros-Ghali, *An Agenda for Peace—Preventive Diplomacy, Peacemaking and Peace-keeping: Report of the Secretary-General Pursuant to the Statement Adopted by the Summit Meeting of the Security Council on 31 January, 1992* (A/47/277-S/24111), June 17, 1992, paragraph 3.

33. Nico Schrijver, "The Changing Nature of State Sovereignty," *The British Year Book of International Law 1999* (Oxford: Clarendon Press, 2000), 69–70.

34. In 2000, the council abandoned its case-specific consideration of these issues in resolution 1296 and recognized the general point that deliberate targeting of civilians, massive and systematic violations of human rights, and the denial or impeding of access by humanitarian organizations all could constitute threats to international peace and security.

35. Kofi A. Annan, "Reflections on Intervention," 35th Ditchley Foundation Lecture (June 26, 1998), in Kofi A. Annan, *The Question of Intervention: Statements by the Secretary-General* (New York: UN, 1999), 6. The reference to peoples here is anomalous, since the relevant articles in the Charter emphasize the sovereign jurisdiction of member states of the organization. See also Javier Pérez de Cuéllar, *Report of the Secretary General on the Work of the Organization* (A/46/1 [1991]), September 13, 1991; and Boutros Boutros-Ghali, *An Agenda for Peace,* paragraph 17.

36. UNDP, *Human Development Report 1994*; UNHCR, *State of the World's Refugees: A Humanitarian Agenda* (New York: Oxford University Press, 1997). See also S. Neil MacFarlane and Yuen Foong Khong, *Human Security and the UN: A Critical History*, a forthcoming volume from the UN Intellectual History Project (Bloomington: Indiana University Press).

37. For an able representative analysis, see Makinda, "Global Governance and Terrorism."

38. The Security Council's resolution 1368 of September 12 recognized the inherent right of individual and collective self-defense, condemned the terrorist attacks as a threat to international peace and security, called on states to cooperate in bringing the perpetrators to justice, and stressed that states and others harboring the guilty would be held accountable. The resolution departs from traditional interpretations of Article 51, which envisage it to apply to relations between states. It deserves to be noted, however, that the United States was careful to ensure that no references to UN or Security Council oversight of its military activities were included in the resolution. On this point see Malone, "US-UN Relations in the UN Security Council," 89.

39. The Secretary-General, "Address to the General Assembly," September 12, 2002. Available online at http://www.globalpolicy.org/secgen/annan/2002/0912ga.htm.

40. "Statement by President Bush, United Nations General Assembly, UN Head-quarters, New York," September 12, 2002. Available online at http://www.un.org/webcast/ga/57/statements/020912usaE.htm.

41. One could of course argue that this is multilateralism à la carte. And so it is. But the United States is no different from most other states in this regard.

42. On the other hand, the resolutions of the 1990s dealing with humanitarian crisis, mass migration, and the overthrow of democratic regimes suggested some dilution of the restriction on the multilateral use of force.

43. The resolution includes the following principles: compliance with prior resolutions; rescinding of actions purporting to annex Kuwait; acceptance "in prin-ciple" of liability for loss, damage, and injury in Kuwait or in third states resulting from the invasion and occupation; release of prisoners and remains beginning with the return of all Kuwaiti property; and provision of information on mines, booby traps, and so forth, in Kuwait and in areas of Iraq where member state forces were cooperat-ing with Iraq.

44. I am indebted to Jennifer Welsh for bringing this point to my attention.

45. The U.S. and British discussion of the legality of the action reminds me of a story about W. C. Fields, who was seen reading the Bible. When asked why he was doing so, he said he was looking for loopholes.

46. As George W. Bush put it on September 12, 2002, "[O]ur greatest fear is that terrorists will find a shortcut to their mad ambitions when an outlaw regime supplies them with the technologies to kill on a massive scale." See also "President Bush Outlines Iraqi Threat," Cincinnati, Ohio. Available online at http://www.whitehouse.gov/news/releases/2002/10/20021007-8.html.

47. George W. Bush, "Introduction," in *The National Security Strategy of the United States of America* (Washington, D.C.: The White House, 2002). See also Section V. Available online at http://www.whitehouse.gov/nsc/nss.html.

48. As one observer commented: "Such an approach renders international norms of self-defense—enshrined by Article 51 of the Charter—almost meaningless." John Ikenberry, "America's Imperial Ambition," *Foreign Affairs* (September/October 2002): 51.

49. See *The National Security Strategy of the United States,* Section V.

50. Preemption involves "striking an enemy as it prepares an attack." Prevention covers "striking an enemy even in the absence of specific evidence of a coming attack." Although there may be place for preemption in *jus ad bellum,* "prevention is a far less accepted concept in international law." Michael O'Hanlon, Susan E. Rice, and James B. Steinberg, *The New National Security Strategy and Preemption,* Policy Brief No. 113 (Washington, D.C.: The Brookings Institution, December, 2002), 4.

51. Ibid., 7.

52. As cited in Elaine Sciolino, "Chirac Offers Iraq Plan," *International Herald Tribune,* 10 September 2002, 1.

53. Condoleezza Rice, "Promoting the National Interest," *Foreign Affairs* LXXIX, no. 1 (2000): 54.

54. Thucydides, *History of the Peloponnesian War* (Harmondsworth: Penguin, 1986), 402. See also Ikenberry, "America's Imperial Ambition," 44.

55. In this context, it should be noted that Security Council resolution 688 concerning the repression of the Kurds and Shiites fell short, as it was not adopted under Chapter VII. I am indebted to Nico Schrijver for this point.

56. For a discussion of this point, see S. Neil MacFarlane, "What the West Can Do to Settle the [Chechen] Conflict," *Central Asia and the Caucasus,* no. 4 (2000): 150–152.

57. Indeed, this was necessitated to some extent by the binding and comprehensive package of measures included in resolution 1373.

58. For a useful summary, see "Security: The Cost for Human Rights," *The Guardian,* 9 September 2002, 5. For an extensive and useful discussion of the evolving situation in the United States, see The Lawyers Committee for Human Rights, *A Year of Loss: Reexamining Civil Liberties Since September 11* (New York: Lawyers Committee for Human Rights, 2002).

59. Cited in Julia Preston, "UN Rights Chief Stepping Down, Criticizes U.S.," *International Herald Tribune,* 13 September 2002, 5. Robinson's expression of such concerns was likely one reason she was not renewed as high commissioner in late 2002.

60. See Article 1.1 of the Convention against Torture and Other Cruel, Inhuman or Degrading Treatment or Punishment (1984), where torture is defined as "any act by which severe pain or suffering, whether physical or mental, is intentionally inflicted on a person for such purposes as obtaining from him or a third person information or a confession, punishing him for an act he or a third person has committed or is suspected of having committed, or intimidating or coercing him or a third person, or for any reason based on discrimination of any kind, when such pain or suffering is inflicted by or at the instigation of or with the consent or acquiescence of a public official or other person acting in an official capacity." Available online at http://www1.umn.edu/humanrts/instree/h2catoc.htm.

61. The quotations in this paragraph are from Dana Priest and Barton Gellman, "For CIA Suspects Abroad, Brass-Knuckle Treatment," *International Herald Tribune,* 27 December 2002, 1, 7.

62. See the January 14, 2003, letter from William Schulz, Ashley Barr, Kenneth Roth, et al. to Deputy Defense Secretary Paul Wolfowitz; available online at http://www.lchr.org/us_law/us_law_let_011403.pdf.

63. See Adam Roberts, "More Refugees, Less Asylum: A Regime in Transformation," *Journal of Refugee Studies* XI, no. 4 (December 1998): 375–395.

64. In Britain, eleven individuals were arrested in late December 2001 on suspicion of terrorism. They have been held ever since in high-security prisons. They were initially denied access to legal counsel. None has been charged, none has been officially interviewed, and none has seen the evidence on which the arrest was made. Under existing legislation, there is apparently no limit to the period of time that they can be held. Audrey Gilian, "No Names, No Charges, No Explanations: The Plight of Britain's Interned 'Terrorists,'" *The Guardian*, 9 September 2002, 5.

65. Matthew Gibney, "Security and the Ethics of Asylum after 11 September," *Forced Migration Review*, no. 13 (2001): 40, 42.

Part II

The "New" International Arena

3

September 11 and Challenges to International Law

Nico Schrijver

The horrifying events of September 11, 2001, challenged some basic notions of international law. Washington[1] and its partners in the North Atlantic Treaty Organization (NATO) and the Organization of American States (OAS) immediately identified the terrorist attacks on the United States as "acts of war,"[2] thereby bringing into play the law of war with its two branches of *jus ad bellum* (law regulating recourse to war) and *jus in bello* (law regulating the conduct of war).[3] The discourse of war, moreover, seemed to have a significant psychological impact on public opinion, thus serving to garner support for the broadening and deepening of executive power not only in the United States but also in allied countries.[4]

But can one identify a terrorist attack by a transnational criminal group against a state as a "war" in terms of the conventional definitions of war in international law, however serious the attack may have been?[5] Upon reflection, the use of the term "war," which is traditionally understood as "a state of force between two or more States with suspension of peaceful relations," was a misnomer. It was most likely employed deliberately to emphasize that the September 11 attacks were so serious that they could be equated with state aggression and that the response might necessitate the use of all available resources—as if we were in a state of war. This is just one of the challenges to international law to which the September 11 attacks gave rise.[6]

This chapter identifies and discusses central challenges and dilemmas emerging from them. First, it briefly reviews what possible responses to the September 11 attacks were available from an international law point of view. Next, it reviews the actual responses from the United States and the international community of states. The chapter then addresses the challenges and dilemmas arising from September 11 and concludes with some final observations about the adequacy of international law as a vehicle for combating international terrorism.

The Options

In case of an armed attack upon a state, a first option of response that comes immediately to the fore is the exercise of the right of self-defense. It is referred to in Article 51 of the UN Charter as an "inherent right." The text is worth citing in its entirety:

> Nothing in the present Charter shall impair the inherent right of individual or collective self-defence if an armed attack occurs against a Member of the United Nations, until the Security Council has taken measures necessary to maintain international peace and security. Measures taken by Members in the exercise of this right of self-defence shall be immediately reported to the Security Council and shall not in any way affect the authority and responsibility of the Security Council under the present Charter to take at any time such action as it deems necessary in order to maintain or restore international peace and security.

This article stipulates that the victim state must report details of the armed attack and the response to it to the Security Council. Furthermore, it emphasizes the primary responsibility of the Security Council for the restoration and maintenance of international peace and security by providing that the right of self-defense of the attacked state can only be invoked until the council itself has taken appropriate measures "necessary to maintain international peace and security." Hence under the Charter, self-defense is construed as a provisional remedy.

Ideally, the Charter foresees that upon an armed attack the Security Council will exercise its primary responsibility in accordance with Article 24.[7] Chapter VII vests the council with the power to take enforcement measures in such a case. This requires, first of all, a determination under Article 39 that a "threat to the peace," "breach of the peace," or "act of aggression" has occurred. Subsequently, the Security Council can take provisional measures under Article 40 (e.g., imposing a cease-fire or call for negotiations), institute sanctions not involving the use of armed force (under Article 41), or take or authorize military enforcement action (under Article 42). In addition, the council can establish international criminal responsibility of those who perpetrated the terrorist acts. However, there is no guarantee, let alone requirement, that it will take such measures, and it often is blocked due to a lack of agreement among its permanent members. Furthermore, not every Security Council "measure" will have the legal effect of suspending or terminating the right of self-defense. In this connection, it is relevant to recall that Article 1 refers to "*effective* collective measures" and Article 51 to "measures *necessary* to maintain international peace and security" (emphases added).

Most important, the Security Council's arsenal of Articles 40–42 has been tailored to interstate disputes or, more recently, to disputes within a state between a government and an identifiable non-state entity in opposition. The presumption is that the aggressor state or rebellious non-state entity can be pressured to terminate its unlawful behavior. Obviously, such a presumption does not apply to the perpetrators of the September 11 attacks.

The Responses

Four consecutive phases can be distinguished in the UN's legal responses to the September 11 attacks: early responses, general anti-terrorism measures, support for the new regime in Afghanistan, and a broadening of the anti-terrorism struggle.

Early Responses

The first phase began on September 12, 2001, when the Security Council unequivocally condemned the previous day's terrorist attacks and labeled such acts as a "threat to international peace and security," thus using the terminology of the opening article of Chapter VII. It did so unanimously, which is quite unusual. In a preambulary paragraph of resolution 1368, the Security Council recognized "the inherent right of individual or collective self-defence in accordance with the Charter of the United Nations." Thus, it legitimized self-defensive military action by the United States, albeit in a somewhat indirect way. No specific reference was made to the September 11 attacks or to the U.S. as the victim state of the aggression. By contrast, during the Gulf War, the council pronounced in August 1990 in resolution 661 that Kuwait was vested with the inherent right of self-defense in response to the armed attack by Iraqi forces.

Furthermore, resolution 1368 expressed in general terms the council's determination to combat "by all means" threats to peace and security by terrorist acts and more specifically its readiness to take all necessary steps "to respond to the terrorist attacks of 11 September 2001." The council did not yet take any steps or measures but called in general terms on states to redouble their efforts to prevent and suppress terrorist acts, inter alia by increased cooperation and full implementation of the relevant anti-terrorism conventions.[8] On the same day, the General Assembly also adopted a resolution on the terrorist attacks. The assembly resolution is cast in somewhat more emotional language than that of the Security Council. Apart from strongly condemning "the heinous acts of terrorism, which have caused enormous loss of human life, destruction and damage," the assembly urgently called for international cooperation to bring to justice "the perpetrators, organizers and sponsors of the outrages of 11 September 2001" and stressed that those responsible for aiding, supporting, or harboring them would be held accountable.[9]

A further Security Council resolution on measures to combat international terrorism was adopted on September 28, 2001, once again with notable unanimity. This time the particular phrase "*acting* under Chapter VII of the UN Charter" was explicitly included in resolution 1373. While the council reaffirmed the right of individual and collective self-defense in general terms, the core of resolution 1373 is a wide-ranging and far-reaching specific list of anti-terrorism measures which all states are legally obliged to implement. As such, it marks the beginning of the second phase.

General Anti-Terrorism Measures

The council decided that all states shall prevent and suppress the financing of terrorist acts, freeze the financial assets of persons and entities involved in the commission of such acts, and prohibit anyone within their jurisdiction from making such assets available for the benefit of persons involved in terrorist acts. The first two paragraphs of resolution 1373 draw clearly on the International Convention for the Suppression of the Financing of Terrorism.[10] All states are obliged to deny safe havens to those involved in such acts, prevent their territories from being used for terrorist purposes, and ensure that any person who participates in such acts is brought to justice. Like the financing convention itself, the resolution does not allow for the "political offense" exception, which seeks to exempt political offenders from extradition. Resolution 1373 was the first legally binding Security Council resolution addressing international terrorism as a global phenomenon without referring to a particular state or region. Through this binding set of anti-terrorism measures, the Security Council took on a quasi-legislative role in a pioneering way.[11] Resolution 1373 also established a committee to monitor actively, on the basis of detailed reporting requirements, the implementation of all these anti-terrorism measures by states. The Counter-Terrorism Committee (CTC) was an important bureaucratic step and was named the "Greenstock Committee" after its first chair, the British permanent representative to the United Nations, Jeremy Greenstock.

Furthermore, the Security Council met at a ministerial level and adopted, once again by unanimity, a Declaration on the Global Effort to Combat Terrorism. This declaration was annexed to resolution 1377 of November 12 and declares, in even stronger terms than resolutions 1368 and 1373, that acts of international terrorism constitute "one of the most serious threats to international peace and security in the twenty-first century" and "a challenge to all

States and to all of humanity." The council stressed that "continuing international efforts to broaden the understanding among civilizations and to address regional conflicts and the full range of global issues, including development issues" will contribute to sustaining the broadest possible fight against international terrorism. In this way, the council put the anti-terrorism struggle in a much wider context.

In the weeks following September 11, a Working Group of the General Assembly's Sixth Committee (Legal) was established to immediately resume talks on the drafting of a comprehensive anti-terrorism convention, an issue which goes back to an initiative by India in 1996 but which had ended in a stalemate in subsequent years.[12] Initially, major progress was made on the basis of the Indian draft, but soon traditional differences of opinion relating to the definition of terrorism and the exception "political offense" came to the fore.[13]

Support for the New Regime in Afghanistan

For many years the United Nations had been advocating a more pluralistic Afghanistan by stipulating that the Kabul government should be broad based, multiethnic, fully representative of all Afghan people, and committed to peace. Various parts of the UN system—including the Security Council, the General Assembly, and the Commission on Human Rights (CHR)—had been severely and routinely criticizing the Taliban regime. For example, as early as October 1996 the Security Council had stated in resolution 1076 that "the continuation of the conflict in Afghanistan provides a fertile ground for terrorism and drug trafficking which destabilize the region and beyond." In December 1998, resolution 1214 demanded that "the Taliban, as well as other Afghan factions, stop fighting . . . and co-operate with the aim of creating a broad-based and fully representative government, which would protect the rights of all Afghans and observe the international obligations of Afghanistan with respect to terrorism." Following the attacks on the U.S. embassies in Nairobi and Dar es Salaam, in October 1999 in resolution 1267 the council referred explicitly to the Taliban's provision of safe haven to Osama bin Laden and determined that the failure of the Taliban authorities to stop providing sanctuary and training for international terrorists constituted "a threat to international peace and security." It demanded in clear terms the extradition of Osama bin Laden without further delay to appropriate authorities in a country where he had been indicted (the United States). In 1999 and 2000, the council also imposed sanctions in resolutions 1267 and 1333, respectively, against the Taliban regime—including an air embargo, the freezing of all financial resources and assets of a number of specified persons and entities, and an arms embargo.

Following the wide-scale strikes by the U.S. and the UK against terrorist targets and against Taliban positions in Afghanistan on October 8, 2001, the Security Council reiterated its calls for a multiethnic regime in Afghanistan and expressed support for consultations to that extent. Such UN-brokered talks were to take place in Bonn in late November and early December. Meanwhile, the Northern Alliance, which was composed of a wide coalition of Afghan anti-Taliban groups and had support from Washington and London, managed to oust the Taliban regime in November and December 2001. On December 5, 2001, nearly all major Afghan factions (with the exception of the Taliban, which was not allowed to participate) agreed to establish an interim regime under the leadership of Hamid Karzai and prepare for democratic elections.[14] Resolutions 1383 and 1386 expressed strong Security Council support for these provisional arrangements in the Bonn Agreement and called on member states to assist with the rehabilitation and reconstruction of Afghanistan and to address immediate humanitarian problems. For this purpose, in early 2002 a major international donor conference was organized in Tokyo. Moreover, the council also authorized the establishment of an International Security Assistance Force (ISAF), which was initially organized and led by the UK. In line with the recommendations of the Brahimi report for more robust peacekeeping and enforcement operations,[15] the force was authorized to take "all necessary measures" to provide for security in and around Kabul.

Expanding the Fight against International Terrorism

Security Council resolutions 1368, 1373, and 1377 obliged states to take a wide range of measures against terrorism in general. This indicated that the anti-terrorism struggle would not be confined to Afghanistan. However, President George W. Bush went considerably farther on September 20, 2001, when he pronounced in an address to a joint session of the U.S. Congress that: "Every nation, in every region, now has a decision to make. Either you are with us, or you are with the terrorists. From this day forward, any nation that continues to harbor or support terrorism will be regarded by the United States as a hostile regime."[16] In his January 2002 State of the Union Address, Bush identified North Korea, Iran, and Iraq as belonging to an "axis of the evil,"[17] which led to a lot of unease, even among faithful allies. Many stated that they were with neither Bush nor bin Laden.

However, attention soon shifted from Al Qaeda and the elusive Osama bin Laden to the "axis of evil," especially to the Saddam Hussein regime in Iraq. Initially, frequent reference was made to the alleged links between Hussein and Al Qaeda. However, little hard evidence was presented and gradually issues of human rights violations, the need for regime change, and weapons of mass destruction (WMD) in Iraq came to dominate the debate.

On November 7, 2002, after seven weeks of intensive debate, the Security Council unanimously adopted resolution 1441. The Security Council decided that Iraq was in "material breach" of its disarmament obligations under previous resolutions, most notably resolution 687, which ended the Gulf War in 1991. However, the council offered Iraq "a final opportunity" and established a tough weapons inspection regime through the United Nations Monitoring, Verification and Inspection Commission (UNMOVIC) and the International Atomic Energy Agency (IAEA). The council warned Iraq once again that it would face "serious consequences as a result of its continued violations of its obligations." When the Security Council reached stalemate on whether or not Iraq had failed to cooperate with the weapon inspections, the U.S., the UK, and Australia unilaterally launched a three-week military strike against Iraq to oust the Saddam Hussein regime in March and April 2003. It is notable that this resolution 1441 made only cursory references to terrorism. In a preambulary paragraph, the council deplored the fact that Iraq had failed to comply with its commitments with regard to terrorism. Resolution 687, in fact, had required Iraq "to inform the Security Council that it will not commit or support any act of international terrorism or allow any organization directed towards commission of such acts to operate within its territory and to condemn unequivocally all acts, methods and practices of terrorism."[18] It is likely that on future occasions the council will link the cause of combating international terrorism to other country-specific situations. However, despite frequent speculation and assertions, among others by Secretary of State Colin Powell in his addresses to the Security Council, so far a clear link between Iraq and Al Qaeda has not been proven.

Challenges and Dilemmas

The September 11 attacks and responses provide ample reason to reflect on current Charter notions of the international management of challenges to peace and on the adequacy of the arsenal of international law to respond to global threats of terrorism. Seven are discussed below.

Conventional Charter Concepts

First of all, it has become obvious that conventional Charter concepts such as "use of force" (Article 2, paragraph 4), "armed attack" and "self-defence" (Article 51), and "threat to peace" and "breach of the peace" (Article 39) are not geared to situations of serious attacks against a state by a group of foreign-based and often loosely organized international terrorists such as the Al Qaeda movement. New interpretations must be developed and new practices must emerge to address situations arising from "terror." In 1945, the drafters of the Charter deliberately employed the terms "force" and "armed attack," as opposed to the term "war," which was used in the Covenant of the League of Nations[19] and the Kellogg-Briand Pact.[20] This was in response to evasive language used by aggressor states in the 1930s, such as Japan's aggression against Manchuria in 1931 and Italy's aggression against Abyssinia in 1936.[21] Yet the Charter concepts are still closely associated with the notion of organized armed groups crossing boundaries.

On previous occasions of acts of international terrorism, it proved to be rather controversial to say that terrorist attacks amounted to an armed attack and activated the right of self-defense. For example, Israel met repeatedly with heavy criticism when it invoked a right of self-defense in response to alleged terrorist attacks by the Palestine Liberation Organization (PLO).[22] Similarly, the United States got little support when it invoked its right of self-defense to legitimize a bombing raid on Tripoli, the capital of Libya, in response to a bomb explosion in a Berlin discotheque frequented by American servicemen.[23] However, few challenged the finding that the September 11 attacks constituted a "threat to international peace" and "armed attack."

Both the Security Council and regional defense organizations, such as NATO and the OAS, affirmed the right of individual and collective self-defense in the sense of Article 51 and the need "to combat by all means the threat to international peace and security caused by terrorist acts."[24] On October 7, 2001, the United States reported to the Security Council that it was exercising its "inherent right of individual and collective self-defense" by military actions "against Al Qaeda terrorist training camps and military installations of the Taliban regime in Afghanistan."[25] Many states participated, directly (United Kingdom) or indirectly (Pakistan, Saudi Arabia, Turkey, and Uzbekistan), in the military action called Enduring Freedom. Other countries, including China and Russia, expressed explicit verbal support.

This may well inaugurate a change of *opinio juris* with respect to the parameters of the norms of use of force and self-defense, triggered by the scale and atrocity of the September 11 attacks which not only resulted in the death of many innocent civilians but also struck at the heart of U.S. national security.[26] No country can be expected to refrain from responding to the sources of such actions. The concept of "armed attack" of Article 51 may well include "armed attacks" by non-state actors such as international terrorists. After all, the text of Article 51 does not stipulate an "armed attack by a state." Hence, the hijacking and deliberately planned and simultaneous use of large passenger aircraft as bombs to attack the Pentagon and the World Trade Center may well be viewed as an "armed attack" against the United States and the civilized world as a whole.

From this fact flows the conclusion that Washington and its allies were justified in taking countermeasures involving the use of armed force until such time as the Security Council acts to restore and maintain peace and security. But how far does the scope of self-defense reach?

The Scope of the Right of Self-Defense

Self-defense has never been an unqualified notion in international law.[27] The 1837 *Caroline* incident at Niagara Waterfalls in the border area of colonial Canada and a newly independent United States gave rise to the doctrine of "a necessity of self-defense, instant, overwhelming, leaving no choice of means, and no moment for deliberation" and the idea that responsive measures may be neither "unreasonable" nor "excessive."[28] What does this imply in the case of the September 11 attacks? Should the United States and its allies have responded by military means immediately rather than nearly one month later, as some have suggested? This appears to amount to an unreasonable curtailing of the right of self-defense. It would also certainly not be in line with the Charter or with the international legal duty to explore all peaceful means of international dispute settlement.[29]

However, it is obvious that self-defense cannot be invoked to do whatever the U.S. and the UK think fit. Any act of self-defense must focus on, if not limit itself to, repelling the armed attack and acute terrorist violence. Hence, a targeted and prudent use of military force to destroy the terrorist infrastructure in Afghanistan in order to repel and prevent further terrorist attacks was certainly legitimate. But a serious question can be raised about whether self-defense through combating international terrorism could legitimately extend to seeking the overthrow by military force of the de facto Taliban authority in Afghanistan and replacing it with a more democratic regime.

This is certainly at odds with the international law of nonintervention, which has evolved considerably since the United Nations was established.[30] Moreover, resolution 1378 only expressed support of the "efforts of *the Afghan people* to replace the Taliban regime" (emphasis added). Nor does the law of self-defense provide a license to victim states to target at their whim other states, including those considered to be part of the "axis of the evil." But considerable controversy exists about whether the Security Council has any supervisory role in assessing the legitimacy of how the right of self-defense is exercised.[31]

Observance of International Humanitarian Law

Jus in bello (international humanitarian law applicable during armed conflict) applies during both interstate and intrastate conflicts. This branch of
law evolved over centuries and reflects the experiences and interests of states,
including their armed forces. Nevertheless, the dominant recurring theme of
the four 1949 Geneva Conventions is the protection of victims of war who
have fallen into the hands of an adversary. While these are written with established armed groups in mind, it can be argued that the obligation to observe
international humanitarian law (IHL) applies equally to the perpetrators of
terrorist acts.[32] The distinctions between combatants and noncombatants and
between civilian and military targets are among the fundamental principles
of international humanitarian law.[33] Quite often terrorist acts are directed
against civilians. Such indiscriminate or deliberate killing or inhumane treatment of civilians constitutes a grave breach of IHL for which the perpetrators
should be held accountable.

Distinguishing between combatants and noncombatants and between civilian and military targets is also a requirement for any exercise of self-defense or
any military action against terrorism.[34] Were these distinctions always scru-
pulously observed as stipulated by the 1949 Geneva Conventions and the additional protocols of 1977 during the Anglo-American military attacks against
Afghanistan? Considerable controversy has emerged about whether the Taliban
soldiers and Al Qaeda fighters would qualify for protection under the Geneva
law. If not at all, are they people deprived of rights and outlawed?[35] There is
reason to differentiate between the Taliban soldiers and the Al Qaeda combatants.[36] The former ought to be accorded the status of prisoners of war,
whereas the latter are just criminals who are still entitled to a fair trial and to
treatment of prisoners as provided for in the UN Covenant of Civil and Political Rights.[37] This also raises the tension between the effectiveness of the
anti-terrorism struggle and the upholding of human rights.

Observance of Human Rights

After September 11 a tendency arose that signaled a willingness to erode standards of human rights and to expand exception clauses for the purpose of combating international terrorism. However, a prime motive of the anti-terrorism
struggle, as exemplified, among other things, in the name "Operation Enduring
Freedom," is the fight for the human right to life, to security and freedom, and—
to quote Franklin D. Roosevelt—to "freedom from fear." It would really not
serve the cause of credibility and legitimacy of the anti-terrorism struggle if

governments in the course of the struggle for "enduring freedom" were to loosen the bonds of the well-established human rights agreements. Fair trial is certainly one such important international human rights value.[38] Furthermore, Article 4 of the International Covenant on Civil and Political Rights includes the possibility for derogation in cases of "public emergency which threatens the life of a nation."[39]

Human duties form the reverse side of the human rights coin, particularly the duty to respect and not to violate the human rights of other individuals. Obviously, acts of international terrorism often result in serious violations of human rights. In certain cases they may even amount to "crimes against humanity."[40] Current international anti-terrorism law is not yet sufficiently developed to designate acts of international terrorism as serious international crimes. Rather, they are viewed as criminal acts giving rise to a crime to be tried on the basis of national law and by domestic tribunals. In this vein, the Security Council has taken steps to oblige all states to cooperate closely in apprehending and prosecuting terrorists. This is necessary to further develop international criminal law, substantively and institutionally, in order to deal with international terrorism at the transnational level in which it increasingly manifests itself. There are good reasons for governments to give renewed thought to the appropriateness of the International Criminal Court (ICC) in this respect. At the future review conference (to be held in 2009, seven years after the entry into force of the Rome Statute), acts of international terrorism should be explicitly included in the statute as "serious crimes of international concern" (Article 1), which will activate the complementary jurisdiction of the ICC. In view of their advance planning, there can be little doubt that the September 11 attacks meet the description of "widespread or systematic attack against any civilian population" in the beginning of Article 7 of the Rome Statute, which features "murder," "extermination," or "other inhumane acts" on the list of crimes within the purview of crimes against humanity. However, the ICC is just becoming operational and cannot function retroactively. Moreover, of all countries, the United States has fervently rejected ratification of the statute. This raises the issue of the need for multilateral cooperation for collective security.

Asserting Collective Security Arrangements

The proceedings on the UN responses to September 11 suggest that the Security Council especially was hobbling between two views: a policy based on the recognition of the right of self-defense of the victim state and its allies and a policy based on collective security arrangements as provided for in Chapter

VII.[41] While the council in general terms responded swiftly and unanimously, upon reflection there may be reason to expect more from the world organization as an active and effective international anti-terrorism agent. The council could have expressed itself more clearly on the applicability of the right of self-defense; Washington and London adequately fulfilled the reporting requirements under Article 51.

However, the council did not respond, let alone exercise control of the military operations in Afghanistan. Nor did the council speak about the alleged link between the anti-terrorism struggle and the question of Iraq. Furthermore, ample reflection is called for on the appropriateness and effectiveness of collective sanctions. Obviously, the sanctions against the Taliban had little effect. What were the reasons for this? Should they have been enforced more forcefully? If the sanctions of resolutions 1267 and 1333 with respect to the Taliban regime in Afghanistan had been fully implemented, would September 11 have happened? In view of the strong and unanimous rhetorical resolve of member states to take the necessary measures to combat international terrorism, it may be wiser to provide more room for collective security through the Security Council than to stretch the confines of the self-defense approach.[42] This would not garner legitimacy for international anti-terrorism measures, but in the long term it might even enhance the effectiveness of such measures.

Attribution and State Responsibility

Another critical issue is the question of state responsibility, and more particularly the question of whether the acts of Al Qaeda and Osama bin Laden could, in part, be attributed to the fact that the Taliban regime harbored, and possibly supported, Al Qaeda. Here we may recall relevant international jurisprudence. In *Nicaragua* v. *the United States* (1986) the International Court of Justice (ICJ) developed the "effective control test."[43] One of the issues at stake was whether the activities of the Nicaraguan "contras" could be attributed to the United States in view of the strong evidence that they were trained, equipped, and armed by Washington. The ICJ concluded that it could not be sufficiently proven that the U.S. government had exercised effective control over the contras to the extent that they could be presumed to act on Washington's behalf. In the Iran hostages case (1980), the ICJ found that the captors of the American hostages held in the U.S. embassy in Tehran could be considered as Iranian agents in a later stage of the hostage-taking and hence that Iran bore responsibility for their acts.[44] In these cases, the ICJ was addressing issues of state responsibility. Pronouncements by the International Criminal Tribunal for the Former Yugoslavia (ICTY), whose mandate relates to issues of individual criminal responsibility and not to state responsibility, are also pertinent. For example, the Tadić case addressed the issue of the close relationship and line of command between the Bosnian Serb forces and the government of the Federal Republic of Yugoslavia. Its Appeals Chamber replaced the ICJ's "effective control" test by a somewhat lower threshold assessment of "*overall control* going beyond the mere financing and equipping of such forces and involving also participation in the planning and supervision of military operations."[45]

Here it is also relevant to refer to the recent Draft Articles on Responsibility of States for Internationally Wrongful Acts, particularly Articles 8 and 11, of the UN International Law Commission. Draft Article 8 on "Conduct carried out or controlled by a State" reads: "The conduct of a person or group of persons shall be considered an act of a State under international law if the person or group of persons is in fact acting on the instructions of, or under the direction or control of, that State in carrying out the conduct." Draft Article 11 on "Conduct acknowledged and adopted by a State as its own" says: "Conduct which is not attributable to a State under the preceding articles shall nevertheless be considered an act of that State under international law if and to the extent that the State acknowledges and adopts the conduct in question as its own."[46] It could be said that the refusal of the Taliban regime to close all terrorist training camps in Afghanistan and turn over the leaders of Al Qaeda came close to tacit support and thus to the acknowledgment and endorsement of the conduct of the Al Qaeda movement. While the September 11 attacks could be imputable to the de facto government of Afghanistan at the time, it is obvious that the current "effective control" or "overall control" tests and the evolving law of state responsibility are insufficient to address threats of terrorism by globally operating criminal groups of stateless individuals.

The Proliferation of Weapons of Mass Destruction and Trade in Small Arms

The September 11 attacks led to the necessity to take the law of arms control much more seriously, including the regulation of the trade in small arms. Apart from the entry into force of the Chemical Weapons Convention and the tough weapons inspections regime under resolution 1441 with respect to Iraq, not much progress has been achieved in this field. The use of certain weapons, most notably biological and chemical weapons, is prohibited. Similarly, certain means and methods of "warfare" that cause unnecessary human suffering are prohibited.

Only recently has the United Nations initiated serious efforts to tackle "the tragedy of the uncontrolled spread of small arms and light weapons." In 2001, the UN adopted a "Programme of Action to Prevent, Combat and Eradicate the Illicit Trade in Small Arms and Light Weapons in All Its Aspects."[47] The council also imposed various arms embargoes and recently adopted a declaration called "Proliferation of Small Arms and Light Weapons and Mercenary Activities: Threat to Peace and Security in West Africa."[48] Among other things, the declaration calls on arms-producing and arms-exporting countries to enact stringent measures to ensure more effective control over the transfer of small arms by manufacturers, suppliers and brokers, and shipping and transit agents. If member states fail to follow up the question of regulation of armaments and the illicit international trade in arms in a committed and active way, we should not be surprised if numerous groups manage to possess and use such weapons and other dangerous materials.[49]

An Agenda for Prevention through Multilateral Cooperation and International Law

Successfully combating international terrorism over the longer term requires a multifaceted and integrated approach that effectively manages sensitive peace and security issues, addresses deep inequalities by promoting social justice and observance of human rights, and stimulates global dialogue among civilizations and religions.[50] Such a long-term approach is reflected in Security Council resolution 1377 of November 12, 2001, which annexes the Ministerial Declaration on the Global Effort to Combat Terrorism, and in resolution 1456 of January 20, 2003, which includes an additional ministerial declaration on the issue of combating terrorism. This huge nonmilitary agenda cannot be pursued unilaterally; it requires a coherent multilateral approach. Since September 11, some progress has been made in this respect, for example at the UN Conference on Financing for Development in Monterrey in March 2002 and at the World Summit for Sustainable Development in Johannesburg in August and September 2002.[51] It is of the utmost importance that a coherent multilateral agenda for preventing terrorism be developed and implemented. As UN Secretary-General Kofi Annan put it: "People who are desperate and in despair become easy recruits for terrorist organizations."[52]

International law, both as a value system and a regulatory system, can be instrumental in pursuing prevention and effectively combating international terrorism. Various provisions of international law are relevant, including those directly or indirectly relating to development, conflict prevention, conflict containment, and post-conflict peacebuilding. They share and are increasingly shaped by key charter values such as peace and security, humanity, and development. This applies just as much to the law applicable during times of armed conflict as it does to the law in times of peace.

There appears to be no reason to call for a fundamental change in the international legal system.[53] Rather, much can be gained by interpreting and applying principles and rules of international law as "living instruments" in order to meet new concerns in present-day circumstances, as demonstrated above with respect to Charter concepts such as armed attack and threat to or breach of the peace. In addition, a further progressive development of international law and organization is called for in such fields as counterterrorism, international criminal responsibility, and international cooperation for development. If applied faithfully and in an interrelated way, the current system of collective security and international economic and social cooperation, as embodied in the UN Charter and general international law, can well serve to combat international terrorism and help contain and eventually prevent it by tackling its root causes. The need for a coherent multilateral approach and for unity of international law poses the enormous challenge to the various branches of international law to effectively converge in order to ensure that public international law with respect to use of force, collective security, responsibility of states for internationally wrongful acts, and conflict management is well coordinated with human rights law, an international criminal law approach with respect to international judicial cooperation, and individual criminal responsibility. A dignified international law response should be made to meet the challenges of September 11.

Notes

1. For example, in his "Address to a Joint Session of Congress and the American People," President Bush declared: "On September 11th, enemies of freedom committed an act of war against our country." September 20, 2001. Available online at http://www.whitehouse.gov/news/releases/2001/09/20010920-8.html.

2. NATO press release for September 12, 2001, "Statement by the North Atlantic Council," available online at http://www.nato.int/docu/pr/2001/p01-124e.htm; NATO press release for October 2, 2001: "NATO-Russia Consultations on Combatting Terrorism," available online at http://www.nato.int/docu/pr/2001/p011002e.htm; Organization of American States, 24th meeting of Consultation of Ministers of Foreign Affairs, "Terrorist Threat to the Americas," resolution 1 in OEA/Ser.F/II.24/RES.1/01, September 21, 2001.

3. This still highly relevant distinction originates from Hugo Grotius's magnum opus *De Iure Belli ac Pacis* (On the Law of War and Peace, 1625); Francis W. Kelsey et al., *Translation of De iure belli ac pacis by Hugo Grotius* (Oxford: Clarendon Press, 1925).

4. See David Abramowitz, "The President, the Congress, and Use of Force: Legal and Political Considerations in Authorizing Use of Force Against International Terrorism," *Harvard International Law Journal* 43, no. 1 (2002): 71–103.

5. See Werner Meng, "War," *Encyclopedia of Public International Law,* vol. IV (Amsterdam: North Holland, 2000), 1334. See also Ingrid Detter, *The Law of War,* 2nd ed. (Cambridge: Cambridge University Press, 2000), 5–26; and Yoram Dinstein, *War, Aggression, and Self-Defence,* 3rd ed. (Cambridge: Cambridge University Press, 2001), Chapter 1.

6. See Antonio Cassese, "Terrorism Is Also Disrupting Some Crucial Legal Categories of International Law," *European Journal of International Law* 12, no. 5 (2001): 993.

7. Article 24: "In order to ensure prompt and effective action by the United Nations, its Members confer on the Security Council primary responsibility for the maintenance of international peace and security, and agree that in carrying out its duties under this responsibility the Security Council acts on their behalf."

8. The relevant texts can be found in *International Instruments Related to the Prevention and Suppression of International Terrorism* (New York: United Nations, 2001); and Peter J. van Krieken, ed., *Terrorism and the International Legal Order* (The Hague: Asser Press, 2002).

9. See "Condemnation of Terrorist Attacks in the United States of America," General Assembly resolution A/RES/56/1, September 12, 2001.

10. This convention was opened for signature on December 9, 1999. It entered into force on April 10, 2002.

11. See also Paul C. Szasz, "The Security Council Starts Legislating," *American Journal of International Law* 96, no. 4 (2002): 901–905.

12. See M. Cherif Bassiouni, "International Terrorism," in Bassiouni, ed., *International Criminal Law,* vol. 1, *Crimes,* 2nd ed. (Ardsley, N.Y.: Transnational Publishers, 1999), 765–801; and Gregory M. Travalio, "Terrorism, International Law, and the Use of Force," *Wisconsin International Law Journal* 18 (2000): 145–191.

13. See, for example, the initial *Report of the Working Group* (A/C.6/56/L.9), October 29, 2001. See also "Working Document Submitted by India on the Draft Comprehensive Convention on International Terrorism," *Indian Journal of International Law* 42, no. 2 (2002): 219–238.

14. See "Agreement on Provisional Arrangements in Afghanistan Pending the Re-establishment of Permanent Government Institutions," S/2001/1154, December 5, 2001.

15. See *Report of the Panel on United Nations Peace Operations* (A/53/305-S/2000/809), August 21, 2000.

16. Bush, "Address to a Joint Session of Congress and the American People."

17. President George W. Bush, "State of the Union Address," January 28, 2002. See the earlier letter dated October 7, 2001, from the U.S. to the Security Council, (S/2001/946), stating: "There is still much we do not know. Our inquiry is in its early stages. *We may find that our self-defense requires further actions with respect to other organizations and other States*" (emphasis added). During a press conference, Ambassador Negroponte further remarked on this sentence: "[W]hen you're talking about the inherent right of self-defense, I don't think that one would want to limit oneself in any particular way. I think one exercises it, when one thinks that is justified and necessary." Text in USUN Press Release 136 (01), October 8, 2001. It is notable that such pronounce-

ments cannot be found in the UK letter to the Security Council of October 7, 2001 (S/20001/947) invoking the right of self-defense following the initiation of military action on that day.

18. Adopted by 12 votes to 1 (Cuba) with 2 abstentions (Ecuador, Yemen).

19. Article 11 of the League of Nations Covenant (1919) said: "Any war, or threat of war, whether immediately affecting any of the Members of the League or not, is hereby declared a matter of concern to the whole League, and the League shall take any action that may be deemed wise and effectual to safeguard the peace of nations."

20. General Treaty for the Renunciation of War as an Instrument of National Policy, commonly known as the Kellogg-Briand Pact, August 27, 1928.

21. See Bert V. A. Röling, "International Law and the Maintenance of Peace," *Netherlands Yearbook of International Law* IV (1973): 81.

22. For example, the bombing of the PLO headquarters near Tunis, Tunisia, by Israeli forces was strongly condemned by the Security Council in resolution 573 (1985), which was adopted 14 to 0, with the United States abstaining.

23. The General Assembly condemned the bombing in A/RES/41/53 (December 3, 1986), whereas a Security Council resolution to that effect met with a veto of the three Western permanent members.

24. In a unique demonstration of solidarity, the nineteen NATO countries declared that the terrorist attacks on the United States were viewed as an armed attack against all NATO member countries pursuant to the collective defense Article V of the 1949 Washington Treaty establishing NATO. Available online at http://www.nato.int/docu/basictxt/treaty.htm.

25. "Letter dated 7 October 2001 from the Permanent Representative of the United States of America Addressed to the President of the Security Council" (S/2001/946), October 7, 2001.

26. See also Sean D. Murphy, "Terrorism and the Concept of 'Armed Attack' in Article 51 of the UN Charter," *Harvard International Law Journal* 43, no. 1 (2002): 47.

27. See, for example, Yoram Dinstein, *War, Aggression, and Self-Defense,* 3rd ed. (Cambridge: Cambridge University Press, 2001).

28. See letter of State Secretary Webster of 1842 in *British and Foreign State Papers* 30 (1841–1842): 193–202; also in Martin Dixon and Robert McCorquodale, *Cases and Materials on International Law,* 4th ed. (Oxford: Oxford University Press, 2003), 529.

29. Article 2, paragraph 3 of the UN Charter reads: "All Members shall settle their international disputes by peaceful means in such a manner that international peace and security, and justice, are not endangered."

30. Key documents in this respect are "Declaration on the Inadmissibility of Intervention in the Domestic Affairs of States and the Protection of their Independence and Sovereignty," adopted by General Assembly resolution 2131 (XX), December 21, 1965; "Declaration on Principles of International Law Concerning Friendly Relations and Co-operation Among States in Accordance with the Charter of the United Nations," General Assembly resolution 2625 (XXV), October 24, 1970; and "Definition of Aggression," annexed to General Assembly resolution 3314 (XXIX), December 14, 1974.

31. See for different views on the one hand Terry D. Gill, "Legal and Some Political Limitations on the Power of the UN Security Council to Exercise its Enforcement Powers under Chapter VII of the Charter," *Netherlands Yearbook of International Law* 25 (1995): 99, and Dinstein, *War, Aggression, and Self-Defense,* 284; and on the other Oscar Schachter, *International Law in Theory and Practice* (Dordrecht: Martinus Nijhoff, 1991), 138–141, and Nico J. Schrijver, "Responding to International Terrorism: Moving the Frontiers of International Law for 'Enduring Freedom'?" *Netherlands International Law Review* 48, no. 3 (2001): 271–291.

32. Frits Kalshoven and Liesbeth Zegveld, *Constraints on the Waging of War,* 3rd ed. (Geneva: International Committee of the Red Cross, 2001).

33. See for a recent confirmation the ICJ Advisory Opinion on the Legality of the Threat or Use of Nuclear Weapons, *I.C.J. Reports 1996,* p. 257, paragraph 78.

34. Adam Roberts, "Counter-Terrorism, Armed Force and the Laws of War," *Survival* 44, no. 1 (Spring 2002): 7–32.

35. This issue arose especially with regard to the status of detainees transferred from Afghanistan to Guantanamo Bay (Cuba) as prisoners of war or noncombatants under the Third Geneva Convention Relating to Treatment of Prisoners of War. See for the relevant texts Adam Roberts and Richard Guelff, *Documents on the Law of War,* 3rd ed. (Oxford: Oxford University Press, 2002).

36. Compare George H. Aldrich, "The Taliban, Al Qaeda, and the Determination of Illegal Combatants," *American Journal of International Law* 96, no. 4 (2002): 891–898.

37. "International Covenant of Civil and Political Rights," General Assembly resolution 2200A (XXI), December 16, 1966. This covenant entered into force in 1976.

38. See International Council on Human Rights Policy, *Human Rights After September 11* (Versoix, Switzerland: International Council on Human Rights Policy, 2002).

39. See Subrata Roy Chowdhury, *The Rule of Law in a State of Emergency* (London: Francis Pinter, 1989).

40. For a recent definition of crimes against humanity, see Article 7 of the Rome Statute for an International Criminal Court, 1998. Text in *International Legal Materials,* 37 (1999): 1004–1005. On the evolution of the concept, see M. Cherif Bassiouni, *Crimes against Humanity in International Criminal Law,* 2nd ed. (The Hague: Kluwer, 1999).

41. See also Danesh Sarooshi, *The United Nations and the Development of Collective Security: The Delegation by the UN Security Council of its Chapter VII Powers* (Oxford: Oxford University Press, 1999).

42. See also Jost Delbrück, "The Fight against Global Terrorism: Self-Defense or Collective Security as International Police Action? Some Comments on the International Legal Implications of the 'War Against Terrorism,'" *German Yearbook of International Law* 44 (2001): 20–22. See also Cassese, "Terrorism Is Also Disrupting Some Legal Categories of International Law."

43. *I.C.J. Reports 1986,* 50–54, paragraphs 106–117.

44. *I.C.J. Reports 1980,* 36, paragraph 74.

45. ICTY, *Prosecutor* v. *Tadić,* Case IT-94-1, Appeals Chamber, 1999, published in *International Legal Materials* 38 (1999): 1546, paragraph 145. Emphasis added.

46. See *Report of the International Law Commission, Fifty-Third Session* (A/56/10), October 30, 2001, 103–109. On December 12, 2001, the General Assembly took note of the draft articles as submitted by its International Law Commission ("Responsibility of States for Internationally Wrongful Acts," A/RES/56/83). See also James Crawford, *The International Law Commission's Draft Articles on State Responsibility—Introduction, Text and Commentaries* (Cambridge: Cambridge University Press, 2002), 110–113.

47. See A/CONF.192/15, July 20, 2001.

48. S/RES/1467, March 18, 2003.

49. See also Article 26 of the UN Charter charging the Security Council with the responsibility to establish a system for the regulation of armaments. So far, this article has remained mainly a dead letter. See Hans-Joachim Schütz, "Article 26," in Bruno Simma, ed., *The Charter of the United Nations: A Commentary* (Oxford: Oxford University Press, 2002), 464–475.

50. See also Delbrück, "The Fight against Global Terrorism," 23–24.

51. See *Report of the International Conference on Financing for Development* (A/CONF.198), available online at http://ods-dds-ny.un.org/doc/UNDOC/GEN/N02/392/67/PDF/N0239267.pdf?OpenElement; and *Report of the World Summit on Sustainable Development* (A/CONF.199/20), available online at http://ods-dds-ny.un.org/doc/UNDOC/GEN/N02/636/93/PDF/N0263693.pdf?OpenElement.

52. "Transcript of Press Conference by President Jacques Chirac of France and Secretary-General Kofi Annan at Headquarters, 19 September 2001." Available online at http://www.un.org/News/Press/docs/2001/sgsm7964.doc.htm.

53. See George Abi-Saab, "The Proper Role of International Law in Combating Terrorism," *Chinese Journal of International Law* 1, no. 1 (2002): 305–327. For a different but thought-provoking view, see Anne-Marie Slaughter and William Burke-White, "An International Constitutional Moment," *Harvard International Law Journal* 43, no. 1 (Winter 2002): 1–21.

4

The U.S., Counterterrorism, and the Prospects for a Multilateral Alternative

Edward C. Luck

It is common wisdom, at least in Western Europe, that Washington's response to the terrorist attacks of September 11, 2001, has confirmed its penchant for unilateralism and its disdain for multilateral processes and institutions. Three-quarters of the respondents to an April 2002 Pew Research Center survey of the four major European countries agreed that in the fight against terrorism "the US is acting mainly on its own interests" rather than "taking into account the interests of its allies."[1] No less a personality than Chris Patten, the European Union's (EU) commissioner for external affairs, warned against Washington's "unilateralist urge" that allegedly holds that "multilateralism is for wimps." The military success in Afghanistan, in his view, "has perhaps reinforced some dangerous instincts: that the projection of military power is the only basis of true security; that the US can rely only on itself; and that allies may be useful as an optional extra but that the US is big and strong enough to manage without them if it must."[2] Such caricatures build on prevalent European skepticism of America's handling of the Arab-Israeli conflict, the war in Afghanistan, and the situation in Iraq.[3]

Both the predilections of the Bush administration and precedents set by earlier administrations would have predicted a predominantly unilateral U.S. response to the terrorist challenge. This administration came into office with a decidedly harsh view of the doctrine of "assertive multilateralism" that was espoused, at times, by the Clinton administration. Its rejection of the Kyoto Protocol on greenhouse gases, the ABM treaty, and the International Criminal Court (ICC) served as a rude rebuke to the kind of international legal and institutional architecture so favored by allies and much of the developing world. In August 2001, prior to the terrorist assault, the Pew Research Center found more than three-quarters of the respondents from Britain, France, Germany, and Italy concurring—as they did when asked the same question eight months later—that President Bush "makes decisions based entirely on U.S. interests."[4] Would not an administration that had demonstrated so little confidence in multilateral arrangements—reportedly seeing them as weak, slow, and fickle— be apt to give them the cold shoulder when it came to meeting such a direct threat to U.S. national security? And would not the temptation to cast diplomacy aside in favor of relying on America's unsurpassed military capabilities prove irresistible, as Patten had cautioned it would?

In looking at the mix of unilateral and multilateral elements in U.S. counterterrorism policies since the horrific events of September 11, this chapter finds a far more calibrated and nuanced response than these simplistic critiques would suggest. Rather than always following its ideological predispositions, the Bush administration's policy choices have been guided primarily by its perceptions of the nature and extent of the threat and of the range and quality of the various policy options available. Its responses, by and large, appear no more unilateralist than those of previous administrations that had to confront terrorist threats, nor was it alone in believing that the possible contributions of the United Nations would be largely confined to the diplomatic and political realms. Modest views of the world body's potential were widely expressed in the scholarly counterterrorism literature long before September 2001. Other countries have been just as reluctant to entrust their defense against terrorism to the UN and other multilateral mechanisms. Nevertheless, the very gravity of the threat to U.S. national security required the Bush administration to set aside some of its ideological baggage and to tone down appeals to more conservative constituencies in the interest of building, domestically and internationally, as broad an anti-terrorist coalition as possible. In the end, it has been sober rationality, not political preference, that has led the administration to give multilateral alternatives greater weight in this issue area than in most others.[5] As much as anything, it has been the political and structural weaknesses of multilateral mechanisms in the field of counterterrorism that have constrained their utilization in this campaign.

At the same time, however, the efforts of the Bush administration to invoke multilateral support for the war on terrorism have been undermined by a series of self-inflicted disabilities. While Washington has talked a lot about the potential role of the UN and other multilateral instruments, it has done far less to provide them with the wherewithal to carry out expanded counterterrorism activities. This ambivalence has also been reflected in its garbled public diplomacy. President George W. Bush and his top advisors appear to have cast their public statements about the potential role of international institutions rather differently for domestic and international audiences. Concerns about the consistency and priorities of U.S. policy have been further fueled by the well-publicized and sometimes public debates among the president's key advisors. Finally, as the skepticism expressed by European critics attests, it is difficult for allies to embrace Washington's desire for multilateral assistance in these matters when it continues to actively oppose their attempts to expand multilateral cooperation in other areas.

Before commencing the analysis, it would be helpful to address some questions of definition that have plagued the unilateralist-multilateralist debate. Some commentators claim that Washington is acting as a unilateralist when it pursues its notion of its national interests in international fora when other countries perceive their interests differently. The U.S. is said to be acting unilaterally, for example, when it dissents from language or provisions that most other states find to be acceptable in the negotiation of a multilateral convention, such as on land mines, the rights of the child, reducing greenhouse gases, or the Rome Statute to establish the International Criminal Court. In such cases, however, it would seem to be more accurate to label Washington's stance "exceptional."[6] Its views may well set it apart from other countries from time to time, its domestic politics may sometimes reward its representatives for going it alone, and its size, traditions, and domestic orientation may make it easier for it to withstand pressures to conform. So the U.S. will act in distinct ways. In general, when what makes it distinct is the substantive content of its policies, it is exceptional. When it is a question of process that sets it apart— that is, when it chooses to act on its own without consulting widely beforehand or seeking to build a broader coalition—then it is indeed acting as a unilateralist. For the purposes of this paper, therefore, the distinction between "unilateral" and "multilateral" will refer to the characteristics of the policy option chosen, not to the nature of the interests pursued through it.[7]

The unilateral-multilateral dichotomy tends to distort our understanding in two other ways as well. First, much of foreign policy is conducted between states, not among them. This has certainly been true of Washington's post–September 11 counterterrorism policies. When one state reaches out to engage the cooperation of a second one, should this be considered a unilateral or multilateral gesture or should it be considered a third category? Multilateral cooperation, after all, is often built one state at a time. At the same time, the content of the bilateral initiative may be coercive or designed to weaken support for a broader multilateral institution or norm, such as the U.S. threat to withhold security assistance to states that ratify the ICC and do not exempt its servicemen from its provisions. Here, the intent and the pattern of a bilateral interaction matter. Second, a wide range of policy options fall on a continuum between the purely unilateral and purely multilateral poles. Most states pick and choose among them as needed, with the relative proportions varying from case to case, time to time, and state to state. Given the urgency of counterterrorism these days, what matters most is which strategy gets the job done as efficiently, as assuredly, and as durably as possible. The latter objective would seem to be suggestive of the value of those international norms and institutions that give the war on terrorism a broader, more global, and more sustainable character.

The remainder of this chapter is divided into three sections, followed by a brief conclusion. The first addresses the strategic and institutional framework that shaped Washington's policy choices after September 11. Particular attention is devoted to growing power asymmetries and to factors conditioning the UN's utility as a vehicle for counterterrorism. The next section relates some of the historical forces and conceptual assumptions that have helped shape U.S. counterterrorism doctrine through the years. The penultimate section, which describes the core initiatives undertaken by the Bush administration after September 2001, finds little basis for the complaint that Washington's approach has been excessively unilateralist. The conclusion suggests that the complaints may relate more to what the Bush administration has not done than to what it has done, and it makes some modest proposals for recasting the transatlantic policy debate. Among these is the need to bolster multilateral capacities so that they will offer more viable and attractive policy alternatives in the future.

The Strategic, Political, and Institutional Context

Neither the U.S. policy choices about how to respond to the terrorist attacks nor the way other countries have evaluated Washington's response can be fully understood without reference to the strategic, political, and institutional framework within which these events have been unfolding. To this end, five factors seem particularly apt: the growing gap between U.S. capabilities, particularly for the projection of military power, and those of other countries; persistent differences in both policy preferences and public attitudes on related issues; the degree to which other countries have employed multilateral or unilateral means to deal with terrorist threats; the way that counterterrorism experts, inside and outside of governments, have viewed the appropriate role for the UN and other multilateral institutions; and the institutional challenges that the struggle against terrorism poses for the UN and other international organizations.

The most obvious and widely noted feature of early-twenty-first-century geopolitics is the growing disparity between the United States and other countries in every traditional measure of national power.[8] Dominance is particularly striking in military affairs, specifically in technology and in the capacity to project and sustain a sizeable and potent force far from home. This is due in part to long-established differences in geography and doctrine and in part to differences in relative willingness to invest heavily in defense preparations since the demise of the Cold War. These discrepancies give Washington a series of policy options that are not open to other capitals. U.S. policymakers, at least in the view of others, may be more prone to think of military responses because they have the capacity to carry them out, whether unilaterally or by assembling a coalition, as in the Iraq war. Others naturally prefer policy options that play to their diplomatic, political, and economic strengths and that will give them a greater voice in determining the course of events.

While it is reassuring that other major countries have apparently been sufficiently comfortable with the way Washington has used its military advantages not to seek to challenge them by engaging in an expensive and fruitless post–Cold War arms race, that comfort level is bound to ebb to the extent that the U.S. is perceived to be forsaking broad consultations and multilateral mechanisms in favor of unilateral go-it-alone strategies. The power disparities, moreover, offer one explanation for differences about the place of international institutions in dealing with threats to peace and security. As one would expect, the dominant military power tends to see the resort to multilateral security institutions as an option rather than as an obligation, as much a potential constraint on its policy choices as a force multiplier. For others, however, international rules and processes offer the best available means both of harnessing the capacities of the dominant power to common purposes and of keeping it from intervening unilaterally in the affairs of others.

Americans, moreover, tend to see the world, and especially international institutions, in distinct ways. Their collective and individual ambivalence toward global organizations has deep roots in the American experience, political culture, and constitutional system.[9] It is a product, as well, of the historic divide within the American body politic between skeptics and enthusiasts of international organization. The U.S. stance on particular substantive issues of relevance to terrorism—such as those relating to the Middle East and Iraq—also tends to set it apart from its partners in Western Europe and Japan. According to summer 2002 polling by the Chicago Council on Foreign Relations and the German Marshall Fund of the United States, Americans are more likely than Europeans to see terrorism as a critical threat and to favor "hard" over "soft" instruments to counter terrorism.[10]

The attacks of September 2001 and the subsequent war in Afghanistan did serve to make Americans more internationalist, but hardly in ways that would narrow the gap on substantive issues with their allies. A comparison of Pew surveys of Americans taken the month before and the month after the attacks showed growing support for Israel's position in its conflict with the Palestinians, for increases in U.S. defense spending, and for the deployment of a national missile defense, coupled with a lower priority after the terrorist attacks to global issues such as HIV/AIDS, hunger, and global warming.[11] Tellingly, in an April 2002 Pew poll, 90 percent of Western Europeans but only 53 percent of Americans approved of President Bush's decision to increase assistance to poor countries, while a majority of Americans and only about one-quarter of Western Europeans approved of his labeling Iraq, Iran, and North Korea an "axis of evil."[12]

The United States, moreover, is hardly the first country to have sought to deal with terrorist threats, at least in part, through unilateral action. Japan, China, Western Europe, Sri Lanka, South Korea, Israel, and Pakistan have not forsaken unilateral responses or turned to the UN as the principal source of assistance in their hours of need following terrorist attacks. Following the October 1983 truck-bomb assaults on U.S. and French troops in the Multinational Force (MNF) in Beirut, France was the first to respond, with an air attack on the bases near Baalbek of a pro-Iranian militia thought to be responsible for the Beirut attacks.[13] India has successfully opposed UN or multilateral involvement in its efforts to overcome terrorist activities related to Kashmir, just as Russia has insisted that the conduct of its war in Chechnya is no one else's business and the United Kingdom has kept the UN out of Northern Ireland. Each defines its terrorist problem as essentially a domestic or localized matter, even when the arms, material, funds, recruitment, and training that fuel it cross borders and even regions. As a general rule, therefore, states prefer to set their own terms for dealing with terrorists, turning to friendly states or functional arrangements for assistance as needed while avoiding the uncertainties of global political fora in most such situations.

Policymakers and diplomats have not been the only ones to see a limited operational role for the UN and other multilateral institutions in the struggle against terrorism. Scholars and policy analysts have virtually ignored the world body in this context, other than as a place to negotiate additional legal constraints or, at times, to provide political backing for national responses. Martha Crenshaw, a longtime student of terrorism, explains this "neglect" by the focus of scholarship on explaining terrorism, by the parochialism of the field, and by the failure of specialists in international relations, foreign policy, and security studies to take terrorism seriously before September 11 as well as by shortcomings in the UN's approach to terrorism. According to her, "a quick non-definitive review of the post-1995 content of the major journal in the field, *Terrorism and Political Violence,* reveals no articles dealing specifically with the UN or with the general subject of international cooperation."[14] In essence, while the scholarly fields of international organization and terrorism studies are both well developed, there has been remarkably little overlap or exchange between them. Prior to September 2001, most experts on the UN paid scant attention to terrorism, and vice versa.

It is not that students of terrorism have foreclosed the possibility of a multilateral response; it is just that they have tended to dismiss its prospects for making a real difference. The view of Paul R. Pillar, a veteran counterterrorism specialist at the Central Intelligence Agency (CIA), is typical: "The counterterrorist diplomacy that matters most is bilateral. . . . In general, the larger the gathering to address terrorism, the less effective it has been."[15] Ruing the General Assembly's sympathy for "national liberation movements" in the 1970s as "the nadir of effectiveness," he complains that even in North Atlantic Treaty Organization (NATO), "the limits to what can be accomplished are set by the state that is least willing to cooperate."[16] Like Crenshaw, Pillar nevertheless finds some uses for multilateral diplomacy through providing support for U.S. efforts, as in Libya; codifying norms; and setting standards for cooperation in certain subjects. The overall message from the specialists, however, has been unambiguous: multilateral approaches, at best, can serve as a supplement to national power and actions. This message has only served to reinforce the existing mind-set among national policymakers in Washington and in other capitals as well. Whether policymakers have influenced the approach of scholars or vice versa, clearly those advocating a central place for multilateral institutions in the war on terrorism have a tough case to make.

The United Nations itself has been anything but enthusiastic about taking on a larger role in countering terrorism, nor has it done much to encourage the member states to have confidence in its capacity to handle such issues competently and fairly. The ambivalence on both sides of this equation is understandable. Terrorism is a topic that is easily politicized—in fact, that is often what the terrorists are seeking. When terrorist tactics are justified as the tool of the weak against the strong, that claim strikes a responsive chord in many parts of the developing world (and apparently among a number of leftist intellectuals and commentators in Western Europe as well).[17] Few bodies are as inherently political, and as easily politicized, as the United Nations. The difficulty the world body continues to have in treating the issues of the Middle East in a balanced and fair manner reflects this underlying problem, as does the assembly's inability to agree on a definition of terrorism even after September 11.[18]

For all the UN's progress in helping to codify a dozen global conventions related to various dimensions of terrorism—no mean feat in the absence of consensus on what the term itself means—it has only sporadically shown any interest in trying to implement their provisions. To scholars of terrorism, according to Crenshaw, "there appeared to be no penalties for non-compliance. Nor were there concrete rewards for cooperation."[19] This could have been said for almost all issues, not just terrorism, during the Cold War years, when the Security Council rarely agreed on enforcement measures. This changed after the collapse of the Soviet Union, however, and the council began to pass Chapter VII enforcement resolutions with unprecedented, even excessive, regularity. The will of states to carry out effective enforcement measures, however, generally lagged far behind their readiness to vote for them.

During the 1990s, for the first time, the council agreed on diplomatic, travel, arms, and/or economic sanctions on three countries—Libya, the Sudan, and Afghanistan—for their alleged support of terrorist groups and activities.[20] It took seven years, from 1992 to 1999, but Libya eventually complied with the Security Council's demand that it turn over the two suspects in the bombing of Pan Am flight 103 and UTA flight 772. In the meantime, the Organization of African Unity (OAU), meeting at the summit level, urged its member states in 1998 to ignore the council-imposed travel ban to Libya.[21] Nevertheless, despite uneven compliance, the UN sanctions are generally credited with being one of a number of factors—including pressure from the major powers—that persuaded Muammar Qaddafi to give up the two suspects for an international trial. The diplomatic sanctions on the Sudan may have served as a signal to the leadership in Khartoum of international concern, but the precise effects in such cases are hard to identify or measure. In Afghanistan, the Taliban regime evidently found Osama bin Laden to be more persuasive than the Security Council, though flouting the latter's edicts no doubt furthered its isolation and bolstered support for the U.S.-led intervention.

Terrorism has also posed a conceptual puzzle for the United Nations and, to a lesser extent, other intergovernmental organs. The UN was founded to forestall war between states, not to protect them from shadowy, ill-defined, and fluid groups of a vaguely transnational character that lack any known structure, affiliation, or address. The world body has adapted to dealing with many forms of intrastate and transnational conflict, so long as the disputes have some geographical definition, some material or political agenda, and some prospect of being swayed by the inducements, incentives, sanctions, and threats that could be wielded by its member states. When terrorist actions are taken to further an identifiable political cause, as has been the case in the Middle East, Kashmir, and Sri Lanka, then international efforts to resolve the larger conflict and to delegitimize the terrorist activities—both goals to which the UN can sometimes make a useful contribution—can make a difference.

It is less clear, though, how—other than through sanctions—the UN should respond to groups, such as Al Qaeda, that reject all the values that the UN stands for: human rights, tolerance, rule of law, democratic values, cooperation among established governments, and the peaceful resolution of differences. It is not surprising, then, that Al Qaeda has dismissed the UN's liberal international-ist agenda and identified the organization and its secretary-general as among its chief enemies. This has been discomforting for some in an organization that has long sought to be liked, or at least tolerated, by all sides and that had not pronounced any doctrine or strategy for dealing with terrorism prior to Sep-tember 2001.[22] Though Secretary-General Kofi Annan has been outspoken at times about the unacceptability of terrorist acts, others within the UN worry that with its higher profile on these issues, the organization has been moving up the list of possible terrorist targets.

The awkwardness of these issues for the UN—member states and Secre-tariat alike—is reflected in the primitive state of its bureaucratic preparations to play an active part in the war on terrorism. It took more than a year after the September 11 attacks for the Secretariat to propose and for the General Assembly to approve any new outlays or posts related to countering terror-ism. The Vienna-based Terrorism Prevention Branch (TPB)—a misnomer by any standard and the only unit in the Secretariat devoted to terrorism—had consisted of two mid-level professionals (a P-5 and a P-4).[23] After some squab-bling, in December 2002 the assembly's Fifth Committee finally approved a less-than-impressive increment of three professionals and two support staff, as the secretary-general had requested more than five months before. The Office for Drug Control and Crime Prevention (ODCCP) within which the TPB is housed, in contrast, has about 400 posts, including sixteen that out-rank that of the head of the TPB.[24]

The Security Council's new Counter-Terrorism Committee (CTC), which, as discussed below, is playing a useful and unprecedented role in encouraging member states to inventory their own executive and legislative preparations for countering terrorism, is staffed by a small team of experts hired on a temporary basis via the fund for special political missions rather than through the regular budget. The notion of a UN trust fund to help those member states needing assistance to upgrade their counterterrorism capacities, an idea once champi-oned by the first chair of the CTC—Jeremy Greenstock, the permanent repre-sentative of the United Kingdom—has been abandoned. He complained that, in terms of Secretariat support, "as a new operation, the CTC tends to be allo-cated the resources that are left over when everything else has been covered."[25] The Department of Political Affairs (DPA) has been designated the UN system's focal point for meeting the terrorist threat, but it has yet to establish an office for this purpose, to receive any new staff, or to reassign existing ones to meet this new mandate on other than a part-time basis.

Claims that the events of September 11 changed the world find little nourishment in the UN's response. For those who felt that the UN would just get in the way of the war on terrorism, it is just as well that its response, outside of the secretary-general's use of his bully pulpit and the work of the CTC, has been so feeble. But for those who insist that the U.S. has been too unilateralist, these developments (or lack of them) pose a deeper dilemma, for they raise doubts about whether an adequate multilateral alternative exists and, if not, what would be required to create one. The reluctance to invest in steps to strengthen multilateral capacities to prevent or respond to terrorist acts also suggests that the complaints about U.S. unilateralism have less to do with developing an effective multilateral response than with giving more countries a say in deciding how the war on terrorism will be conducted.

The U.S. and Terrorism prior to September 2001

To claim that the U.S. response to September 11 has been shaped by an unusual degree of militarism and unilateralism because of its increasingly dominant position in the world and the conservative politics of the Bush administration, one would need to demonstrate that Washington's counterterrorism strategies before the attacks were markedly more prone to use diplomacy and multilateral machinery. In fact, there is little evidence that this was the case. Almost two decades ago, Secretary of State George P. Shultz outlined the Reagan administration's strategy in "the war against terrorism."[26] It stressed preemption, unpredictability, surprise, and the unfettered use of military force as needed to strike at terrorists. These are precisely the elements, of course, that have most disturbed critics of the "new" Bush doctrine. In Shultz's view, "the rule of law is congenial to action against terrorism," and he urged, presciently, the employment of international sanctions "to isolate, weaken, or punish states that sponsor terrorism against us." At other points, U.S. permanent representatives to the UN William A. Scranton and Vernon Walters defended the "well-established right" to use military force to protect its nationals threatened by terrorists "where the state in whose territory they are located either is unwilling or unable to protect them" or "in very narrow counterterrorism cases" to intercept a civilian aircraft thought to be carrying terrorists.[27] The U.S. did the latter following the hijacking of the *Achille Lauro* in 1986, and the Carter administration tried to use force to extricate the U.S. hostages in Tehran in 1980, after having failed to get Security Council approval of sanctions against Iran.

U.S. strategies for countering terrorism have never relied heavily on multilateral approaches, and the policies of the Clinton and Bush administrations in that regard have a good deal more in common than either would care to admit. Over the past two decades, U.S. forces, facilities, and citizens have been the target of international terrorist assaults scores of times, more often than those of any other major power. On only four occasions, however, did the U.S. retaliate with a military strike against the terrorists or their state sponsors. In some cases this reflected self-imposed restraint, in others uncertainty about the perpetrators or their whereabouts, and in others the existence of more appropriate and promising courses of action. In only one of the four cases did Washington seek the backing of the Security Council prior to its military response, since its consistent position has been that it has ample justification under international law, including under Article 51 of the UN Charter, to pursue those who have assaulted its territory and/or citizens. That one case, of course, was the Bush administration's response to the attacks of September 2001.

Of the other three solely unilateral military retaliations, two were by the Clinton administration and one by the Reagan administration. In response to the April 1986 bombing of a Berlin nightclub packed with off-duty U.S. soldiers, President Reagan ordered a large-scale bombing raid of military installations in Libya and one of Qaddafi's homes there. Though this unilateral action was widely criticized around the world, many in the counterterrorism community believe that it had a more profound impact on Qaddafi's retreat from terrorism than did the multilateral course of UN sanctions and international diplomatic pressures pursued after the bombing of Pan Am flight 103. A 1990 presidential commission established by President George H. W. Bush to investigate the latter incident urged the U.S. to launch "pre-emptive or retaliatory military strikes" against known terrorists and the states that harbor them.[28] Ten years later, the National Commission on Terrorism expressed frustration with what it called the law enforcement approach to counterterrorism. In the Lockerbie case, it concluded, "prosecuting and punishing two low-level operatives for an act almost certainly directed by Qaddafi is a hollow victory."[29] At the same time, the involvement of Libyan agents in the downing of Pan Am flight 103 two and a half years after the bombing raid on Libya suggests that the latter's deterrent effect was delayed at best.

For all its rhetoric about "assertive multilateralism," the Clinton administration resorted to unilateral military retaliation within its first six months in office. On June 26, 1993—ironically, UN Charter Day—U.S. cruise missiles struck the headquarters of Iraqi intelligence in response to evidence that Iraq had tried to assassinate former President Bush. Asserting its right to "the exercise of self defense in such cases," the Clinton administration requested an emergency meeting of the Security Council, but only after the strike on Baghdad was completed.[30] It had been carefully targeted and timed at night to minimize civilian casualties, but whether it had any dampening effect on terrorism against the United States was questionable. The World Trade Center was bombed later that year, the Riyadh and Khubar Tower attacks on U.S. forces in Saudi Arabia followed in 1995 and 1996, and the U.S. embassies in Nairobi and Dar es Salaam were destroyed in 1998.

To retaliate for the embassy bombings, the Clinton administration again chose a unilateral cruise missile attack, this time on Osama bin Laden's training camps in Afghanistan and a Sudanese pharmaceutical plant suspected of aiding in the production of chemical weapons. Once again, the strikes were widely criticized by other capitals, and their ultimate effects on deterring Osama bin Laden were doubtful, given his subsequent involvement in the October 2000 attack on the USS *Cole* and in the events of September 11 of the following year. In his speech to the American people, President Clinton invoked neither Article 51 nor international law to justify the U.S. action.[31] When he addressed the General Assembly the next month on terrorism, President Clinton avoided any reference to the Security Council or to a political or security role for the United Nations—two big omissions when speaking in the General Assembly Hall.[32]

The declaratory policy of the Clinton administration, especially after the embassy bombings, also foreshadowed that of its successor. The terrorists, warned Secretary of State Madeleine K. Albright, "have basically declared war on all Americans."[33] Clinton, like his successor, also saw this as a Manichaean struggle between good and evil, telling the American people that "this will be a long, ongoing struggle between freedom and fanaticism, between the rule of law and terrorism."[34] With the cruise missile attacks, one journalist was inspired to declare that President Clinton had "launched a new War on Terrorism."[35] Accordingly, U.S. expenditures to combat terrorism rose from $6.1 billion in FY 1998 to $9.7 billion in FY 2001; $10.3 billion was requested for FY 2002.[36] Clearly, the fiscal and political foundations for President Bush's war on terrorism were laid long before September 2001 and well before his inauguration.

But if unilateral military responses to terrorism have had such an uncertain record, why do successive administrations keep resorting to them as the most visible component of their counterterrorism strategies? One part of the answer is public opinion. According to Philip B. Heymann, "[I]n the aftermath of our bombing of Libya, only 30 percent of those interviewed by a *Washington Post/ ABC* poll believed that our action would reduce terrorism, but 76 percent approved of the bombing."[37] Retaliation, seen as punishment for those responsible for killing innocent American civilians, serves a clear emotional and political purpose at home, whatever its effects on terrorists abroad.[38] A 1998 survey by the Chicago Council on Foreign Relations is particularly instructive in that regard. Generally the survey found a marked preference for multilateral co-operation to deal with a wide range of issues and a reluctance to deploy U.S. troops abroad. In fact, the only scenario in which a majority of the public favored using ground troops was against terrorist training camps.[39] About three-quarters, moreover, approved of U.S. airstrikes "against terrorist train-ing camps and other facilities." Taken after the embassy bombings, the survey found that concern over the threat of terrorism had grown substantially since a similar poll in 1994. The results also suggested that this is a bottom-up phe-nomenon, as the "public" respondents showed a keener sensitivity to the ter-rorist threat than did the "leaders" group on several questions. A quick review of other surveys since the mid-1980s also reveals steady majorities in favor of military strikes against terrorists and the countries that shield them. It may be, as critics have charged, that the U.S. is too ready to resort to military op-tions in response to terrorism. But if so, this is neither a new phenomenon nor one tied uniquely to Republican administrations.

The U.S. Responds

Accounts of President Bush's thinking and of his deliberations with his top advisors in the hours following the terrorist assaults of September 11, 2001, suggest that the global dimensions and dynamics of their policy choices were much on their minds from the very beginning. Apparently Bush was well aware of the critiques of his alleged unilateralist leanings and of his low poll ratings in Western Europe. In a series of interviews with Bob Woodward of the *Wash-ington Post* in 2001 and 2002, he repeatedly returned to the resentments of other countries, to America's unique leadership position, and to the uni-lateralist charges. "I know the world is watching carefully," he commented, but others "would be impressed and will be impressed with results achieved."[40] In his view, "[C]onfident action that will yield positive results provides kind of a slipstream into which reluctant nations and leaders can get behind." Ac-cording to Bush, "[P]eople respect us, but they like to tweak us. . . . People respect America and they love our values, but they look for every excuse in the world to say that, because we don't do exactly what, you know, the inter-national community wanted, we became unilateralist."[41] He went on to la-ment that no one knew "what it's like to have a commander in chief tested under fire like this."

Given these concerns, it is understandable that the twin themes of being tested and of seeking international support and understanding surfaced re-peatedly in the president's initial public and private statements. He concluded his first televised remarks, at Barksdale Air Force Base in Louisiana just three

hours after the terrorist attacks, by declaring that "the resolve of our great nation is being tested, but make no mistake: We will show the world that we will
pass this test."[42] That night, he noted in his daily diary that "my hope is that this
will provide an opportunity to rally the world against terrorism."[43] According
to the *Washington Post*, President Bush told his advisers that first evening that
"the crisis was not only a challenge but also an opportunity, a chance to change
relationships with many countries."[44] And in his speech the next day, he told the
nation that "we will rally the world." When his speechwriters proposed referring to "our way of life" in that address, reportedly it was the president who
inserted the phrase "and to all nations that love freedom."

The effort to build a broad-based international coalition against terrorism, moreover, commenced less than twenty-four hours after the attacks. One
of the president's first acts on his first full day back in the White House was an
early morning call to British Prime Minister Tony Blair, in which they agreed
to seek NATO and UN support. This was followed by two calls to President
Vladimir Putin of Russia, and one each to President Jacques Chirac of France,
Chancellor Gerhard Schröder of Germany, Prime Minister Jean Chrétien of
Canada, and President Jiang Zemin of China. As the president told the *Washington Post*, "[M]y attitude all along was, if we have to go it alone, we'll go it
alone; but I'd rather not."[45] When the National Security Council (NSC) convened that afternoon, one of the principal items on its agenda was the nature
of the coalition. According to the *Washington Post*, "[E]veryone believed that
a coalition would be essential, particularly to keep international opinion behind the United States." Though the president was confident "that the right-
ness of the cause would bring other nations along," he had no doubts about
the nation's absolute right to defend itself "no matter what others thought."
All agreed, moreover, "that the coalition should be a means to wiping out
terrorism, not an end in itself."[46] Ten days after the attacks, the president reportedly told an NSC meeting that the war against terrorism "requires a coalition, it can't be done without one."[47]

President Bush and his aides did not see any inherent contradiction between the vigorous but measured use of military force and the effort to gain
multilateral support for the struggle against terrorism. In fact, they believed
that a strong, persistent, and determined U.S. response was essential for sustaining international support and participation. In late October, as the Afghanistan campaign was unfolding, Bush reportedly was advised by a European
leader that the key to a durable coalition was to hold many consultations and
to demonstrate responsiveness to the views of others in the group. He apparently replied that he was convinced that "the best way that we hold this coalition together is to be clear on our objectives and to be clear that we are

determined to achieve them. You hold a coalition together by strong leadership and that's what we intend to provide."[48] To him, the key is "being clear that we are going to win."[49]

This would require, in his view, a much more concerted military response than his predecessor had attempted. "The antiseptic notion of launching a cruise missile into some guy's, you know, tent, really is a joke," asserted the president, "I mean, people viewed that as the impotent America . . . of a flaccid, you know, kind of technology competent but not very tough country. . . . It was clear that bin Laden felt emboldened and didn't feel threatened by the United States."[50] There was never any question in the administration, moreover, about the notion that the U.S. was at war with terrorism. As the president told the *Washington Post*, his initial thought on hearing of the terrorist strikes was that "they had declared war on us, and I made up my mind at that moment that we were going to war."

But what kind of a war did the administration envision? Did the use of the rhetoric and image of war suggest that the critics' worries about a militaristic America were well founded? On September 12, President Bush cautioned that "the American people want a big bang. . . . I have to convince them that this is a war that will be fought with many steps." He underlined that "I don't want a photo-op war."[51] As he confided to the *Washington Post*, he "instinctively knew that we were going to have to think differently" about how to fight terrorists. In a phone conversation as the president flew back to Washington on the fateful day, Secretary of Defense Donald Rumsfeld contended that a war on terrorism must use every tool available—legal, financial, diplomatic, and intelligence— not just military ones.[52] On September 20, in his first post-attack address to the Congress and the American people, President Bush asserted that "we will direct every resource at our command—every means of diplomacy, every tool of intelligence, every instrument of law enforcement, every financial influence, and every necessary weapon of war—to the disruption and to the defeat of the global terror network."[53]

He and his advisors were convinced not only that this was war but that this was an unambiguously just and moral war in which all but a few rogue nations had an important stake. Whatever the surveys of Western European opinion indicated about the pursuit of unilateral U.S. interests through the war on terrorism, Washington policymakers appear to have made little distinction between U.S. and global interests in this area. Noting that the citizens of eighty other nations had lost their lives in the attacks,[54] the president noted that this is not "just America's fight. And what is at stake is not just America's freedom. This is the world's fight. This is civilization's fight. This is the fight of all who believe in progress and pluralism, tolerance and freedom. We ask every nation to join us." In classic collective security terms, he declared that "an attack on one is an attack on all. The civilized world is rallying to America's side." Warning that "we will pursue nations that provide aid or safe haven to terrorism," President Bush stressed that "every nation, in every region, now has a decision to make. Either you are with us, or you are with the terrorists." While this stark approach no doubt made a number of capitals uncomfortable, especially because multilateral diplomacy generally features shades of gray, it did flow both from the administration's wartime mentality and from the high priority assigned to building a reliable and truly working coalition. Washington policymakers wanted to know on whom they could count in a crunch situation.[55]

Several pieces of evidence suggest that the administration's concern about gaining broader international support for the war on terrorism extended well beyond the level of rhetoric. It moved quickly to convince Congress to fill three glaring gaps in U.S. policies toward the UN: the approval of $582 million in arrears payments promised in the December 2000 agreement among UN member states on the adjustment of assessment scales, the Senate confirmation of John Negroponte to be permanent representative to the world body, and the holding of hearings and eventual Senate consent to ratification of the International Convention for the Suppression of Terrorist Bombings and the International Convention for the Suppression of the Financing of Terrorism. It welcomed the quick and unanimous resolutions of the General Assembly and Security Council condemning the terrorist strikes and worked hard to ensure that Security Council resolution 1373, which established the Counter-Terrorism Committee, both had teeth and achieved unanimity among the council members. The CTC was given the essential task of identifying where the efforts of individual member states to deny individuals or groups the funds, support, shelter, space, or movement required to carry out terrorist acts need patching and to match up these needs with the states or institutions that could assist with such capacity-building.

The U.S., in addition, pursued a series of multilateral avenues outside the UN system to further these ends. For example, less than two weeks after the attacks, President Bush announced that in terms of tracking the money flow, "[W]e're working with friends and allies throughout the world to share information. We're working closely with the United Nations, the EU and through the G-7/G-8 structure to limit the ability of terrorist organizations to take advantage of the international financial systems."[56] With U.S. encouragement, the G-8 undertook a broad range of cooperative efforts to counter terrorism, and the U.S. and EU enhanced their information-sharing and targeting of terrorists and their supporters, their law enforcement cooperation, and their nonproliferation export-control assistance to third countries.[57] By the end of October, the Financial Action Task Force on Money Laundering had prepared eight special recommendations on terrorist financing.[58] NATO, in an unprecedented move, declared the attack on the United States to be an attack on all its members under the terms of Article V of its charter. And Secretary of State Colin Powell reported to the Security Council that "every single regional and subregional organization represented at this world body condemned the attacks."[59]

Indeed, as these examples suggest, the Bush administration made a full-court press to gain the support of multilateral institutions for the war on terrorism. This went far beyond window dressing, because Washington policymakers recognized that a number of the key fronts in this war—especially those related to denial of the means to carry out acts of terrorism, and dissuasion—had to be handled through some form of multilateral cooperation, whether through established institutions or through ad hoc arrangements. As the president told the General Assembly in November, "[T]he conspiracies of terror are being answered by an expanding global coalition. Not every nation will be part of every action against the enemy. But every nation in our coalition has duties."[60] This notion of creating what presidential aides called the "variable geometry" of coalitions was first voiced in an NSC meeting the day after the attacks by Secretary of State Powell and then endorsed by Secretary of Defense Rumsfeld, who called for a "coalition of coalitions."[61] Citing Security Council Resolution 1373 in some detail, President Bush told the General Assembly in his November speech that "the most basic obligations in this new conflict have already been defined by the United Nations."

Though clearly gratified that the UN had laid down such an unambiguous legal and moral foundation for the war on terrorism, the administration never questioned that it was up to Washington, not Turtle Bay, to determine how the "variable geometry" of coalitions should be defined and operate in practice.[62] There had been a decade, after all, of precedents for such a division of labor in UN-authorized missions involving military enforcement actions. Over these post–Cold War years, the distinct geometry of each of these coalitions of the willing reflected both the mix of states and institutions required to get the particular job done and the evolving balance of power among member states. In many, but certainly not all, cases, America's increasingly dominant power position, particularly in terms of the capacity to project and sustain military power far from home, had made Washington the logical and widely accepted locus for decision-making on such matters. The fact that the most horrific terrorist strikes had been carried out against civilian and government targets on U.S. soil only reinforced this conclusion.

For the Bush administration, as for the Clinton administration before it, there was no automatic assumption that broad-based multilateral responses were always preferable for carrying out UN mandates. As Richard Haass put it, Washington's desire to build coalitions "does not mean we will always agree with our partners or adopt what we consider wrong policies in the spirit of 'going along to get along.' In such cases, it is not a question of multilateralism versus unilateralism, but of the specific details of the multilateral approach in question."[63] Likewise, though the administration understood that a global coalition needed to be built through one bilateral relationship after another, its partners needed to understand Washington's determination to respond to the terrorist threat one way or another. As President Bush told a special session of the German Bundestag, "America will consult closely with our friends and allies at every stage. But make no mistake about it, we will and we must confront this conspiracy against our liberty and against our lives."[64] Earlier, in his State of the Union Address, he noted that "many nations are acting forcefully. . . . But some governments will be timid in the face of terror. And make no mistake about it: If they do not act, America will."[65]

The most direct response to the September 11 attacks—the intervention in Afghanistan—produced a series of intracoalition controversies, much as had been the case with previous coalitions of the willing. But it also reflected such an intricate and nuanced division of labor among countries, groups, and organizations as to make labels such as "unilateral" or "multilateral" seem both crude and of marginal relevance. The most sensitive issues had to do with who would do the fighting, how command relationships would function, and how targeting and war goals should be determined. The Bush administration, like its predecessors, displayed considerable ambivalence about the prospects of fighting alongside a broad and diverse coalition. Initially the forces on the ground were limited to the U.S., the UK, Canada, and Australia, but in early November the administration agreed to a somewhat more diverse force.[66] As President Bush told a White House gathering of allies in March 2002, "[M]ore than half of the forces now assisting the heroic Afghan fighters, or providing security in Kabul, are from countries other than the United States."[67] And, as he had pledged to the General Assembly in November, the U.S. looked to the UN and multilateral development banks to play leading roles in the political, economic, social, and humanitarian reconstruction of Afghanistan. He also told the assembly that "every known terrorist camp must be shut down, its operators apprehended, and evidence of their arrest presented to the United Nations."

It would appear that the Bush administration has envisioned three primary roles for the UN and other multilateral institutions and arrangements in the war on terrorism: to help dissuade groups from adopting terrorist tactics by underlining that such acts are not morally, legally, or politically acceptable to the international community; to be part of the effort to deny terrorists the funds, materials, arms, space, shelter, secrecy, or movement required to carry on their activities effectively; and to provide the political, legal, and institutional basis for sustaining cooperation in a broadly based international anti-terrorist coalition. These roles are precisely the ones that the secretary-general's own Policy Working Group came up with for the world body.[68] As noted earlier, the U.S. and other member states could have done a good deal more to bolster the UN's capacity to play an effective part in operational matters relating to capacity-building and denial strategies. Overall, however, it appears that the Bush administration has included multilateral options as an integral part of its strategy for the war against terrorism from day one.

Though the content of Washington's approach no doubt has been exceptional in some respects and its style has often been abrupt, it is hard to sustain the argument that the U.S. has sought to carry out this struggle solely or even largely through unilateral action. To the contrary, some may charge, as they did in the debate on Iraq, that the problem instead has been Washington's determined exploitation of multilateral machinery for its own purposes. Given existing power asymmetries and the president's perception that U.S. national security is at stake, critics are bound to see U.S. policies as either ignoring international institutions or dominating them. Assuming that most other states share Washington's core goal of eliminating the terrorist threat, however, the ultimate test will be strategic, not tactical: Will the war on terrorism, with U.S. leadership, succeed? While this chapter argues that American counter-terrorist policies since September 2001 have been neither unusually unilateralist in method nor exceptionalist in content, it lacks a crystal ball regarding future results. If terrorism does not subside, then future generations will care relatively little whether the form of our response fell more on the unilateral or multilateral side of the spectrum of policy options.

Things Not Done

In sum, this chapter finds little basis for the prevalent complaints about excessive unilateralism in the U.S. response to the terrorist attacks of September 11. If its approach appears obsessive or headstrong, some allowance might be made for the circumstances. Many worried at the time, it should be recalled, that the U.S. response would be far less discriminating. As we go to press, President Bush's conduct of the war on terrorism, moreover, remains quite popular at home a year and a half after the attacks.[69] Events surely have served to confirm the inflated sense of exceptionalism, of being special, that has proven so engaging to both the public and policymakers in the U.S. But they have also reminded Americans of the value of international cooperation and of how much they have in common with peoples around the world who have long faced the terrorist menace. Perhaps allied capitals—other than London—feel that consultations have been perfunctory or inadequate. But historically, this has been the case more often than not, especially on issues so close to U.S. national security and on which its public is so engaged.

If the sources for the more severe unilateralist critiques are hard to find in what the Bush administration has done, then perhaps they lie more in what it has not done. Four interrelated possibilities suggest themselves.

First, style points count for a lot these days, especially in the way that others judge the lone remaining global power. Multilateralism is about form as much as substance. Americans tend to care more about results than process, while less powerful countries, for understandable strategic reasons, put considerable stake in the smooth and reliable functioning of multilateral mechanisms. Because other member states have come to expect only episodic interest from Washington in the daily functioning of the UN system, a new administration has to work extra hard to overcome such perceptions and expectations. While the Bush administration has not been notably hostile toward the world body, it certainly has not made the cultivation of the UN community a priority either. It was not lost on other member states that it did not push very hard to get the second payment of arrears paid or Ambassador Negroponte's nomination confirmed until after September 11. Nor has it made the kind of commitment to other items on the UN's agenda that matter to other member states—such as development, environment, health, human rights, and the Middle East. Washington's multilateral agenda is even more narrow and selective than usual. And, as noted above, the U.S. has not chosen to invest in enhancing the UN's operational capacities to assist with counterterrorism efforts.

Second, the willingness of the president and his aides to invoke the importance of multilateral institutions and processes in the war on terrorism has varied with his audience. In private, the need to build a global coalition and to fully utilize international institutions was candidly acknowledged early on. From the president's two addresses to the General Assembly—in November 2001 and September 2002—it would have appeared that the UN was absolutely central. Yet in his two addresses to the Congress—in September 2001 and January 2002—the world organization was not even mentioned. Such unevenness only encourages skepticism about Bush's commitment to multilateral policy alternatives, especially in light of his unwillingness to take on congressional critics of the world body on a range of issues.

Third, the Bush administration has done little to meet allied concerns about its policies toward a host of largely unrelated multilateral issues, ranging from the Kyoto Protocol on greenhouse gases to the International Criminal Court, on which the West is deeply divided. On some of these issues, Washington's stance could fairly be characterized as both unilateral and exceptional; the president's position is less reflective of public opinion and his policies are different in some important respects from those of his predecessors. These disputes may have conditioned publics and officials in other countries to expect the Bush administration to adopt unilateral and exceptional positions in other areas of public policy, such as counterterrorism, as well. These perceptions and linkages could help explain why the administration's efforts to pursue multilateral as well as unilateral responses to terrorism have been so little appreciated by so many.

Fourth, others are likely to worry as much about what a dominant power might do as about what it has done or is doing. As the debate about the war in Iraq illustrated, this is particularly true when it comes to the use of military force—who is next?—and to any possible adjustments in widely accepted norms and rules about its use. Though, as noted earlier, there was considerable relief in allied capitals when the Bush administration demonstrated restraint in its immediate military response, there has been substantial wariness about its subsequent talk of adapting existing norms and doctrines on the use of force to the new demands posed by the escalating terrorist threat, including, most sharply, by the prospect of terrorists acquiring weapons of mass destruction (WMD). The National Security Strategy statement issued in September 2002 called pointedly for proactive WMD counterproliferation efforts, for the adaptation of the concept of imminent threat under international law, and for an operational policy of preempting emerging threats.

As President Bush told the Warsaw Conference on Combating Terrorism in November 2001, "[W]e will not wait for the authors of mass murder to gain the weapons of mass destruction. We act now, because we must lift this dark threat from our age and save generations to come."[70] In his State of the Union Address two months later, he cautioned that "I will not wait on events, while dangers gather. I will not stand by, as peril draws closer and closer. The United States of America will not permit the world's most dangerous regimes to threaten us with the world's most destructive weapons." He went on to tell the 2002 West Point graduates that "the war on terror will not be won on the defensive. We must take the battle to the enemy, disrupt his plans, and confront the worst threats before they emerge."[71] Evidence uncovered in the caves of Afghanistan, after all, had documented Al Qaeda's interest in acquiring weapons of mass destruction, and the attacks on the World Trade Center confirmed its readiness to inflict large-scale civilian casualties.

The National Security Strategy concluded, as had Secretary Shultz in 1984, that traditional security concepts such as deterrence did not appear to apply to shadowy, non-state foes with a zealot's single-minded determination and a penchant for self-destruction. But for all the logic behind preemption as a tool for dealing with terrorists, others fret that such a doctrine virtually precludes multilateral decision-making processes and is a worrisome departure from past self-defense norms. While these concerns are understandable, the stakes involved in this new phase of national security planning are so high and so urgent as to make it a new game that demands new rules.

The Bush administration could do much better, however, on the other three factors. It would be advised to review its statements and actions toward global issues and institutions with a view to seeing whether there might not be some low-cost ways of narrowing its differences and cooling the rhetoric with key allies. In some cases, such as on the International Criminal Court, a less aggressively antagonistic style on both sides would help. The president has taken some positive initiatives: he announced plans to reenter the UN Educational, Social and Cultural Organization (UNESCO); he has pledged to both expand and reform development assistance; and he outlined a major HIV/AIDS program in his January 2003 State of the Union Address. Yet, given the depth of skepticism in many other capitals about the general orientation of the Bush administration, these efforts appear to have won relatively few hearts and minds at Turtle Bay. If the Bush administration fails to cement and sustain the anti-terrorism coalition, therefore, it will be more because of style than because of substance.

For their part, allies in Europe and elsewhere need to do the opposite—to begin to pay more attention to substance and less to style and process. Some allied leaders have allowed their uncertainty about how to deal with U.S. power and their discomfort with military force to lead them to focus on secondary questions, missing the mark in terms of the core security challenges posed by this generation of terrorists. They are right about the need for Washington to remain more closely engaged in Middle Eastern diplomacy, but their one-sided approach makes their appeal for Washington to be more even-handed ring hollow. It would be helpful, moreover, if they would encourage their publics to pay more attention to the evil that terrorists do than to the causes they claim to represent or to the imperfections of the policies adopted in response. Terrorism, after all, is less a challenge to U.S. power than to widely shared liberal democratic values. As the Secretary-General's Policy Working Group on the United Nations and Terrorism put it, "[T]errorism is, and is intended to be, an assault on the principles of law, order, human rights and peaceful settlement of disputes on which the world body was founded."[72]

At the end of the day, those concerned about Washington's power and unilateralist tendencies should be the first to candidly assess the weaknesses of existing multilateral alternatives and the first to take steps to correct them. Those who are uncomfortable with U.S. military dominance should expend the resources and political capital to develop an alternative military capacity that could be put at the Security Council's disposal. Over time, it is important to deal with root causes, but that should not distract attention from the urgent priority of defeating the existing terrorist rings. In that context, to deny the necessity of using brute force at times to deal with terrorists whose only mode of operation is to kill innocent civilians, who have established well-armed training camps, who covet weapons of mass destruction, and whose reach is global is to badly misjudge, even deny, the scale of the problem. To assert that the UN should be the centerpiece of the global campaign against terrorism and yet to take no steps to provide it with the tools required to get the job done—not even significant new funding or posts—is no favor either to the world body or to the effort to overcome terrorism. It suggests a lack of seriousness about either enterprise.

Even the Bush administration, despite its penchant for unilateral action and its misgivings about the world body, has come to recognize that broad-based multilateral cooperation is an essential component of a successful war on terrorism. Yet at times it must be asking whether a workable multilateral alternative really exists. Perversely, an unusual degree of international cooperation and commitment—led by those who habitually champion multilateralism—is necessary to repair the leaks in existing institutions so that one can begin to give an affirmative response to this core question.

Notes

1. "Americans and Europeans Differ Widely on Foreign Policy Issues: Bush's Ratings Improve But He's Still Seen as Unilateralist," Pew Research Center multinational survey conducted with the International Herald Tribune and in association with the Council on Foreign Relations, April 20, 2002. Available online at http://people-press.org/reports/print.php3?ReportID=153.

2. Chris Patten, "Jaw-Jaw, Not War-War," *Financial Times*, February 15, 2002.

3. See, for example, The German Marshall Fund of the United States, *Worldviews 2002: European Public Opinion and Foreign Policy*, 23–24, which presents the results of a six-nation survey carried out in June and July 2002. Available online at http://www.worldviews.org/detailreports/europeanreport.pdf.

4. "Bush Unpopular in Europe, Seen as Unilateralist," Pew Research Center multinational survey conducted with the International Herald Tribune in association with the Council on Foreign Relations, August 15, 2001. Available online at http://people-press.org/reports/display.php3?PageID=36. See also Adam Clymer, "Surveys Find European Public Critical of Bush Policies," *New York Times*, August 16, 2001.

5. The decisions of the Bush administration in the fall and winter of 2002–2003 to seek a UN role in addressing the attempts by Iraq and North Korea to acquire weapons of mass destruction would seem to reflect a similar logic. These matters, however, are not addressed directly in this paper, since they involve issues well beyond the war on terrorism. For the debate within the Bush administration on whether to seek another Security Council resolution on Iraq that fall, see Bob Woodward, *Bush at War* (New York: Simon & Schuster, 2002), 344–349; and Edward C. Luck, "Bush, Iraq, and the UN: Whose Idea Was This Anyway?," in Thomas G. Weiss, Margaret E. Crahan, and John Goering, eds., *Wars on Terrorism and Iraq: Human Rights, Unilateralism, and U.S. Foreign Policy* (London: Routledge, 2004), which grew from seminars co-sponsored by the Ralph Bunche Institute for International Studies and the Center for the Humanities.

6. Edward C. Luck, "American Exceptionalism and International Organization: Lessons from the 1990s," in Rosemary Foot, S. Neil MacFarlane, and Michael Mastanduno, eds., *U.S. Hegemony in an Organized World: The United States and Multilateral Institutions* (New York: Oxford University Press, 2003), 25–48.

7. For perceptive accounts of the realist underpinnings of Washington's turn toward multilateral institutions following World War II, see John Gerard Ruggie, *Winning the Peace: America and World Order in the New Era* (New York: Columbia University Press, 1996); and G. John Ikenberry, *After Victory: Institutions, Strategic Restraint, and the Rebuilding of Order after Major Wars* (Princeton, N.J.: Princeton University Press, 2001).

8. American advantages in hard power may encourage others, as they did in the 2003 debate over the use of force in Iraq, to seek to counterbalance Washington with "soft power" appeals centered in diplomacy that seek to influence U.S. domestic politics. For a discussion of soft power, see Joseph S. Nye, *The Paradox of American Power: Why the World's Only Superpower Can't Go It Alone* (New York: Oxford University Press, 2002).

9. See Edward C. Luck, *Mixed Messages: American Politics and International Organization, 1919–1999* (Washington, D.C.: Brookings Institution Press, 1999).

10. German Marshall Fund, *Worldviews 2002,* 11–13.

11. "America's New Internationalist Point of View," survey conducted by the Pew Research Center for the People and the Press in association with the Council on Foreign Relations, October 24, 2001. Available online at http://people-press.org/reports/display.php3?PageID=18.

12. "Americans and Europeans Differ Widely on Foreign Policy Issues."

13. Thomas L. Friedman, "French Jets Raid Bases of Militia Linked to Attacks," *New York Times,* November 18, 1983.

14. Martha Crenshaw, "The 'Terrorism Studies' Community and the UN Role in Counter-Terrorism," paper prepared for the Project on the United Nations and Terrorism, the Center on International Organization, Columbia University, May 2, 2002, 1. The preliminary results of a survey undertaken for the center by Columbia graduate students of the literature in fifteen other languages suggest that the neglect of the potential UN role in resisting terrorism is a global phenomenon, not just an American one.

15. Paul R. Pillar, *Terrorism and U.S. Foreign Policy* (Washington, D.C.: Brookings Institution, 2001), 75.

16. Ibid., 75–76.

17. See, for example, "The World Responds to September 11," *Correspondence: An International Review of Culture and Society* 9 (Spring 2002), available online at http://www.cfr.org/pdf/correspondence/correspondence_Spring2002.php; Social Science Research Council, "Perspectives from the Social Sciences," available online at http://www.ssrc.org/sept11/; Rosemary Righter, "Why It Is Right to Join America's Fight," *The Spectator,* March 16, 2002; and Mark Gilbert, "Superman Versus Lex Luther: British Anti-Americanism since September 11," *World Policy Journal* XIX, no. 2 (Summer 2002): 88–92.

18. For further discussion of the effect of Middle Eastern politics on the UN's response to terrorism, see Edward C. Luck, "Trouble Behind, Trouble Ahead? The UN Security Council Tackles Terrorism," in David M. Malone, ed., *The UN Security Council: From the Cold War to the 21st Century* (Boulder: Lynne Rienner, forthcoming).

19. Crenshaw, "The 'Terrorism Studies' Community and the UN Role in Counter-Terrorism," 2.

20. David Cortright and George A. Lopez, *Sanctions and the Search for Security: Challenges to UN Action* (Boulder: Lynne Rienner, 2002), 47–60 and 115–132.

21. For the decision adopted at the Assembly of Heads of State and Government of the Organization of African Unity, held in Ouagadougou, Burkina Faso, June 8–10, 1998, see Gus Constantine, "UN Travel Ban on Libya Collapsing: Egypt's Mubarak Latest African Dignitary to Visit Gadhafi," *Washington Times,* July 10, 1998; and Office of the Spokesman, U.S. Department of State, "Rubin Statement: OAU Resolution on Libya," June 16, 1998.

22. In an effort to correct this doctrinal lapse, in October 2001 the secretary-general convened a Policy Working Group on the United Nations and Terrorism. The report of this group, on which this author served, takes a useful first cut at the question of how the UN might best assist the struggle against terrorism; it identified dissuasion, denial of the means to commit terrorist acts, and sustaining cooperation as the UN's areas of comparative advantage. It is hoped that the report will spur a broader dialogue on these issues and will be just the initial step toward developing a UN strategy for dealing with terrorism. *Report of the Policy Working Group on the United Nations and Terrorism,* (A/57/273, Annex), September 10, 2002.

23. In July 2002, almost ten months after the attacks, the secretary-general finally proposed expanding the TPB by adding three professional posts (a D-1, a P-4, and a P-3) and two support staff. Its mandate would be enlarged to include some capacity-building and legislative assistance for member states concerned with the linkage between terrorism and related crimes. Report of the Secretary-General, *Strengthening the Terrorism Prevention Branch of the Secretariat* (A/57/152), July 2, 2002. Also see "Draft Resolution: Strengthening the Terrorism Branch of the Secretariat," A/C.5/57/L.47, December 12, 2002.

24. "Proposed Programme Budget for the Biennium 2002–2003," Part IV, Section 14, "Crime Prevention and Criminal Justice" (A/56/6 [Sect. 14]), March 20, 2001, 2–3, 11. For suggestions on how UN efforts and structures might be revamped, see Steven R. Ratner,

"Capacity-Building to Fight Terrorism: Finding the UN's Comparative Advantage," paper prepared for the Project on the United Nations and Terrorism, Center on International Organization, Columbia University, April 29, 2002.

25. On the trust fund, see Security Council, 4453rd meeting, S/PV.4453, January 18, 2002, 4; available online at http://www.un.org/Docs/pv4453e.pdf. For quotation, see Security Council, 4512th meeting, S/PV.4512, April 15, 2002, 4; available online at http://www.un.org/Docs/pv4512e.pdf.

26. "Shultz Says U.S. Should Use Force Against Terrorism," and "Excerpts from Shultz's Address on International Terrorism," both in *New York Times*, October 26, 1984, A1 and A12, respectively.

27. William W. Scranton, quoted by Kathleen Teltsch, "Rescue by Israel Acclaimed by U.S. at Debate in U.N.," *New York Times*, July 13, 1976, 1; and Vernon A. Walters, quoted by Milt Freudenheim, James F. Clarity, and Richard Levin, "Israel Stops the Wrong Jet," *New York Times*, February 9, 1986, section 4, page 2 (second quote from Vernon A. Walters).

28. Lionel Barber, "US Urged to Strike Air Terrorist Bases: Lockerbie Bomb Commission Demands Tougher Action from Bush," *Financial Times*, May 16, 1990, section I, page 1.

29. National Commission on Terrorism, *Countering the Changing Threat of International Terrorism* (Washington, D.C.: U.S. Government Printing Office, June 7, 2000).

30. Excerpts from speech of U.S. Permanent Representative Madeline K. Albright to the Security Council, "Raid on Baghdad: Excerpts from UN Speech: The Case for Clinton's Strike," *New York Times*, June 28, 1993, A7.

31. "Our Objective Was to Damage Their Capacity to Strike," *Washington Post*, August 21, 1998, A17.

32. "Remarks by the President to the Opening Session of the 53rd United Nations General Assembly, 21 September 1998." Available online at http://www.un.int/usa/98_154.htm.

33. Brian McGrory and Chris Black, "US Hits Suspected Terror Sites," *Boston Globe*, August 21, 1998, A1.

34. Ibid.

35. Tom Bowman, "Embassy Bombings Force U.S. to Focus on Terrorism Threat," *Baltimore Sun*, August 23, 1998, A24.

36. U.S. Office of Management and Budget, *Annual Report to Congress on Combating Terrorism* (Washington, D.C.: U.S. Government Printing Office, August 2001), 100.

37. Philip B. Heymann, *Terrorism and America: A Commonsense Strategy for a Democratic Society* (Cambridge, Mass.: MIT Press, 2000), 75.

38. Long before the U.S. interventions in Afghanistan and Iraq, opinion polls showed strong public support for using military force as a tool to suppress terrorism. See, for example, Adam Clymer, "A Poll Finds 77% in U.S. Approve Raid on Libya," *New York Times*, April 17, 1986, A23; and Adam Nagourney and Michael R. Kagay, "High Marks Given to the President But Not the Man," *New York Times*, August 22, 1998, A1. After the September 11th attacks, support among Americans for the use of force against terrorists, of course, became even more pronounced. See poll sponsored by the Chicago

Council on Foreign Relations and the German Marshall Fund, *Worldviews 2002,* www.worldviews.org/detailreports/usreport.pdf, p. 23.

39. John E. Rielly, ed., *American Public Opinion and U.S. Foreign Policy, 1999* (Waukegan, Ill.: Lake County Press, 1999), 27. Diplomatic and juridical approaches to addressing terrorism were also popular.

40. Woodward, *Bush at War,* 341.

41. Bob Woodward and Dan Balz, "'We Will Rally the World': Bush and His Advisers Set Objectives, But Struggled with How to Achieve Them," *Washington Post,* January 28, 2002, A1.

42. Dan Balz and Bob Woodward, "America's Chaotic Road to War; Bush's Global Strategy Began to Take Shape in the First Frantic Hours After Attack," *Washington Post,* January 27, 2002, A1.

43. Ibid.

44. Ibid.

45. Ibid.

46. Ibid.

47. Woodward, *Bush at War,* 113.

48. Ibid., 281.

49. Ibid.

50. Balz and Woodward, "America's Chaotic Road."

51. Ibid.

52. Ibid.

53. President George W. Bush, "Address to a Joint Session of Congress and the American People, 20 September 2001." Available online at http://www.whitehouse.gov/news/releases/2001/09/20010920-8.html. In an April 2002 speech, Richard N. Haass, director of the state department's policy planning staff, went even farther regarding the global campaign against terrorism: "[O]ver the long haul the military tool will almost certainly *not* be the most important contributor to our success. Instead, a combination of diplomatic, economic, intelligence, financial and law enforcement means—along with military—will make the difference." Richard N. Haass, "Defining U.S. Foreign Policy in a Post-Post–Cold War World," Remarks to the Foreign Policy Association, April 22, 2002. Available online http://www.state.gov/s/p/rem/9632.htm. Emphasis in the original.

54. That number has since been raised to ninety, according to official counts.

55. For an explication of the conceptual and strategic basis for the Bush administration's approach to foreign policy that centers on integration, see Richard N. Haass, "From Reluctant to Resolute: American Foreign Policy After September 11," June 26, 2002. Available online at http://www.state.gov/s/p/rem/11445.htm.

56. White House Press Release, "President Freezes Terrorists' Assets," September 24, 2001. Available online at http://www.whitehouse.gov/news/releases/2001/09/20010924-4.html.

57. U.S. Department of State Fact Sheets, "G8 Counter-Terrorism Cooperation Since September 11," June 26, 2002; and "U.S.-EU Summit: Counterterrorism Coopera-

tion," May 2, 2002, available online at http://www.state.gov/e/eb/rls/fs/11477.htm and http://www.state.gov/p/eur/rls/fs/9920.htm, respectively.

58. Financial Action Task Force, "Special Recommendations on Terrorist Financing," October 31, 2001. Available online at http://www1.oecd.org/fatf/SRecsTF_en.htm.

59. U.S. Department of State Press Release, "Remarks of Secretary of State Colin L. Powell to the Security Council of the United Nations," September 11, 2002. Available online at http://www.un.int/usa/02clp-sc-0911.htm.

60. White House Press Release, "President Bush Speaks to United Nations," November 10, 2001. Available online at http://www.whitehouse.gov/news/releases/2001/11/20011110-3.html.

61. Woodward and Balz, "America's Chaotic Road." For a description of six distinct coalitions needed for a successful war on terrorism, see Andrew J. Pierre, *Coalitions: Building and Maintenance, Gulf War, Kosovo, Afghanistan, War on Terrorism* (Washington, D.C.: Institute for the Study of Diplomacy, Georgetown University, 2002), 39–72.

62. Turtle Bay is the name of the neighborhood in New York City where UN headquarters are located.

63. Haass, "From Reluctant to Resolute."

64. White House Press Release, "President Bush Thanks Germany for Support against Terror," May 23, 2002. Available online at http://www.whitehouse.gov/news/releases/2002/05/20020523-2.html.

65. White House Press Release, "President Delivers State of the Union Address," January 29, 2002. Available online at http://www.whitehouse.gov/news/releases/2002/01/20020129-11.html.

66. David E. Sanger and Michael R. Gordon, "A Nation Challenged: The White House; U.S. Takes Steps to Bolster Bloc Fighting Terror," *New York Times,* November 7, 2001, A1; and Editorial, "Coalition Maintenance," *New York Times,* November 8, 2001, A26.

67. White House Press Release, "President Thanks World Coalition for Anti-Terrorism Efforts," March 11, 2002. Available online at http://www.whitehouse.gov/news/releases/2002/03/20020311-1.html.

68. The Policy Working Group, of course, did not advocate that the UN take part in intelligence-sharing or joint policing and law enforcement activities, which are important components of Washington's agenda for international cooperation.

69. Polls conducted during the last quarter of 2002, in fact, gave the president a 70 percent or higher approval rating for his handling of terrorism and one of 60 percent or more for his overall handling of his office.

70. White House Press Release, "President Bush: 'No Nation Can Be Neutral in This Conflict,'" November 6, 2001. Available online at http://www.whitehouse.gov/news/releases/2001/11/20011106-2.html.

71. U.S. Department of State, "Answering the Call of History," June 1, 2002. Available online at http://www.state.gov/r/pa/ei/wh/rem/10648.htm.

72. *Report of the Policy Working Group on the United Nations and Terrorism* (A/57/273-S/2002/875, Annex), paragraph 11, p. 4.

5

Improving the International Response to the Transnational Terrorist Threat

Karin von Hippel

In the immediate aftermath of the attacks on September 11, many commentators proclaimed a new and unprecedented era in international cooperation. Not only had consensus been reached that terrorist networks had to be eliminated, but the United States welcomed support from all corners of the globe. In what would soon become the most ephemeral expression of French solidarity in recent times, *Le Monde*'s famous headlines read, "We are all Americans now," and 800 million people in forty-three European countries observed several minutes of silence. Even Muammar el-Qaddafi and Fidel Castro expressed their outrage and offered limited assistance.

This consensus soon turned into diplomatic and military resolve as Washington built a broad global coalition against terrorism and prosecuted a determined military campaign against the Taliban and Al Qaeda in Afghanistan. The resistance of the latter rapidly crumbled in the face of a remarkable U.S.-led military campaign, one that has already changed the way that the U.S. military thinks about fighting future wars. At the start of 2003, there were still 70 countries supporting the military "war against terror" in Afghanistan to eliminate remaining Al Qaeda fighters, 160 countries working to freeze terrorist funds, 90 countries cooperating in law enforcement and intelligence-sharing, and internal reforms initiated in most states to "root out terror." In addition, almost every multilateral institution and arrangement—the United Nations, the European Union (EU), the Organization for Security and Co-operation in Europe (OSCE), the Organisation for Economic Co-operation and Development (OECD), the Organization of American States (OAS), the World Bank, the International Monetary Fund (IMF), North Atlantic Treaty Organization (NATO), and Group of Seven/Eight (G-7/G-8)—have their own special counterterrorist agendas to link to this international campaign.

Yet despite these rosy figures, more than a year after the attacks, a number of problems threaten the coalition. The question that arises is whether the obstacles are serious enough to undermine the campaign. In other words, while it may be self-evident that the transnational Al Qaeda terrorist threat can be defeated only through a robust, long-term global response, whether this is a realizable aspiration is unclear. As articulated by David Veness, the United Kingdom's assistant police commissioner, the challenge before the coalition is to "out-globalize Al Qaeda."[1]

The modus operandi of Al Qaeda's fanatical, fluid, secretive, ever-evolving, unpredictable, and multipronged network can be sharply contrasted with the heavily bureaucratic, open, and lumbering procedures of most multilateral efforts and organizations, not to mention similar national systems. The U.S. government experienced enormous internal problems harnessing intelligence information prior to September 11, as described in one of the reports of Senate hearings: "[A] range of political, cultural, jurisdictional, legal and bureaucratic issues are ever present hurdles to information sharing."[2] These problems are intrinsic to international endeavors as well. Indeed, achieving effective integration of activities and analysis at the international level may be possible only in certain spheres in the near term, such as in blocking terrorist financing or in civil emergency response and planning, and for others, particularly intelligence and police cooperation, a longer time frame may be necessary. A closer examination of coordination efforts within this broad U.S.-led counterterrorist coalition illuminates the advances and the challenges thus far.

This chapter analyzes the effectiveness of international counterterrorist coordination through a discussion of three interlocking themes. The first concerns the complicated transatlantic relationship and the problems that need to be resolved between the major players for the campaign to succeed. The second emerges from the first and is based on the lack of a common analytical framework. The third examines the role of the United Nations, which, as the global organization responsible for peace and security, should be the ultimate arbiter of transnational efforts and should be entrusted with attacking fundamental root causes and facilitators for terrorism.

The United States and Europe:
Transatlantic Cooperation and Tension

Strong relationships and coordination at the inner core between the United States and European states are crucial components of a successful counterterrorist campaign. These countries have the best chance of harmonizing their work because of their similar cultures, their overall long-standing good relations, and their requisite resources and expertise. If European and American states were to adhere to a tight and comprehensive counterterrorist agenda, it would allow energies to be fully dedicated to the most difficult countries and intractable problems and to maintaining the broader coalition. Reforms within the U.S. have been well documented, but what has been happening in Europe? More specifically, how has cooperation been enhanced across Europe and what can be done to resolve the transatlantic dispute that has been in evidence since the end of the Cold War, which was reinvigorated after President George W. Bush's "axis of evil" speech in January 2002, and which potentially reached an apex just prior to the war in Iraq that began on March 20, 2003?

European Union member states have been reorganizing their counterterrorist infrastructures at the national level in the aftermath of September 11, and the EU has attempted to incorporate these recent changes in a larger and more comprehensive counterterrorist framework, which, if successful, will also streamline cooperation between Europe as a bloc and Washington. The EU divided its program into five thematic divisions: 1) police and judicial cooperation; 2) bilateral relations with non-EU member states and other regions (e.g., the Middle East, Euro-Mediterranean partnership, reconstruction of Afghanistan, humanitarian aid); 3) air transport security; 4) economic and financial measures; and 5) emergency preparedness. Only the third was a direct response to September 11; the rest were already in the pipeline to improve coordination. The response is thus not a novel program of action to counter the "new terror" but rather an enhancement of the old program. The EU has also developed a 69-point "road map"—a "Plan of Action of the Extraordinary European Council" that embodies the changes under way.

Europeans began to coordinate counterterrorism in 1976, with the establishment of the Terrorism, Radicalism, Extremism, and International Violence (TREVI) group[3] within what was then the European Community to promote regular sharing of information on security and terrorism issues between some ministers of justice and interior and police. TREVI evolved into the third pillar of the European Union; it dealt with Justice and Home Affairs and led to the establishment of European Police (EUROPOL), whose budget has doubled since September 11. Its current mandate only allows the agency to provide intelligence support to law enforcement agencies and prevents it from engaging in more robust enforcement activity.

Within the larger counterterrorism framework, regular meetings have been taking place to assess and manage progress from the ministerial level down to bureaucrats from different ministries of the member states. For example, European health ministers meet regularly to share information about how to improve the capability to respond to biological weapons attacks, including the stockpiling of vaccines. This same format is replicated for the Group of 8 (G-8) meetings to ensure that these concerns are internationalized. At home, health ministers are now playing a role in counterterrorist working groups, as are ministers in charge of defense, internal security, intelligence, and judicial affairs. It is interesting to observe that their inclusion is not always popular with traditional security types. It is not surprising that EU coordination is at its best in the nonpolitical arena of health and worst in the most sensitive intelligence-sharing.

Beyond the five themes noted above, additional work is under way in the European Council and the European Commission. Javier Solana, the council's high representative for a Common Foreign and Security Policy (CFSP), has been trying to develop a specific European analytical capability to combat terrorism across Europe that combines civilian crisis management, police, military, and intelligence capabilities in one unit. If he succeeds, this would be an important new development of the European Security and Defense Policy (ESDP), which currently does not include terrorism in its core tasks; the so-called Petersburg tasks are humanitarian assistance, crisis management, and peacekeeping.[4] Finally, the appropriateness of embedding counterterrorism within the new constitution, the European Convention, is being considered in the Working Group on Defense, which would also be a significant step forward. The convention should also harmonize the potential replication of efforts between the council and the commission, as the latter has also been developing a rapid-response capacity.

Despite the importance of these Europe-wide reforms, the counterterrorist successes thus far have been achieved primarily through bilateral initiatives or between a small number of states (e.g., between the United Kingdom, Spain, Germany, France, and the U.S.), especially concerning intelligence and police work. One senior German intelligence official noted that he did not anticipate this practice of limited cooperation changing for at least a decade.[5] Security and intelligence chiefs in European member states and in the U.S. worry about the variability inherent in multinational fora and the lack of cohesion on crucial issues.

Moreover, some Europe-wide reforms are not popular with all member states, which worry about transferring sovereignty to the supranational level on issues related to crime and terrorism. For example, the common European Arrest Warrant, due to be operational by the end of 2003, has made most states nervous that this new legislation may make it easier for the United States to extradite a suspect and potentially use the death penalty against him, which all European states oppose. Negotiations with Washington have, however, been under way since early 2002. Another thorny issue relates to data protection. Germany—perhaps the most protective European country of the right to privacy—is fearful that harmonization within Europe would facilitate U.S. interference in national matters.[6] Yet it is not just concerns about the use of the death penalty but rather more fundamental differences that have been impeding the relations between the United States and most European states since the end of the Cold War.

Although Henry Kissinger once wryly noted that "one country's perception of unilateralism is another's perception of leadership," in times of war, anti-Americanism and accusations of unilateralism inevitably surface in Europe.[7] Obvious examples include World War II and, more recently, the 1999 Kosovo war. Similar tension arises concerning terrorism, as Bruce Hoffman noted in 1999: "Terrorism has long been a source of friction between the United States and Europe."[8]

European governments have historically adopted a more tolerant approach to dealing with terrorist-sponsoring states than Washington has for three reasons. First, Europeans considered it better to maintain a dialogue than not. Second, certain countries have wanted to protect foreign investment opportunities, particularly in the oil and gas industries. Third, many of these same European countries are home to large Muslim populations and therefore have been fearful of a domestic backlash if harsh action were to be taken.

Thus, recent transatlantic tension,[9] which is well documented by a number of scholars and policymakers,[10] is consistent with past experience. This time, however, the combination of the war in Afghanistan, a larger war in Iraq, different approaches to the Middle East conflict,[11] the "axis of evil" speech, *and* terrorism has deepened the rift. Major European states assisting in the campaign against terrorism are also annoyed because they feel they are excluded from the decision-making process. The oft-heard French complaint that the "Americans want to do the cooking and have us do the dishes" reflects this tension.

European insecurity over the widening gap in military capabilities also underlines this tension. Since the end of the Cold War, European states have greatly reduced defense spending and have shifted funds to social infrastructure. The 2001 U.S. defense budget, on the other hand, was more than double that of all EU countries together ($310 billion versus $144 billion). And after Bush's request for 2004 is approved at $379 billion, the biggest increase in defense spending in twenty years, the gap will widen even farther.

European reductions in defense spending have taken place under the protective umbrella of long-standing U.S. defense agreements. U.S. officials have continually expressed their anxiety over this gulf, and they are disinclined to take European criticism seriously until they see bigger commitments. Significant pressure on European counterparts to increase defense spending is unlikely to bear fruit in the near future. One Spanish diplomat remarked that "our budget process does not allow for the type of deficit spending so common in the United States."[12] Europeans do not necessarily need to spend significantly more at the national level; an efficient pooling of resources and manpower Europe-wide could drastically alter the gap.[13]

Beyond undertaking necessary military reforms, Europe would become more than an economic power if counterterrorism could be institutionalized in the ESDP and enshrined in the European Convention. The hope is that the added political weight could help to counter unilateralist tendencies by the United States. Such changes would facilitate a more robust global response to the transnational threat and assist in overall crime reduction because terrorism spills over into other areas.

For its part, Washington also needs to utilize European experience with terrorism in a more substantive fashion. Many European states have developed considerable counterterrorist and anti-terrorist infrastructures as the result of coping with terrorism for over thirty years, even if the threat has been largely of a different character than that represented by Al Qaeda. Beyond the more familiar left-wing or ethnonationalist terrorist groups, such as Brigate Rosse (Red Brigades) in Italy or the Provisional Irish Republican Army (PIRA), European states have also borne the brunt of attacks by some form of Islamic extremism on their airports, airlines, and embassies since the late 1960s, even if they were mostly directed at Israeli targets.[14]

Moreover, not only France but also Germany, the Netherlands, Spain, and the UK are home to large Muslim populations. Terrorist cells have been able to blend in without being detected or infiltrate and use local Mosques, community centers, and *madrasas* as bases for recruitment; and they have even operated, on occasion, with the tacit knowledge of the government. The attitude of the UK security services prior to September 11, for example, was that the presence of a fairly sizeable number of known hard-line radical Islamic extremists, such as Abu Hamza al-Masri, the London-based radical imam, was not necessarily harmful.

The government was aware that hard-line radical Islamic extremists were living in UK cities, where they were planning operations and using their adopted cities for logistics and financing for attacks. The misconception and assumption, which is now recognized as incorrect, was that they would only be attacking targets back at home, not in the United Kingdom.[15] Even during this period, London still monitored their activities with intelligence and police assets. At the same time, the French, who often referred to "Londonistan" (because they were annoyed with British policy), had a deeper understanding of the extremist Islamic terrorist threat because of their long-standing experience with North African terrorism and insurgency movements.

Finally, particular European states have better political and economic relationships than the United States with a number of key developing states (e.g., Iran, Libya, and Syria), which can help to ensure the maintenance of such a large coalition. If Washington can thus partner its considerable resolve and resources with the experience, intelligence, and expertise of these European states, the campaign would have a far greater likelihood of achieving success.

A Common Analytical Framework

As noted, the counterterrorism campaign has been hurt because of European annoyance at being excluded from decision-making, differences over foreign policy, and the spillover from the gap in military capability. Equally significant, Europeans and Americans appear to be talking past each other; all states have been responding in a more reactive manner that focuses on crisis management rather than on prevention. A second related obstacle impeding an enhanced response, therefore, is the lack of a common analytical framework among major actors and a concomitant agreed-upon methodology to challenge the threat.

It is generally recognized that Al Qaeda is trying to fulfill the dream of a pan-Islamic superstate and considers war with the United States necessary because the U.S. is hindering its ambitions in a number of ways. As Daniel Benjamin explained:

> After decades in which jihadists were defeated by security services in their home countries, Osama bin Laden and his followers decided that they would attack the "far enemy," the United States, which they believe is the primary source of strength for the secularist regimes in the Arab world. If the United States withdrew its support, the "near enemy" that holds power in Muslim capitals would be unable to defend itself.[16]

There is further consensus that Osama bin Laden and the leadership of Al Qaeda are not interested in negotiations—evidenced by bin Laden's 1998 fatwa to kill all Americans, Christians, and Jews—especially given that the rewards for this brand of jihad will come only in the afterlife.[17] The motto for Sheikh Abdullah Azzam, bin Laden's teacher at King Abdul Aziz University and his mentor for some time, was "Jihad and the rifle alone: no negotiations, no conferences, and no dialogues."[18]

Where the consensus breaks down is over the grand strategy to counter this threat.[19] The disagreement centers on whether the appeal and influence of bin Laden and Al Qaeda can be fundamentally reduced through the introduction of a number of political and socioeconomic reforms. The first school—which consists primarily of hawkish members of the Bush administration—argues that Al Qaeda's claims in support of the Palestinian cause or in favor of the removal of U.S. troops from Saudi Arabia are merely masks to cover the movement's real global ambitions. Proponents of this school of thought argue that even if significant efforts could be made to redress Al Qaeda's grievances, they would not be realizable. At crucial moments, extremists would act as spoilers and undermine any advancements made in order to maintain a high level of tension. If anything, honing in on the Middle East would be an unnecessary distraction. This school advocates an aggressive military, police, and investigative campaign throughout the world to eradicate terrorists and their bases of support.

The other school—represented by European states, institutions, and some members of the U.S. State Department as well as some U.S. Democrats—does not necessarily disagree with the use of force as part of the campaign; however, proponents of this school would also advocate an equally aggressive attack on root causes and facilitators. Representatives from this school assert that if significant progress could be made toward finding a peaceful resolution in the Middle East (and the spoilers were blocked), if U.S. and other Western troops could be removed from Gulf states (or at least from Saudi Arabia), and if serious efforts could be dedicated to implement the Millennium Development Goals, then the platforms and justifications for violence that find resonance in a broad section of the Muslim community worldwide could be removed, even if Al Qaeda cannot be appealed to directly.

Frustration is so strong that we often hear two entirely different and competing versions of events. Conspiracy theories abound as to who really committed recent terrorist attacks. Accusations that the Central Intelligence Agency (CIA) and the Federal Bureau of Investigation (FBI) were behind the Bali bombing or the attacks on the World Trade Center are perpetuated by extremist religious leaders. These beliefs are cleverly exploited by the Al Qaeda leadership and fed to populations that are already disillusioned and distrustful of the intentions of the West and discontented with their own governments.

Moreover, these populations read and hear about generous Western financial support for the impoverished but rarely see evidence that the money reaches their poor. This is not necessarily the fault of donors, who are often forced to work with corrupt governments or are unable to spend funds that have been committed because of a paucity of legitimate partners on the ground. Nevertheless, the inability of developed states to realize international development goals contributes to disillusionment and resentment in many developing countries and allows more and more ordinary citizens to become susceptible to conspiracy theories.

This is the "complicit society" and the "enabling environment" that concern the second school.[20] Its approach would thus serve to reduce the seemingly endless stream of recruits from disaffected Muslim communities. It would help to remove the perceptions of bias and unequal treatment and go some way toward addressing snowballing anger and resentment.

Two further areas interfere with a common approach. First, since the majority of European Union reforms were under way before September 11, they were designed primarily to counter "old" terrorism. Though the dividing line between international and some national terrorist groups is beginning to blur, there are clear distinctions between old and new.[21] Indeed, the term "new terrorism" signifies a brand of transnational terrorism in which the terrorists aspire to cause massive devastation and many casualties. They are often described as fanatics who have exploited religious fervor through the use of suicide bombing. To the extent that they have a political agenda, it has been transformed into absolute religious imperatives and thereby rendered nonnegotiable, in practical terms. They aim not only to acquire and use high-tech weapons of mass destruction but also to creatively adapt other technologies (e.g., an airplane or a box cutter). They shrewdly manipulate and harness the benefits of globalization through the use of fluid transnational networks with cells that can be activated immediately or remain dormant for extended periods. Finally, their attacks are often executed simultaneously in a well-rehearsed and choreographed manner (e.g., Kenya and Tanzania, New York and Washington).

Despite European expertise and experience, a successful counterterrorism campaign that can undermine new terrorism will require a holistic response and not just a tweaking of existing counterterrorist infrastructure. Some states have already shown that they can adapt old terrorist tools to confront the new terrorist threat. For example, all Spanish provinces have a counterterrorist infrastructure in place, which varies depending on the region. In Basque country, for obvious reasons, the focus is on the Basque Fatherland and Liberty (ETA), while in Almeria it is more geared to confront Islamic threats.

The second conceptual difference occurs within Europe, where governments are divided about whether they consider their own cities, civilians, and assets targets for future attacks or if they assume that only Americans and their assets abroad are primary targets. If they assume the latter, they will not respond in a comprehensive manner until they are themselves victims of an attack. But even for those who fall into the former category and have a significant counterterrorist infrastructure in place, it is not entirely obvious what additional measures they could take on their own beyond tightening their internal security. One senior Spanish official remarked, "I don't know what else we can do in Spain that we are not already doing to protect ourselves."[22]

Indeed, Spain can be placed on one end of the continuum as a country that views terrorism as a major threat. Prime Minister José María Aznar has repeatedly declared that his first priority is the fight against terrorism, which, although focused mostly on ETA, also includes Al Qaeda. France too has recognized the seriousness of this threat and has given it due priority in government because of the numerous attacks by subgroups of Al Qaeda over the last decade. In December 1994, for example, an Algerian terrorist group planned to crash an Air France jet into the Eiffel Tower, an early and overlooked indication that fully fueled airplanes would be used as weapons.

Situated at the other end of the spectrum are countries such as Sweden or the Netherlands, which regard the terrorist threat as important but not a top priority. However, the recent attacks in Bali and Mombassa serve as harsh reminders to even the more complacent countries that their citizens are also targets. Even these countries are now aware that most European countries served as financial and logistical bases for Al Qaeda and its affiliates in the 1990s. The Netherlands, for example, had been a preferred site for banking and has been used as a base to launch attacks on France.[23]

If a new and more comprehensive response could be based on the assumption that all Western states and their civilians and assets at home and abroad are potential targets, and if it could be developed in conjunction with Europeans and North Americans and could incorporate a robust effort to counter root causes and facilitators, a more effective counterterrorist program could be implemented. Only when both the U.S. and European governments agree on an overriding strategy will there be less acrimonious debate over responses and next steps. The alliance could then be concerned with the real challenges beyond defeating Al Qaeda, such as how to rebuild Afghanistan and Iraq. A strong transatlantic alliance is also instrumental to preserving the broader coalition, the collapse of which would seriously undermine the campaign.

Safeguarding the coalition also requires a strong international effort at the United Nations, which is the only forum in which a common conceptual strategy and standards could be advocated and the implementation managed. Utilizing the UN for this purpose would also serve to prevent some states from exploiting the counterterrorist campaign as an excuse to clamp down on domestic opposition. Is the institution equipped for this role?

The United Nations

It is essential that the United States and major European countries resolve their differences and work closely together to develop a common analytical framework that can successfully undermine Al Qaeda. Unless this happens, the responsibilities assigned to the Security Council will not be realizable, because tensions among the Permanent Five (P-5) members spill over into the work of the organization and damage its credibility and effectiveness (assuming that the damage caused by the decision to go to war in Iraq is reparable). Beyond the P-5, the counterterrorist campaign would gain legitimacy from the majority of member states if it was enshrined in international law and was not perceived to be operating at the whim of the sole remaining superpower.

The kind of cooperation that is required would be encouraged if Washington was seen as respecting UN decisions. Even in the debate over the use of force in Iraq in late 2002, most states indicated they would support force if the Security Council agreed to use it. How has the United Nations responded thus far?

Immediately after September 11, the Security Council played a critical role when it passed resolution 1373, which mandated all members to initiate a specified number of counterterrorist measures and submit progress reports concerning these changes to its newly established Counter-Terrorism Committee (CTC). As of April 16, 2003, 190 states had submitted their first-round reports (plus four from non-member states and observers), while 134 had submitted second reports and 27 had submitted third reports. Never before have so many members responded in such a rapid fashion to a request by the Security Council.

The speed with which member states submitted their reports to the Counter-Terrorism Committee testified to the effectiveness of the new international coalition. But some states responded from a fear of being attacked (for example, Libya). Other developing states (Somalia's embattled Transitional National Government, for instance) used this as an opportunity to submit their "wish list," because one of the promised outcomes is assistance to improve internal responses to terror.[24] At the same time, the wealthier developed states do not trust the UN enough to send substantial information relevant to terrorism, even though the committee has provided mechanisms for handling confidential reports.

The reports from industrialized states—in particular, the United States—therefore read as a combination of affirmations of government attention and veiled threats about how the reporting government will respond if others do not make certain cooperative changes in their own procedures. One could therefore argue that these reports are hardly helpful and, if anything, put the UN in a difficult position since the process raises the expectations of a number of poorer states that they will receive development and other aid that is unlikely to be available. On the positive side, the report submission process has achieved an increased level of compliance with the Security Council and raised awareness among most countries about the requirements of an effective counterterrorist campaign. Even though some argue that this is a new form of intrusiveness by the Security Council, it demonstrates the importance of multilateralism; it would not have been possible for the U.S. government to have achieved a similar outcome on its own.

Beyond the work of the council, other organizations in the UN system have also begun reorganizing activities and strategies, from the International Maritime Organization's efforts to confront threats to shipping, to the World Health Organization's efforts to prepare for potential chemical and biological weapons attacks, to the International Civil Aviation Organization's efforts to improve airport and airline security. The UN secretary-general established eight subcommittees to promote reforms and greater understanding between the different international secretariats.[25]

Compliance with the Security Council has been an important advance. However, beyond the whirlwind of activity and organizational reforms, it is far from clear whether these changes are underpinned by substance or whether they consist mainly of rhetoric. The common perception among most of the Western powers is that the UN is unreliable and tends toward the lowest common denominator. Moreover, and practically speaking, member states have yet to see UN resolutions fully implemented.[26] The view is that if the General Assembly cannot even agree on a definition of terrorism, how is it possible for the organization to be responsible for counterterrorism worldwide? Given the inherent constraints of the world organization, what responsibilities should be entrusted to it?

Not only should the Security Council retain the authority for maintaining the broader coalition but the UN should also be entrusted with directing the attack on root causes and facilitators of religious extremist terrorism with a primary focus on four issues. The first is the complicated link between terrorism and poverty. Since September 11, a number of politicians, including President George W. Bush, have made a direct connection between poverty and terrorism.[27] Although conventional wisdom argues in favor of a correlation between poverty and terrorism, available evidence does not lend credence to this proposition. If anything, it supports the opposite.[28] Indeed, if poverty really were the root cause of terrorism, terrorists would mostly come from the poorest parts of the world, namely sub-Saharan Africa. Thus far, this has not been the case.

Even if it may be true that in general terrorists are neither poor nor uneducated,[29] they tend to use the plight of the poor as one justification for committing violence and for broadening their appeal. They often claim to speak on behalf of the poor, just as other middle-class well-educated ideologues have done in the past. Therefore, as noted in the previous section, a serious effort to fulfill the Millennium Development Goals would help remove the appeal of one of the platforms commonly used by terrorists.

Strengthening weak states and rebuilding collapsed ones should be a second area of responsibility for the UN. When discussing the environment in which terrorism flourishes, a further theory links "failed" states to terrorism.[30] Even if they are not the real breeding grounds for terrorists—and there is little hard evidence to support such allegations—they could become more attractive territories for terrorists if their networks in other states were to be eliminated or threatened. And terrorists may also use them for financing through the transshipment of goods, people, and other economic activity.

Where the threat of terrorist penetration may be more manifest is in weak and fragile states. Here, governments are often corrupt and they still retain some control over security structures, which would allow terrorists to operate in a protected environment. It is for this reason that the more plausible Al Qaeda spottings have been identified in places such as Kenya, Mozambique, Angola, Liberia, and Sierra Leone or in the tri-border area between Paraguay, Brazil, and Argentina. A serious effort to strengthen governance and security sectors in such places would make a substantial difference to the campaign.

A third area where the UN could play a role is in helping to end wars perceived as threatening Islam, which have been exacerbated due to the participation of "foreign volunteers," many of whom have links to Al Qaeda. This penetration occurs much in the same way that past ideological wars have attracted foreign recruits (e.g., in the Spanish Civil War). Bin Laden and other Al Qaeda members—the so-called Afghan Arabs—fought against the Soviet occupation of Afghanistan, which took place during the time period when Al Qaeda was founded. More recently, Muslim mercenaries have fought in conflicts in Kashmir, Chechnya, and Bosnia, and they unsuccessfully tried to do so in Kosovo. Participation by the Al Qaeda movement can also transform these territories into breeding grounds for terrorists, as occurred in Afghanistan during the late 1990s. Ayman al-Zawahiri, Osama bin Laden's top lieutenant, wrote that he once visited Chechnya with the intention of establishing it as another training base.[31] Again, the UN can play a pivotal role in attempting to resolve these conflicts before they are corrupted in this manner.

The fourth area, blocking terrorist financing, is one in which the UN is already playing an important role, along with the Financial Action Task Force (FATF) of the Organisation for Economic Co-operation and Development (OECD). Despite the advances made thus far, a greater effort needs to be placed on disrupting the fundamentalist charities. A distinction needs to be made here between Islamic charities such as the Aga Khan Foundation, which provide critical health services and education in neglected rural areas, and other charities that promote a more radical agenda. Indeed, one of the basic tenets of Islam is charity, given in a way that does not humiliate the receiver. This discreet method of delivery, however, complicates matters because some Islamic charities, along with such governments as Iran, propagate their extremist ideology through their aid.

In Somalia, for example, the influence of Islamic movements has increased, although not yet to a significant degree throughout the country. A recent International Crisis Group (ICG) report noted that the fundamentalist movements inside Somalia "owe their rapid growth since 1990 less to genuine popularity than [to] access to substantial external funding."[32] However, Western assistance is insignificant (it totaled only $48 million in 2002). The funds come mainly from a variety of legitimate and illegitimate Islamic sources. Islamic charitable assistance is rarely taken into account in UN appeals for Somalia. Moreover, few Islamic countries or organizations actively participate in the Somalia Aid Coordination Body that was established to serve as the permanent coordination body for donors, UN agencies, and NGOs.

It is not just the extreme Islamic groups that utilize this method of influence. Christian fundamentalist organizations in the United States, for example, have been supporting certain sides in conflicts that are perceived as threatening to Christianity; southern Sudan is the most obvious example. President Bush is now openly supporting the southern Sudanese in this long-standing conflict, primarily due to the influence of the Christian fundamentalist lobby.[33]

These four areas—poverty, weak and collapsed states, wars exploited by Islamic extremists, and fundamentalist charities—play a central role in facilitating terrorist attacks and help to recruit new "martyrs" and members of Al Qaeda. They perpetuate the enabling and complicit environment noted earlier. Reducing poverty and conflict and rebuilding effective government worldwide should therefore become the priorities of the world organization.

Conclusion

Because of their expertise, experience, and common cultures, European states need to be closely aligned with the United States to assist in directing the counterterrorist campaign. Both sides must work together to resolve their differences if this is to happen, and the development of a common analytical framework and strategy is a necessary component. Only then can these states enable the UN to participate in a meaningful way.

A strong UN, in turn, would help remove the general perception that Washington is forcing its standards on others. While the enormous support the United States received in the immediate aftermath of the attacks may have waned, it has not disappeared entirely. According to a recent Pew study, "There is broad support for the U.S. goal of combating terrorism, with the notable exception of those countries in the Middle East/Conflict Area." This same study points out, however, that "there is an equally strong global consensus that the United States disregards the views of others in carrying out its foreign policy."[34]

Terrorist cells with plans to target U.S. and other "infidel" assets have been found in friendly European countries (Germany, the UK, France, and Spain), in friendly developing states (Egypt and the Philippines), and in not-so-friendly developing countries (Sudan, Lebanon, Libya, and Iran). Recent attacks have taken place in the United States and in Kenya, Indonesia, Yemen, Jordan, and Tunisia. It follows that the U.S. can not eradicate Al Qaeda and its affiliates without assistance from friendly states. Already suspected Al Qaeda members have been arrested by Italian, French, Spanish, German, and Swedish authorities, among others. Further, if Washington wishes to remove an unfriendly leader, it will need help from a broader support base. Finally, if it wants to prevent attacks from occurring in any part of the world, the U.S. government, along with its partners, needs to provide necessary assistance to developing states.

There is no doubt that this campaign will be a lengthy one. Al Qaeda's spectacular attacks were planned years in advance and were meticulously designed, thereby attesting to the organization's incredible patience and capabilities. Members also truly believe that they can and will defeat the remaining superpower. The organization has demonstrated an astonishing capacity for entrepreneurship in financing its activities, in choosing targets, and in executing plans. Indeed, Al Qaeda always appears to be a step ahead while Western governments scurry to keep up.

While it is extremely unlikely that Al Qaeda will defeat the United States or indeed establish an Islamic caliphate over the Muslim world, it is very probable that the organization and movement will continue to cause immense damage and undue suffering until they are decisively defeated. To achieve this, the coalition will have to demonstrate a similar degree of flexibility, fluidity, and adaptability, particularly in terms of improved coordination at many levels. As noted in the U.S. Senate Intelligence Committee hearings, "As terrorist groups increasingly associate with and support each other, information sharing and overarching strategic analysis is critical to success in counterterrorist efforts."[35]

Notes

1. Remark made by David Veness, in charge of specialist operations, including counterterrorism, "Roundtable Discussion," November 15, 2002, New Scotland Yard, London.

2. "Counterterrorism Information Sharing with Other Federal Agencies and with State and Local Governments and the Private Sector," Eleanor Hill, staff director, Joint Inquiry Staff, October 1, 2002, 4. Available online at http://fas.org/irp/congress/2002_hr/100102hill.html.

3. The French acronym for "Terrorism, Radicalism, Extremism, and International Violence."

4. In June 1992, foreign and defense ministers of the Western European Union met to define the role and tasks of the WEU. This resulted in the Petersburg Declaration, which outlined steps for the WEU's future development. The declaration reaffirmed NATO's responsibility for collective self-defense and defined its own roles as humanitarian assistance, crisis management, and peacekeeping. The Petersburg tasks are included in the Treaty of Amsterdam.

5. Interview with the author, the Chancellery, Berlin, February 18, 2002.

6. An additional major challenge for the EU is how to help accession countries (countries that are candidates for accession into the EU) develop similar counter-terrorism infrastructures.

7. "Answering the 'Axis' Critics," *Washington Post,* March 5, 2002.

8. Bruce Hoffman, "Is Europe Soft on Terrorism?" *Foreign Policy* 115 (Summer 1999): 64.

9. In 1998, French foreign minister Hubert Vedrine proclaimed that American power represented a problem for the world and labeled U.S. foreign policy heavy-handed. Since the "axis of evil" speech, these differences have only become more pronounced. On February 6, 2002, Vedrine remarked in reference to the United States, "We are today threatened by a new simplism [*sic*] which consists in reducing all the world's problems to the battle against terrorism. That's not a responsible approach. . . . Today there is clearly a radical difference between our approach and that of the U.S. administration." U.S./France interview given by Minister of Foreign Affairs M. Hubert Vedrine to France-Inter's "Question Directe" radio program (excerpts), Paris, February 6, 2002. And it is not just the French. Chris Patten, commissioner of the EU in charge of external relations, not only accused the United States of imperialism but also criticized America's "dangerous instincts." German editorials have also decried American isolationism and hegemonism. "Europeans Ease Criticism of Washington," *International Herald Tribune,* March 5, 2002.

10. See, for example, Joseph Nye, "The New Rome Meets the New Barbarians," *The Economist,* March 23, 2002, 23–25, and "Answering the 'Axis' Critics," *The Washington Post,* March 5, 2002; Robert Kagan, "Power and Weakness," *Policy Review* 113 (June/July 2002): 3–28; or Chantal de Jonge Oudraat, *The New Transatlantic Security Network,* Policy Papers 20 (Washington, D.C.: The American Institute for Contemporary German Studies, Johns Hopkins University, 2002).

11. The dispute between the major European states and the United States over policy toward the Middle East conflict peaked in March and April 2002, when Israeli forces temporarily reoccupied areas of the West Bank.

12. Interview with author, Madrid, May 7, 2002.

13. See Michael Alexander and Timothy Garden, "Counting the Cost of Europe's Security Needs: The Arithmetic of Defence Policy," *International Affairs* 77, no. 3 (July 2001): 509–529; and Timothy Garden, "Military II: EU vs US: Closing the Capability Gap," in Karin von Hippel, ed., *The European Counter-Terrorist Response* (forthcoming).

14. See Juan Aviles, "Es Al-Qaida una amenaza para Europa?" Real Instituto Elcano, documentos de trabajo/working papers, 20 de diciembre de 2002.

15. As explained by David Veness, "Roundtable Discussion."

16. Daniel Benjamin, "Saddam Hussein and Al Qaeda Are Not Allies," *New York Times,* September 30, 2002.

17. "Fatwa Urging Jihad Against Americans," published in *Al-Quds al-ʿArabi,* February 23, 1998.

18. Lawrence Wright, "The Man Behind Bin Laden: How an Egyptian Doctor Became a Master of Terror," *The New Yorker,* September 16, 2002, 72. According to Wright, bin Laden and Azzam finally split because "bin Laden envisioned an all-Arab legion, which eventually could be used to wage jihad in Saudi Arabia and Egypt. [Azzam] strongly opposed making war against fellow-Muslims. Zawahiri undermined Azzam's position by spreading rumors that he was a spy." On November 24, 1989, Azzam and his two sons were killed by a car bomb.

19. Similar strands compete within the extremist Islamic movement about ideology, strategy, and tactics.

20. The terms "complicit society" and "enabling environment" both come from Harvard professor Louise Richardson.

21. For more information, see Walter Laqueur, *The New Terrorism: Fanaticism and the Arms of Mass Destruction* (Oxford: Oxford University Press, 1999); or Ian Lesser, Bruce Hoffman, John Arquilla, David Ronfeldt, and Michele Zanini, *Countering the New Terrorism* (Santa Monica, Calif.: Rand, 1999).

22. Interview with the author, Madrid, May 7, 2002.

23. See Rohan Gunaratna, *Inside Al Qaeda: Global Network of Terror* (London: Hurst and Company, 2002), 126. On 114–131, Rohan documents the role Europe played in supporting Al Qaeda—unwittingly and often even with the knowledge of the government.

24. See http://www.un.org/Docs/sc/committees/1373/ for country reports (click on "Documentation," then "Reports and Related Documents").

25. They are International Legal Instruments and International Criminal Justice Issues, chaired by Hans Corell; Media and Communications, chaired by Edward Mortimer; Human Rights and Terrorism, chaired by B. G. Ramcharan; Weapons of Mass Destruction, Other Weapons and Technologies, chaired by Jayantha Dhanapala; Ongoing and Possible Future UN System Activities, chaired by Michael Doyle; The Uses (and Misuses) of Religion, chaired by Ibrahim Gambari; Security Council's 1373 Committee, chaired by Danilo Turk; and Non-UN Multilateral Initiatives, chaired by Michael Sheehan.

26. Information gleaned from interviews with the author and representatives of the major European states and officials in the Bush administration and at the United

Nations throughout 2002 as part of a MacArthur-funded project at King's College to examine the European counterterrorist response.

27. For example, at the March 2002 World Development Summit in Monterey, Mexico, world leaders declared that the fight against poverty was intrinsically linked to the fight against terrorism.

28. See, for example, "Education, Poverty, Political Violence and Terrorism: Is There a Causal Connection?" Alan B. Krueger, Princeton University and National Bureau of Economic Research, and Jitka Maleckova, Charles University, Working Papers, Research Program in Development Studies, Woodrow Wilson School, Princeton University, May 2002.

29. A caveat must be noted here because there is evidence to suggest that some suicide bombers volunteer (or are volunteered by their families) because of the financial rewards that will accrue to the family. Moreover, many poor parents send their children to extremist *madrasas* because the children receive education, food, books, and clothing free of charge. In these *madrasas,* children learn few practical skills to equip them for the modern world and instead learn a violent version of jihad. Most members of the Taliban were educated in these *madrasas,* though the September 11 hijackers were not. See Jessica Stern, "Pakistan's Jihad Culture," *Foreign Affairs* (November/December 2000): 115–126; and Stern, "Meeting with the Muj," *Bulletin of the Atomic Scientists,* 57, no. 1 (January/February 2001): 42–51.

30. See, for example, "Banks-to-Terror Conglomerate Faces US Wrath," *The Daily Telegraph,* September 28, 2001. This article claimed that "between 3,000 and 5,000 members of the al Qaᶜeda and al-Itihad partnership are operating [in Somalia], with 50,000 to 60,000 supporters and reservists."

31. As cited in Wright, "The Man behind Bin Laden," 80–81.

32. *Somalia: Countering Terrorism in a Failed State,* ICG Africa Report no. 45, May 23, 2002, 13.

33. For more information on root causes, see Karin von Hippel, "The Roots of Terrorism: Probing the Myths," in Lawrence Freedman, ed., *Superterrorism: Policy Responses,* Special Issue of *Political Quarterly* 73, no. 3, Supplement 1 (September 2002): 25–39.

34. The Pew Research Center for the People and the Press, "What the World Thinks in 2002," The Pew Global Attitudes Project, How Global Publics View: Their Lives, Their Countries, the World, America, December 4, 2002, 57. Available online at http://people-press.org/reports/display.php3?ReportID=165.

35. "The FBI's Handling of the Phoenix Electronic Communication and Investigation of Zacarias Moussaoui Prior to September 11, 2001," Eleanor Hill, staff director, Joint Inquiry Staff, September 24, 2002, 3. Available online at http://fas.org/irp/congress/2002_hr/092402hill.html.

6

The Inherent Difficulties of Interinstitutional Cooperation in Fighting Terrorism

Thierry Tardy

In the aftermath of the events of September 11, 2001, the debates about how to respond to the attacks on the United States broadly acknowledged that the fight against terrorism had to be global and that it had to encompass as many political entities as possible. Every structure involved in activities related to the fight against terrorism—at the state, substate, or interstate levels—had to be mobilized. The global nature of the threat implied the necessity of a global response.

Global mobilization implies cooperation. International organizations (IOs) have a particular role to play, not only as forums for discussion but also as independent agents of interinstitutional cooperation. This chapter focuses on cooperation between and among formal IOs that have a central political and security—rather than economic or financial—agenda. The essay focuses on the four most important and well-financed of these entities: the United Nations (UN), the North Atlantic Treaty Organization (NATO), the Organization for Security and Co-operation in Europe (OSCE), and the European Union (EU).

Security institutions are created and mandated to collectively address the threats faced by their member states. The end of the Cold War placed all existing institutions in a new situation; thus, their mandates, their composition, and even their raisons d'être had to be reconsidered. Activities were reoriented to match the needs of the new international milieu: the UN embarked upon a new generation of peacekeeping and peacemaking operations; NATO struggled to redefine its purpose and moved away from its collective-defense dimension to embrace crisis-management activities; the OSCE developed its competency in the field of human rights, institution-building, and electoral supervision; and the EU expressed the will to become a security actor through the Common Foreign and Security Policy (CFSP), which had newly found capacities in the field of crisis management. While these institutions found themselves interacting more and more frequently, competition forced them to think more seriously about their respective comparative advantages.

Like the end of the Cold War, the events of September 11 have had an impact on security institutions. Even though none of them have an explicit mandate to fight terrorism, the advent of threats from non-state actors obliges these institutions to demonstrate their relevance to member states as they face a "new" challenge.[1] The transnational nature of the threat, the magnitude of the attacks, and, at least in part, the place of the United States in the international system have all contributed to the turn of states and IOs toward the idea of enhanced interinstitutional cooperation.

Interinstitutional cooperation is multifaceted. It may take place at the tactical and strategic levels in both the short and long term. It may include normative and legal issues as well as operational matters such as raising public awareness, sharing of information by the police and intelligence services, providing mutual assistance and support to third parties, developing joint bodies, and appointing liaison personnel. Operational cooperation among security institutions may also include actions to deal with the consequences of terrorist attacks and dismantling terrorist cells, possibly with the use of force.

This chapter argues that interinstitutional cooperation among security institutions in the fight against terrorism is weak, unstructured, and unlikely to be significantly developed in the medium term. In spite of the official discourse that followed the tragic events of September 2001, security institutions barely cooperate with one other. What cooperation there is is unstructured because there is no overriding central mechanism to coordinate or facilitate it. The interinstitutional environment cannot be considered a "social network" with "recurrent transactions," to use the usual terms employed by analysts. Interinstitutional cooperation among security institutions is unlikely to become an effective channel of the fight against terrorism because few elements conducive to meaningful collaboration are present.

The first part of this chapter examines and questions the official discourse of the UN, the OSCE, the EU, and NATO about interinstitutional cooperation. The second and the third parts then look at two sets of reasons that explain the shortcomings of interinstitutional cooperation: the nature of interinstitutional cooperation under what international relations specialists call "anarchy," and the specific character of the fight against terrorism.

Interinstitutional Cooperation in Fighting Terrorism: Discourse versus Reality

In the first months following September 11, the secretariats of IOs as well as state officials issued a spate of declarations strongly advocating international cooperation and, to a lesser extent, interinstitutional cooperation, as channels of the fight against terrorism. The UN, the OSCE, the EU, and NATO have added to the discourse with different levels of conviction. Not only has the need for interinstitutional cooperation been unequally perceived, in practice such cooperation remains undeveloped. Each of these four institutions is discussed in turn.

The UN: Uniquely Placed?

In accordance with its principal purpose of maintaining international peace and security, the UN is, in the words of the executive director of the UN Office for Drug Control and Crime Prevention (ODCCP),[2] "uniquely placed to foster international and regional cooperation [in the fight against terrorism], together with regional organizations which have been working for years in this field, or have been taking new initiatives since September 11."[3] The legitimacy of the UN as *the* coordinating body of the interstate and interorganizational response to September 11 has been widely recognized.

Almost by definition, contemporary terrorism cannot be fought effectively by a few actors in isolation. Every state and international institution should contribute to the overall response. The numbers of actors involved in the response as well as the nature of the threat to the core values embodied by the UN Charter give a central role to the world organization in fostering cooperation and coordination at all levels. Well before the attacks of September 11, a number of different UN bodies (depicted in Figure 6.1) regularly stressed the need for enhanced cooperation among international organizations on terrorism, but this necessity became even more acute after September 2001.[4]

According to a representative of the Terrorism Prevention Branch (TPB) of the UN Centre for International Crime Prevention (CICP), in addition to its ability to "[establish] . . . international legal and behavioral norms" and to "[strengthen] . . . the capacity of the Member States to meet new challenges," the UN has comparative advantages in the fight against terrorism in the areas of "fostering international coordination" and "enhancing international cooperation."[5] The *Report of the Policy Working Group on the United Nations and Terrorism*[6] sees "efforts to sustain broad-based international cooperation in the struggle against terrorism" as one dimension of a tripartite strategy to be followed by the UN.[7] The report also assures that a more systematic "cooperation between the UN and other international actors" is a condition of the effectiveness of any international action. Similarly, the UN Plan of Action on terrorism (adopted in April 2002 in the framework of the Vienna Declaration on Crime and Justice)[8] recommends that the CICP play a central role in fostering "cooperation with other relevant international and regional organizations."[9]

Figure 6.1. The UN and Terrorism

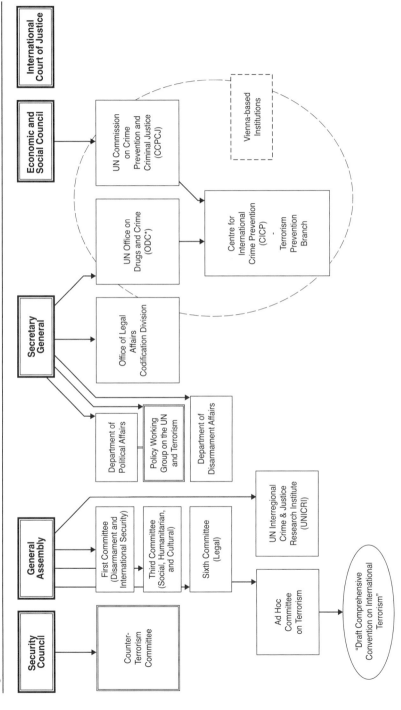

International Court of Justice

Economic and Social Council
— UN Commission on Crime Prevention and Criminal Justice (CCPCJ)

Vienna-based Institutions

Secretary General
— Office of Legal Affairs Codification Division
— UN Office on Drugs and Crime (ODC*)
— Centre for International Crime Prevention (CICP) - Terrorism Prevention Branch
— Department of Political Affairs
— Policy Working Group on the UN and Terrorism
— Department of Disarmament Affairs

General Assembly
— First Committee (Disarmament and International Security)
— Third Committee (Social, Humanitarian, and Cultural)
— Sixth Committee (Legal)
— UN Interregional Crime & Justice Research Institute (UNICRI)
— Ad Hoc Committee on Terrorism
— "Draft Comprehensive Convention on International Terrorism"

Security Council
— Counter-Terrorism Committee

——— Bodies created after September 11, 2001

*The UN Office for Drug Control and Crime Prevention (ODCCP) was renamed Office on Drugs and Crime (ODC) as of October 1, 2002.

Beyond the general commitment to the principle of interorganizational cooperation, the role of regional organizations is particularly stressed.[10] In his opening address to the symposium on "Combating International Terrorism: The Contribution of the United Nations," the ODCCP's executive director stated that "many initiatives have been taken to deal with terrorism. Now it is time to coordinate them. The synergy we seek is, in the first instance, within the United Nations. Secondly, it is coordination with other international organizations, especially those which represent regions and sub-regions." Hence, the Policy Working Group on the United Nations and Terrorism has established four principles that should underpin UN efforts to enhance cooperation and coordination with regional mechanisms:

- Current ad hoc interaction between the UN and regional organizations should be made more systematic.
- Coordination mechanisms already in place should be used to avoid duplication of efforts and waste of resources.
- Where possible, the UN should help regional organizations involved in counterterrorism to develop a division of labor based on comparative advantage.
- Better flow of information among regional organizations and the UN should be established.[11]

More specifically, ODCCP representatives have launched "initiatives to increase the synergy" with organizations such as the Association of Southeast Asian Nations (ASEAN), European Justice (EUROJUST), the League of Arab States, the African Union,[12] the Organization of American States (OAS), the Organization of the Islamic Conference, and the OSCE.[13] The role of the OSCE is particularly emphasized, as both a partner of cooperation—especially in Central Asia—and as a regional coordinator.

In February 2002, the annual High-Level Tripartite Meeting between the UN,[14] the OSCE, and the Council of Europe, with participation by the European Commission, the International Organization for Migration (IOM), and the International Committee of the Red Cross (ICRC), focused its discussion on collective responses to terrorism. The agenda item on "Coordinating action in the aftermath of 11 September" stressed "comparative advantages." The importance of intercultural and interreligious dialogue was also emphasized, which might involve "such organizations as the Organization of the Islamic Conference and the Arab League."[15]

Most significant, the Counter-Terrorism Committee (CTC) created by Security Council resolution 1373 of September 28, 2001, has been implicitly mandated to play a key role in cooperation and coordination. Although the resolution does not specifically address interinstitutional cooperation—it only specifies state cooperation—the process has a direct link with interinstitutional cooperation. This is further advocated by resolution 1377 (2001), which invites the CTC to "explore with international, regional and sub-regional organizations" ways to facilitate the implementation of resolution 1373. The CTC's first chair, Britain's permanent representative Jeremy Greenstock, describes it as a "switchboard, a catalyst and a driver of other institutions to do their work in a globally coordinated way" and states that it is the CTC's job to "make sure that Member states contribute to this activity, that international institutions coordinate with each other in a global system."[16]

The OSCE: The Recurrent Will to Be a Regional Coordinator

Along with the UN, the OSCE is undoubtedly the organization that has made the greatest effort to enhance interorganizational cooperation in the fight against terrorism. The "Bucharest Plan of Action for Combating Terrorism"[17] adopted in December 2001, and the "Programme of Action" adopted at the Bishkek conference co-organized by the OSCE and the UN's ODCCP[18] call for enhanced cooperation and coordination between the OSCE and other intergovernmental organizations.[19] The OSCE convened a meeting in Lisbon in June 2002 that gathered representatives of the UN, NATO, the EU, the Council of Europe, and other organizations.[20] The chairman-in-office of the OSCE, Antonio Martins da Cruz, supported the idea of the "development, under the aegis of the United Nations, of an efficient and articulated strategy that avoided duplication and reinforced cooperation, while building on the expertise and individual strengths of each organization."[21]

The OSCE's role in coordinating subregional organizations in particular was stressed and was further discussed at a Vienna meeting in September 2002 that gathered about ten subregional organizations and initiatives[22] of the OSCE area and representatives of the UN, the OSCE, NATO, the EU, and the Council of Europe.[23] An Action against Terrorism Unit was also created, with a mandate to foster working-level collaboration of various types. The unit is to establish a list of measures taken by international organizations within the OSCE area, in "close consultation with the UN Counter-Terrorism Committee."[24]

As a regional arrangement under Chapter VIII of the UN Charter, the OSCE reported[25] to the CTC as required by resolution 1373 and consistently refers to the UN in official statements, and the CTC is explicitly asking for OSCE assistance to states in the implementation of the dispositions of the resolution.[26] At the same time, the OSCE has displayed a clear will to be seen as *the* coordinator of other organizations in the OSCE area. The Bucharest Plan of Action for Combating Terrorism states that "the OSCE can take on a coordinating role for inter-and intra-regional initiatives" as it "reaches out through close contacts to non-governmental organizations, civil society and parliamentarians, creating an ever-closer network for the international coalition against terrorism."[27] Favored by the UN, this coordinating role for the OSCE was already outlined in the 1999 Platform for Cooperative Security of the Charter for European Security.[28]

All these elements were integrated into the OSCE Charter on Preventing and Combating Terrorism adopted at the Porto Ministerial Council in December 2002. The adoption of this charter is considered a solid achievement. The imperative of "responding to change" was stressed, as well as the need to "reinforce regional and global cooperation in support of the UN anti-terrorism strategy," as "no organization or state can meet this challenge on its own."[29] The OSCE has a comparative advantage in operational matters in four strategic areas: policing, border security, anti-trafficking, and exposing and eliminating the financial resources of terrorists.[30] OSCE institutions and field missions will be required to adapt or maintain their mandates and activities to reflect such comparative advantages.

The European Union: High Politics Moves to the Forefront

Within the context of this chapter, the European Union is considered to be a security institution because a significant number of activities within its remit directly relate to security of its member states, even beyond the process initiated at Saint-Malo in December 1998 around the concept of a European Security and Defense Policy (ESDP).

Institutional cooperation *within* the organization is as relevant as potential collaboration with other security institutions in addressing terrorism. Taken broadly, interinstitutional cooperation within the EU involves the following levels:

- Between the three pillars of the EU structure,[31] especially CFSP with Justice and Home Affairs
- Between different agencies within each pillar—for example, EUROPOL (European Police) with EUROJUST
- Between national institutions (for instance, police and intelligence services or judicial authorities) through EU channels (essentially EUROPOL and EUROJUST)
- Between the Commission and the Council
- Between individual member states and the Brussels-based institutions

The idea behind the construction of the European Union is more about integration—implying some transfer of sovereignty to a higher body—than it is about mere intergovernmental cooperation among member states. The second and third pillars of the structure established at Maastricht are clearly governed by intergovernmental approaches, but the intrusive type of interstate cooperation that takes place in those two pillars is very different from the cooperative processes observed in other intergovernmental bodies. Insofar as terrorism is concerned, another peculiarity of the EU is the establishment of an area of free movement of persons, which has proven to be a favorable environment for the development of terrorist groups. Interstate and interinstitutional cooperation within the EU has therefore become indispensable.

At the internal level, the great majority of the measures taken by the EU after September 11 (in the Plan of Action adopted on September 21, 2001) fall within the framework of the third pillar. In addition to decisions on the European Arrest Warrant and on a common definition of terrorism,[32] efforts were made to improve cooperation between intelligence services, law enforcement agencies, and judicial authorities. This was done through strengthening and expanding the mandate of EUROPOL and, most important, through the creation of EUROJUST,[33] while cooperation between those two institutions was enhanced. A debate on the protection of the EU's external borders was also launched, which included the idea of creating a European corps of border guards to foster closer cooperation of police institutions throughout the EU, especially an enlarged EU.

As far as interpillar cooperation is concerned, the events of September 2001 have revealed in no uncertain terms the deleterious compartmentalization of the EU pillars structure.[34] Communication among the three pillars remains difficult and constrained. The institutions created under each pillar have developed their own cultures and working methods.

The European Union's rhetorical commitment to cooperate with other IOs is not matched by implementation. The EU has, of course, made regular references to the role of the UN in the fight against terrorism. A report[35] was submitted to the CTC in response to resolution 1373, although the EU was not required to do so.[36] At the Security Council, a EU representative stated: "The international coalition against terrorism must include us all, since the enemy is also common to all of us. Relevant international organizations, including the World Bank, the International Monetary Fund (IMF) and the Financial Action Task Force (FATF), should also be involved in the struggle against terrorism, and should coordinate their efforts in this field with those of the United Nations as a whole."[37] In a similarly innocuous fashion, the EU Declaration on the contribution of the CFSP/ESDP in the fight against terrorism stated that "The Union will seek to further contribute to these international efforts, both internally and in its relations with third countries and international organizations, such as the

UN, NATO and the OSCE." The Declaration went on to say that "promoting coordinating work within bodies and with relevant international organizations, notably the UN and NATO" was important "to increase the effectiveness of the contribution of CFSP, including ESDP, in the fight against terrorism."[38]

Interestingly, neither the Plan of Action adopted on September 21, 2001, nor the conclusions of the EU Council held the day before made explicit reference to cooperation with IOs but rather emphasized closer cooperation with the United States.[39] Similarly, while EUROPOL and the United States reached an agreement on December 6, 2001, on police cooperation and terrorism,[40] the EUROPOL-INTERPOL agreement of November 5, 2001 (which was largely negotiated before September 2001) does not specifically deal with terrorism.[41]

NATO: The Reluctant Partner

In spite of the historical first invocation of Article V of the Washington Treaty, NATO has been outside the military response to September 11. The leitmotiv "adapt or be marginalized" has dominated discussions within NATO and provided new momentum to the sensitive debate about its raison d'être after the Cold War. Logically, cooperation with other IOs might be one of the necessary steps of the adaptation process, but NATO has been traditionally very reluctant to constrain itself through interorganizational cooperative activities. At the same time, NATO's need to display its own comparative advantages vis-à-vis other organizations may lead to increased competition among institutions, thus hindering cooperation further.

A few weeks after September 11, one of the conclusions of a ministerial meeting of the North Atlantic Council was that "military tools alone are not sufficient to combat terrorism effectively. The response must be multi-faceted and comprehensive." The final communiqué included a clear reference to the importance of interinstitutional cooperation:

> [W]e support the efforts of the United Nations and its central role in [the fight against terrorism], and undertake to fully implement UN Security Council Resolution 1373. We also support the efforts of the EU, the OSCE, the G-8 and international financial institutions to combat terrorism. We believe it will be essential to continue to develop cooperation between international organizations in this multifaceted campaign, taking into account their respective responsibilities. In this context, NATO and the European Union are exploring ways to enhance cooperation to combat terrorism.[42]

The same day, a joint meeting of NATO and EU foreign ministers concluded that "following the horrifying attacks on 11 September, cooperation between NATO and the European Union was vital to the fight against terrorism."[43] It was agreed that the two organizations should act "in close consulta-tion" and benefit from their respective comparative advantages. Later, NATO's Secretary-General Lord Robertson mentioned the term "cooperative security" as an important tool of the fight against terrorism, by which he meant "good working ties with international organizations operating in the same or simi-lar fields." He then referred to the existing and forthcoming cooperation with the UN, the OSCE, and the EU and briefly summarized the contacts with each and linked them with the "real and effective working partnership" that routinely takes place on the ground in the Balkans. Lord Robertson feels that the NATO contribution to the implementation of Security Council resolu-tion 1373 should be facilitated because NATO is "particularly well placed to help tackle the intersection between terrorism and transnational organized crime, including the illegal movement of nuclear, biological and chemical materials."[44] In the field of international disaster relief, links have been estab-lished between NATO's Euro-Atlantic Disaster Response Coordination Cen-tre (EADRCC) and the UN Office for the Coordination of Humanitarian Affairs (OCHA). Such links could be activated when dealing with the conse-quences of terrorist attacks on civilians.[45]

In the OSCE, cooperation takes place within the framework of the Platform for Cooperative Security, where the two organizations are "exploring how [they] can better work together in the fight against terrorism, given the considerable overlap in membership . . . between the OSCE and the EAPC [Euro-Atlantic Partnership Council]." As for the EU, it emphasizes civil emergency planning as "a particularly promising avenue for practical cooperation, given the consider-able expertise and capabilities available through NATO on this issue, and the possibility of involving Home Affairs and other Ministries and Agencies in the EU context." Coordination between the European Commission and the EADRCC has been required on both sides. At the military level, NATO also plans, as is already the case for ESDP, to make its assets and capabilities available to support "operations undertaken by or in cooperation with the EU or other international organizations or coalitions involving Allies."[46]

The Persistent Weakness of Interinstitutional Cooperation

Interinstitutional cooperation in the fight against terrorism is, at best, in the very initial phase of its development; the idea is more to explore in what ways co-operation is possible than to implement any defined policy. To date, cooperation appears to be more a rhetorical than a practical achievement. Interorganizational cooperation has undoubtedly been an object of concern, especially for the orga-nizations that have expressed the will to ensure some form of coordination, but it is only one dimension of the overall fight against terrorism.

Security institutions have not established visible and meaningful links between themselves, and the interinstitutional environment can hardly be compared to a "social network" defined as "a patterned set of relationships among actors or groups in a social space."[47] Such a weak "structure of recurrent transactions" means that security institutions have not yet entered into "strategic interdependence,"[48] which would imply recurrent and unavoidable transactions. For the same reasons, the interinstitutional environment cannot be considered an international regime, which is defined as "principles, norms, rules, and decision-making procedures around which actor expectations converge in a given issue-area."[49] No such features currently exist in the interinstitutional environment of the fight against terrorism.

The UN has tried to foster interorganizational cooperation through regular high-level meetings with regional organizations, which have focused on conflict prevention and peacebuilding.[50] For peace support operations, a common presence in different operations by the UN, the OSCE, NATO, and the EU has led to better coordination, both at the level of headquarters and in the field.

These initiatives have, however, produced no major results at the political level. The difficulties observed in the field of crisis management between NATO and the UN or between the EU and NATO (in the context of the development of ESDP) suggest little or uneasy political cooperation. Security institutions do not really know each other, and they barely communicate.[51]

This situation did not fundamentally change after September 11. When they exist, the linkages between IOs are unstructured. Transactions take place more on an ad hoc than a recurrent basis. In the aftermath of the terrorist attacks of September 2001, the great majority of official statements stressed the need to foster cooperation among IOs while simultaneously acknowledging the paucity of such cooperation.

In spite of the official declarations, interinstitutional cooperation has not been a priority. From April 30 to May 2, 2002, the follow-up meeting[52] to the Fourth High-Level Meeting between the UN and regional organizations focused its work not on terrorism but rather on conflict prevention and peacebuilding, as scheduled. A few months later, the *Report of the Policy Working Group on the United Nations and Terrorism* suggested that the "next High-Level Meeting between the UN and regional organizations in 2003 should establish terrorism as an agenda item, with the goal of developing an international action plan."[53] If interorganizational cooperation was a priority, would it not have made sense to propose an emergency meeting on the question? Or change the agenda for the one planned for April–May 2002?

In the same vein, the various institutional documents issued after September 11 were not ambitious or clear about who should do what in the overall fight against terrorism. In most cases, documents dwell on the macrolevel or

multilateral level and do not specifically deal with interinstitutional cooperation, and when they actually do, they almost always confine themselves to a
call for enhanced cooperation without putting forward precise recommendations. This also means that the areas of possible cooperation among security
institutions are not clearly identified. The *Report of the Policy Working Group
on the United Nations and Terrorism* states that the UN is not "well placed to
play an active operational role in efforts to suppress terrorist groups, to pre-
empt specific terrorist strikes, or to develop dedicated intelligence-gathering
capacities."[54] The OSCE is hardly better. These two institutions are most likely
to cooperate on normative issues and actions such as raising public awareness, providing legal assistance to states, training, or creating long-term policies that address the "root causes" of terrorism. At the same time, the
collaboration between NATO and the EU might well address more operational issues—for instance, sharing information, setting up databases, and
dismantling terrorist cells.

But the mandates and roles of coordinating bodies need to be further defined. The roles of the UN's ODCCP,[55] CICP,[56] and Terrorism Prevention
Branch in fighting terrorism have not been clearly established, much less their
role in fostering interorganizational cooperation. To say the least, the mandate given by the Vienna Action Plan to the CICP ("VII. Action against Terrorism") is not ambitious.[57]

The UN-OSCE Bishkek conference in December 2001 can be seen as a good
start because the two institutions focused on a particular area, Central Asia.
But the OSCE is clearly limited in its endeavor by its limited capacity to play
a significant operational role in fighting terrorism. And therefore it is limited
as a driving force in cooperating with others.

As far as cooperation between the EU and NATO is concerned, the joint
press statement by NATO's secretary-general and the EU presidency of May
2002 reveals the timidity of the two organizations. Ministers only *hope* that
"useful consultations on several questions" relating to the fight against terrorism will continue between the two organizations.[58] For the two institutions, the
threat embodied by the September 2001 attacks has led to a prioritization of
activities that is inward looking. In this constrained environment, the development of organizational capacities clearly prevails over interinstitutional
cooperation. Finally, other organizations that theoretically have a security dimension, such as the African Union, the Arab League,[59] the Organization of
the Islamic Conference, or ASEAN,[60] have barely explored what can be done
in the field.

Thus, there is no evidence of the emergence of an effective interinstitutional cooperative process. Major security institutions need to adapt to a situation and develop proper capacities before cooperation with other entities

can be seriously considered. Beyond this, however, the nature of cooperation among international organizations and the nature of the fight against terrorism further complicate the prospects for meaningful collaboration. It is to these additional issues that the analysis now turns.

The Difficulties of Interinstitutional Cooperation under Anarchy

For neoliberal institutionalists, cooperation between political entities in a system characterized by anarchy is possible if certain conditions are met.[61] For Robert Axelrod and Robert Keohane, "cooperation can only take place in situations that contain a mixture of conflicting and complementary interests . . . when actors adjust their behavior to the actual or anticipated preferences of others."[62]

For Kenneth Oye, three elements explain why and when cooperation occurs: the "payoff structure," the "shadow of the future," and the "number of players." The payoff structure affects the possibility of cooperation between two actors because they consider it necessary for their "mutual benefit." The shadow of the future can positively affect the likelihood of cooperation because it implies an iterative process without which "defection would emerge as the dominant strategy." Finally, the number of players matters because the "prospects for cooperation diminish as the number of players increases." In other words, "the complexity of N-person situations militates against identification and realization of common interests."[63]

In the absence of a central authority, neoliberal institutionalists therefore consider cooperation possible. According to neoliberals, the possibilities for cooperation among states are enhanced by international organizations, which "provide information, reduce transaction costs, make commitments more credible, establish focal points for coordination, and in general facilitate the operation of reciprocity."[64] International regimes may also play a role through norms and rules, which are internalized by states, as well as through the alteration of "states' understanding of their interests."[65] Within the framework of anarchy, the difficulties of interinstitutional cooperation are best discussed under two categories: the dual nature of international organizations and weak incentives.

The Two-Level Equation of Interinstitutional Cooperation

The level of analysis is peculiar in this exploration of the fight against terrorism because our reference is not the state but rather the international organization. The analysis of cooperation among IOs has to take into account their dual nature as semi-autonomous actors of the international system and as an expression of state will. In short, an international organization is already the product of cooperation among its member states but also has an existence on its own.[66] Interinstitutional cooperation therefore takes place in a two-level environment: first, the level of the states that decide whether to go through international institutions to implement a particular policy; and second, the level of IOs that must display the will and the ability to deliver in a particular field. Only after those conditions are met does interinstitutional cooperation become possible as the product of both state and organizational policies.

If interinstitutional cooperation is dependent upon state and organizational policies, this two-level equation is likely to further decrease the likelihood of cooperation in the fight against terrorism. If states are lukewarm about multilateral cooperation to address terrorism, as we saw earlier, the likelihood that IOs themselves will take the initiative to cooperate with one other will be low. In other words, substantial and effective interinstitutional cooperation that is not grounded in a firm commitment to interstate cooperation is not feasible.

Moreover, security institutions need to demonstrate their competence and comparative advantages before interorganizational cooperation is even a possibility. Yet any analysis of the role of IOs in fighting terrorism, individually or collectively, has to begin with the fact that no existing international organization is specifically mandated to address the issue of terrorism. Thus, there is prima facie evidence that states are more reluctant to cooperate in matters concerning military, police, and intelligence. While NATO might play a role in the coming years in addressing some of the elements of the overall response to terrorism (as was stated at the November 2002 Prague Summit),[67] it clearly did not appear as an appropriate tool in the days and weeks following the terrorist attacks of September 2001. The roles of the UN and the OSCE are also likely to be confined to normative rather than operational roles. The EU is a particular case, however, as the all-purpose regional organization will be theoretically the most involved in fighting terrorism, especially through its third pillar. But the likelihood of a truly European policy is in this field constrained by the nature of the threat and by the way that it jeopardizes perceived vital interests of the states. Hence, even here the "multilateral reflex" is not obvious.

Weak Incentives for Cooperation and Leadership

Given that the propensity of IOs to cooperate is dependent upon state approaches to the role that these institutions should play in the fight against terrorism, what are the chances that the four security institutions under review could develop their own agenda, have their own interests, and pursue policies aimed at defending them? Two general concerns are pertinent here: the weak incentives for cooperation and the absence of strong leadership.

Beyond state policies, the willingness of an institution to cooperate depends on its own capacities as well as upon internal factors that might not be related to the fight against terrorism. Organizations care about their resources, their identities, and their survival.[68] Such interests may lead institutions to cooperate or to compete, depending upon the case. Depending on the circumstances, they may pursue policies that eclipse mere "efficiency concerns."[69]

In spite of their differences, the UN, NATO, the OSCE, and the EU are in a peculiar situation in the fight against terrorism because cooperation and competition are simultaneously at stake. September 11 gave rise to a renewed competition among international actors. Institutions could simply not remain aloof and not actively participate in the global response. Each institution had to adapt to the new situation and be seen as doing something, and if possible doing more than the others, while simultaneously opening up avenues for cooperation with other institutions. A careful reading of documents suggests an emphasis on comparative advantage; but this essential element of efficiency is quite unlikely to enhance the prospects for cooperation among actors constantly attempting to demonstrate their "uniqueness" on the international scene. Competition is more likely to lead to defection unless cooperation is a means to participate in a process from which an institution would be otherwise excluded.

Yet in the fight against terrorism, cooperation does not appear to be an indispensable way to achieve most objectives. For instance, the post–September 11 context highlighted once again NATO's relevance as a collective defense and security institution. NATO officials—especially its secretary-general—have visibly displayed a desire to engage in counterterrorism.[70] However, this activism has not led NATO officials to favor cooperation with other institutions. In any case, the need to justify budgets or to assert identity has led security institutions, as a matter of priority, to look at what was feasible by each institution individually rather than collectively. In other words, it is difficult to identify in what sense cooperation would pay off and in what sense defection would be costly.

Another complicating factor is that the interinstitutional environment is characterized by the absence of leadership. There is no "linking-pin organization"[71] that would have "extensive and overlapping ties to different parts of [the] network" and would be the "node through which a network is loosely joined."[72] Nor are there enforcement mechanisms through which sanctions could be decided and enforced.[73]

In spite of the lofty prose of its Charter, the UN does not play such a role globally, nor does the OSCE regionally. In the fight against terrorism, in addition to the political reasons often mentioned in explaining the UN's limited operational capabilities, the UN is not equipped to play the role of the interinstitutional coordinator. The Counter-Terrorism Committee is an ad hoc body primarily created to coordinate states and only secondarily to coordinate international organizations. Furthermore, it was established in a system that already had many overlapping entities, as we saw earlier in Figure 6.1. The ill-defined division of labor was underlined during the June 2002 Vienna symposium on "Combating International Terrorism: The Contribution of the UN," whose objective was to "clarify the role of the Vienna based UN entities in relation to the overall efforts of the Organization to combat terrorism."[74] Most important, the permanent members of the Security Council clearly wish to keep control over the actions of the UN and the CTC; within this context, it is hardly a foregone conclusion that they will welcome a more important role for the world organization. In the highly sensitive issue of the fight against terrorism, the tension created by the twofold nature of IOs is obvious because states, and especially the most powerful, are reluctant to relinquish their prerogatives.

Finally, while this analysis has been focused mainly on cooperation processes among security organizations, one of the most formidable challenges lies in ensuring cooperation *within* particular organizations—that is, among different bodies of an organization—as well as between an organization and its member states. For example, within the UN, the relationship between the CTC and the CICP and between them and member states is a striking challenge. Within the EU, the issue of the interpillar cooperation remains paramount.[75] For both of these key organizations, the diversity of the bodies possibly involved in the fight against terrorism impinges on the cohesion of institutional policy as well as on the prospects of cooperation.

The EU case is particularly revealing about the inherent difficulties of cooperation in fighting terrorism. For instance, EUROPOL has no direct access to the databases of the Schengen Information System. Stressing the difficulties that the EU encounters in fighting terrorism within its own member states, Paul Wilkinson notes that "when one takes into account that the EU has the most fully developed structures for regional integration in the world, it is evident that international police and intelligence cooperation on terrorism and related matters in other parts of the world is going to remain fairly limited in scope."[76]

Within the UN, Secretary-General Kofi Annan has stressed that "[w]e must ensure closer coordination between different UN bodies."[77] In its review of UN system activities, the Policy Working Group on the United Nations and

Terrorism recognized that "the Organization's terrorism-related efforts would be more effective if better coordinated, supported by modestly enhanced resources, and shaped by a more sharply defined strategy and priorities." In this respect, the creation by the great majority of international organizations of special units to address the consequences of the events of September 11 may permit better cooperation. As the *Report of the Policy Working Group on the United Nations and Terrorism* notes, "such steps establish clear delineations of responsibility, especially for facilitating inter-organizational cooperation."[78] But those units will not suffice to solve the internal coordination issue.

The Peculiarity of the Environment of the Fight against Terrorism

Cooperation between actors is largely determined by the nature of the environment in which cooperation occurs. Players will be more inclined to cooperate as the environment in which they operate offers good prospects for organizational profit. To restate the theory, cooperation has to pay off in the long run. Yet the environment of the fight against terrorism does not appear to be the most conducive environment for cooperation. In this regard, Malcolm Anderson writes:

> [E]ffective and continuing cooperation [in the field of the fight against terrorism] is almost impossible to achieve because there must be substantial agreement between governments of the member states on political rather than criminal law enforcement objectives, and because mutual assistance is also complicated by the diverse contexts in which transnational violence takes place, the difficulty of conceptualizing terrorism, the problematic legal basis of counterterrorism, differing articulation of the security agencies involved in different countries, and the unwillingness of national authorities to share intelligence.[79]

Terrorism is undoubtedly a most sensitive issue for which the exchange of information poses problems. Actors may see cooperation as necessary but still remain reluctant to embark upon a policy path that would prove to be counterproductive from a narrow institutional perspective. For example, the difficulties encountered by INTERPOL in the criminal field are well known and predictable. Sovereignty is also at stake because the attacked state may legitimately judge its existence to be threatened; hence, the response is inherently a "state issue." In addition to the problems analyzed earlier, this section adds two more complicating factors to the difficulties of interinstitutional cooperation in the fight against terrorism. The environment is unusual because of the ambiguity behind the very notion of terrorism, which is exacerbated because of the position of the United States in the contemporary international system.

The Blurred Notion of the "Fight against Terrorism"

What precisely is meant by "terrorism" and the "legitimacy" of the ways that it can be fought? The answer has implications for the prospects for interinstitutional cooperation in the fight against terrorism. Specific answers to such questions are problematic for a single state and consequently are problematic for IOs. I do not wish to enter the debate about the various controversial definitions of terrorism, but it clearly has been conceptualized differently within the UN, the EU, and NATO—not to mention the African Union, the Arab League, and ASEAN. Furthermore, states have different approaches within each of these organizations. The events of September 11 may give the impression that terrorism is a well-defined concept and Al Qaeda its best illustration. No matter how extensive the Al Qaeda network, or transnational terrorism in general, may be, terrorism is inevitably perceived by states and regional organizations through "parochial" lenses.

Questions of definition are key because they determine the types of priority responses by security institutions and therefore where interinstitutional cooperation is needed and where it is possible. A careful scrutiny of the official documents produced by security institutions following September 11 does not help much in identifying the ways in which IOs can contribute to the overall fight against terrorism. Logically, the ambiguity about the notion of terrorism leads to ambiguities about the ways it should be fought.

The fight against terrorism combines actions aimed at "suppressing" terrorist groups and addressing the "root causes." Along with the normative dimensions of actions by the UN, the OSCE, and the EU and a possible role for NATO in suppressing terrorism, one field in which security institutions would certainly have a role to play is long-term policies that address "root causes." Here again, issues of definition arise; consensus within IOs about what can be said to constitute a root cause would make it difficult even without the sensitivity of the United States—and other countries[80]—to imply any justifications of the September 11 attacks. Nonetheless, if poverty, social inequalities, political oppression, and uneven access to resources can be breeding grounds for terrorist groups, or for their sympathizers, then international organizations are likely to play an essential role in addressing such issues.

However, in addition to the disputed link between so-called root causes and terrorism,[81] security institutions outside Europe are weak precisely in the regions where breeding grounds exist. The UN may try to play a role, together with the OSCE (in the Balkans, the Caucasus, or Central Asia) or the EU (through political processes or aid programs), but prospects of cooperation with regional security institutions in Africa, Asia, and the Middle East will remain very low.

An additional problem with the identification of measures would fall within the category of the "fight against terrorism." If IOs were to become involved in long-term policies aimed at combating what appears to be root causes of terrorism, it is doubtful that the activities those policies generate will be labeled as such. In other words, can educational programs in the Gaza Strip be considered as interinstitutional cooperation in the fight against terrorism? Given the links between transnational organized crime and terrorist organizations identified in numerous UN resolutions, would activities led by the UN, the OSCE, or NATO in fighting transnational organized crime in Kosovo or Bosnia and Herzegovina be seen as part of the fight to address root causes?

Distinctions between long-term and short-term policies, and between normative and operational activities, will differ depending upon specific circumstances, as will the potential role for individual security organizations. Activities to combat existing terrorist groups or to raise public awareness are different from activities to address root causes. They require different capacities and different kinds of political backing from states. Furthermore, if no other major attack occurs, attention to long-term policies will inevitably wither. Wilkinson calls this phenomenon the "politics of the latest outrage," by which "in the wake of a major atrocity, public outrage is reflected in numerous promises of major governmental and international action to ensure that 'it never happens again.'" However, "once the memory of the atrocity begins to fade the public begins to lose interest in measures against terrorism."[82] Such a loss of momentum is already being observed in the case of September 11. This reality is likely to affect the prospects for an increased role for IOs and therefore for interinstitutional cooperation.

Threat Assessment: The Centrality of the U.S. Position

Cooperation among states and among international organizations will be facilitated to the extent that a consensus exists about the threat and the nature of a legitimate response to it. For obvious reasons, the fight against terrorism is dominated by the United States and its own evaluation of the situation. The United States does not particularly count on security institutions to fight terrorism and relies even less on interinstitutional cooperation. The U.S. perception directly affects the whole environment of the war on terrorism and consequently the prospects for interinstitutional cooperation.

One corollary is the important divide between the official consensus—which is strongly inspired by the United States—by which international terrorism is a global threat that has to be fought globally by all and the threat assessment and effective commitment of various actors. This divide partly comes from divergences of approach to the threat and, more broadly, to what is meant by "international security."

The secretary-general of the League of Arab States, Amre Moussa, asks: "What is the definition of international terrorism that you want us to fight for years to come? . . . When Western countries define international security, and the threats to it, do they take into consideration the security of others as defined by them and not as defined for them? Africa considers that the main threats to its security lie in extreme poverty, in diseases, and the resulting social collapse in many societies." Moussa concludes, "We cannot, at least from our standpoint, agree to the proposition that international security is being tied down only to or only threatened by international terrorism."[83]

In other words, terrorism might not appear to everyone as the clear threat that the United States wants everyone to believe. Such divergences seem somewhat less evident within NATO, the EU, and the OSCE than within the Arab League or other regional organizations. Nonetheless, these three Western security organizations and their member states have substantially different perceptions about threats than those in Washington. At the Prague summit, the reluctance of some NATO countries to see the alliance building "new capabilities for new challenges,"[84] among them terrorism, under American pressure is revealing. Divergences can also be found in the case of the EU and its member states, which have not displayed the same eagerness to fight terrorism as Washington, partly because of a different assessment of the threat and partly because of a fear of becoming a target.

Differences follow in the policy responses, and subsequently in the evaluation of the payoff structure of cooperation, at all levels. What are the incentives for and the prospects of cooperation between the EU with NATO (or of the League of Arab States or the African Union with NATO) if these organizations and/or their member states have different perceptions about the threat, about its urgency, and about what is to be done?[85] These reservations will undoubtedly be exacerbated by any unilateral action undertaken outside the Security Council, especially by Washington.

Conclusion: Back to the Realist Paradigm?

The peculiar character of the contemporary environment of the fight against terrorism inherently leads to confused calculations about the costs and benefits of interinstitutional cooperation. The gains are difficult to identify, and so are the possible costs of noncooperation. Faced with the multifaceted terrorist threat, international organizations have few incentives to cooperate. Yet, noncooperation is not cost effective; defection does not seem to offer a greater payoff than cooperation.

This observation leads to a reconsideration of the overarching theoretical framework. Interinstitutional cooperation clearly falls within the neoliberal institutionalist paradigm, which contends that anarchy is not an insurmountable obstacle to cooperation among rational actors. But one could also argue that the events of September 11 and the fight against terrorism are characterized by the domination of realist perspectives. The war on terrorism is arguably shaped by the notion of self-help, the domination of the United States and unilateral approaches to the use of force, short-term analysis of national interests, and state survival.

Even before the September 2001 attacks, Paul Wilkinson wrote: "The huge gulf between the rhetoric and the reality of international cooperation against terrorism is a powerful illustration of the extent to which the realist paradigm actually dominates and shapes the perceptions of the majority of political leaders and their citizens in the contemporary international state system." He went on to contend that "the realist paradigm is all too clearly inherently incapable of contending with new transnational threats to human rights and security posed by international terrorism." But if "ideally all countries should cooperate fully to ensure that those involved in terrorist crimes are brought to justice, . . . in practice, the anarchic nature of the international system and the fact that there are states that use, sponsor, support and sympathize with specific terrorist groups are basic reasons why terrorism is likely to remain the most ubiquitous form of political violence well into the future."[86]

Conceptually as well as practically, the major obstacle to interinstitutional cooperation in the fight against terrorism is the fact that the environment is largely dominated by states. One lesson of the immediate aftermath of September 11 is that multilateral security institutions were not considered as appropriate tools to fight terrorism. Their role was rhetorically praised, but in practice, the response had to be primarily led by states, at least in the short run. Similarly, security institutions have not been able to shape the behavior of states, or even to convincingly orient the debate on terrorism. They have not played a significant role in "fixing the meanings . . . establish[ing] the parameters, the very boundaries, of acceptable action."[87] This obviously limits the prospects of interinstitutional cooperation and takes us back to the debates on the relationship between the state and IOs and the role of IOs in bringing responses to international/transnational security issues.

Consequently, the conditions for effective and coherent cooperation among international organizations in general, and security institutions in particular, in the fight against terrorism are far from being met. Sporadic interinstitutional cooperation has occurred and will undoubtedly occur in the future, but it is likely to remain isolated. States and international organizations alike are trying to define how they can respond to the events of September 2001, but interinstitutional cooperation has not yet appeared as a priority.

Moreover, the peculiarity of the environment of the fight against terrorism reduces still further the prospects for such collaboration. In spite of the gravity of the tragic events of September 11, states and security institutions have not only faced difficulties in conceptualizing terrorism and in defining coherent and coordinated responses to the attacks, but they also have been reluctant to cooperate in this sensitive arena. Furthermore, the U.S.-inspired consensus by which terrorism is a global threat that has to be fought globally by all has not moved from the rhetorical to the operational level. The UN, the OSCE, NATO, and the EU are not in agreement about what can be done, by whom, and how. Consequently, the terms of interinstitutional cooperation remain to be defined, as do the details of genuine operational cooperation.

Notes

The author would like to thank particularly Neil MacFarlane, Susan Woodward, and Jeffrey Laurenti for their comments and advice on earlier drafts of this chapter.

1. The point is not to argue that transnational terrorism is a new phenomenon but that the way the attacks were executed is new.

2. The UN Office for Drug Control and Crime Prevention (ODCCP) was renamed Office on Drugs and Crime (ODC) as of October 1, 2002.

3. Antonio Maria Costa, Opening Address to the Symposium entitled Combating International Terrorism: The Contribution of the United Nations, Vienna, June 3–4, 2002.

4. The interinstitutional cooperation emphasized in UN declarations and documents contains references to *international* cooperation rather than to *interorganizational* cooperation. The latter is usually mentioned as part of a general process, and the potential coordinating role of the UN is rarely addressed straightforwardly. See "Strengthening International Cooperation in Combating Terrorism," in Commission on Crime Prevention and Criminal Justice, Economic and Social Council, *Report on the Eleventh Session (16–25 April 2002)* (E/2002/30-E/CN.15/2002/14); available online at http://www.unodc.org/pdf/crime/commissions/11comm/14e.pdf.

5. Alex Schmid, "What Role for the UN in Fighting Terrorism?" Academic Council on the United Nations System Fifteenth Annual Meeting, Cascais, Portugal, June 21–23, 2002. The coordination role of the UN was also stressed at a UN symposium organized by ODCCP entitled "Combating International Terrorism: The Contribution of the United Nations," Vienna, June 3–4, 2002. See in particular opening remarks by Federal Minister for Foreign Affairs Benita Ferrero-Waldner of Austria.

6. The mandate of the Policy Working Group is to "identify the longer-term implications and broad policy dimensions of terrorism for the UN and to formulate

recommendations on steps the UN system might take to address the issue." *Report of the Policy Working Group on the United Nations and Terrorism* (Annex to A/57/273-S/2002/ 875), June 16, 2003. Available online at http://www.un.org/terrorism/a57273.htm.

7. The two other dimensions are about "dissuad[ing] disaffected groups from embracing terrorism" and "deny[ing] groups or individuals the means to carry out acts of terrorism." *Report of the Policy Working Group on the United Nations and Terrorism* (S/2002/875), August 6, 2002, 2–3.

8. The Vienna Declaration on Crime and Justice was adopted on December 4, 2000, at the time mainly to deal with organized crime.

9. "Plans of Action for the Implementation of the Vienna Declaration on Crime and Justice: Meeting the Challenges of the Twenty-first Century" (VII. Action against Terrorism) (A/RES/56/261), April 15, 2002. The CICP (and its Terrorism Prevention Branch) is regularly cited as a body that should play a role in enhancing cooperation, although the documents that address the issue of the role of the CICP usually do not specifically refer to cooperation between international institutions. On the role of the CICP, also see *Work of the Centre for International Crime Prevention, Report of the Executive Director, Economic and Social Council* (E/CN.15/2002/2), February 26, 2002; and Commission on Crime Prevention and Criminal Justice, "Strengthening International Cooperation and Technical Assistance," in *Report of the Eleventh Session (April 16–25, 2002)*.

10. See Schmid, "What Role for the UN in Fighting Terrorism?"; and Commission on Crime Prevention and Criminal Justice, "Strengthening International Cooperation and Technical Assistance," in *Report on the Eleventh Session (16–25 April 2002)*, 43–44.

11. *Report of the Policy Working Group on the United Nations and Terrorism*, 14.

12. In September 2002, a representative of the ODCCP attended the High-Level Intergovernmental Meeting of the African Union on Terrorism in Algiers. Areas of cooperation between the two organizations were explored.

13. See ODCCP, "The Way Ahead," summary of the symposium entitled Combating International Terrorism: The Contribution of the United Nations, Vienna, June 3–4, 2002, SYMP/TERR/1, May 24, 2002.

14. Apart from representatives from the Secretariat (in New York and Geneva), the HCR, the HCHR, UNICEF, the UNDP, and UNESCO were also represented. Held in Strasbourg on February 8, 2002.

15. See "Chairman's Conclusions," Strasbourg, Council of Europe, February 8, 2002. Available online at http://www.reliefweb.int/w/rwb.nsf/o/e7c62a2200d29a50 c1256b810045915e?OpenDocument.

16. Quoted in "Vienna Symposium on Terrorism Adds More Momentum to Global Fight Against Terrorism" (UNIS/CP/413), June 6, 2002. Also see Jeremy Greenstock, presentation at the symposium entitled Combating International Terrorism: The Contributions of the UN, Vienna, June 3–4, 2002.

17. "Bucharest Plan of Action for Combating Terrorism," OSCE Ninth Meeting of the Ministerial Council, Bucharest, December 2001, Annex to MC(9).Dec/1; available online at http://www.osce.org/docs/english/1990-1999/mcs/9bucho1e.htm#22.

18. The goal of the Bishkek conference, held in December 2001, was to discuss ways to provide practical support to the five Central Asian OSCE participating states. See UN Office for Drug Control and Crime Prevention and Organization for Security and Co-operation in Europe, *Summary Report: Bishkek International Conference on Enhancing Security and Stability in Central Asia: Strengthening Comprehensive Efforts to Counter Terrorism,* December 13 and 14, 2001. Available online at http://www.osce.org/events/bishkek2001/documents.

19. In late January 2002, the chairman-in-office appointed Jan Troejborg as his personal representative for preventing and combating terrorism. Troejborg has displayed his will to cooperate better with NATO and the EU. See "Address by Jan Troejborg, Special Meeting of the Permanent Council on Combating Terrorism," CIO.GAL/19/02, April 12, 2002. Available online at http://www.osce.org/press_rel/documents/2002-158-adv-speech.pdf.

20. The ICRC, the European Commission, the UN ODCCP, and the Financial Action Task Force on Money Laundering.

21. See "OSCE Chairman Co-ordinates Role of International Bodies in Global Fight against Terrorism: Meeting in Lisbon Unites Organizations in Comprehensive Campaign," *OSCE Newsletter* IX, no. 6 (June 2002): 2.

22. The subregional organizations included the Southeast European Cooperative Initiative (SECI), the Council of the Baltic Sea States (CBSS), the Central European Initiative (CEI), the Central Asian Cooperation Organization (CACO), the Black Sea Economic Cooperation (BSEC), and the GUAM Group (the GUAM Group consists of Georgia, Ukraine, Azerbaijan, and Moldova).

23. See opening address by the OSCE Secretary-General, Ambassador Ján Kubis, "OSCE Meeting with Regional and Subregional Organizations and Initiatives on Preventing and Combating Terrorism," Vienna, September 6, 2002.

24. On the mandate of the unit, see "Statement by Jan Troejborg, Personal Representative of the Chairman-in-Office, OSCE Meeting with Regional and SubRegional Organizations," Vienna, September 6, 2002.

25. *Report to the Counter-Terrorism Committee with Regard to the Implementation of Resolution 1373 (2001)* (S/2002/34), December 19, 2001.

26. See the presentation by Ambassador Curtis A. Ward, advisor on technical assistance of the CTC, "Building Capacity to Prevent and Combat International Terrorism: The Role of Regional and Subregional Organizations," Vienna, September 6, 2002.

27. See "IV. Action under the Platform for Cooperative Security. Cooperation with other Organizations," Bucharest Plan of Action for Combating Terrorism; also see "I.5. External Cooperation" ("Ensuring Close Cooperation and Coordination with the UN"; "Strengthening Cooperation and Coordination With Relevant Organizations and Institutions Within the OSCE Area"; and "Broadening Dialogue with Partners Outside the OSCE Area") in *OSCE Action Against Terrorism: Status Report on Implementation of the Bucharest and Bishkek Documents,* Lisbon, June 12, 2002.

28. OSCE, Charter for European Security, SUM.Doc/1/99, November 19, 1999. Available online at http://www.osce.org/docs/english/1990-1999/summits/istachar99e.htm.

29. See OSCE chairman-in-office speech, Tenth Ministerial Council, Porto, MC.DEL/7/02, December 6, 2002. Available online at http://www.osce.org/events/mc/portugal2002/documents/files/mc_1039171001_e.pdf.

30. See *OSCE Action Against Terrorism*.

31. The first pillar is Communities Policies; the second is Common Foreign and Security Policy (CFSP); and the third is Justice and Home Affairs.

32. See European Union Council, "Council Framework Decision on the Fight against Terrorism" (6128/02), April 18, 2002.

33. EUROJUST was created at a Justice and Home Affairs Council on February 28, 2002. EUROJUST is mandated to support cooperation and coordination between judicial institutions of the EU member states.

34. See Jolyon Howorth, "The European Union, Peace Operations and Terrorism," in Thierry Tardy, ed., *Peace Operations after 11 September* (London: Frank Cass, forthcoming).

35. *Report of the European Union to the Security Council Committee Established Pursuant to Resolution 1373 (2001) Concerning Counter-Terrorism* (S/2001/1297), December 28, 2001.

36. Without submitting a formal report, ASEAN, SADC, and the Rio Group have transmitted some information on their activities to the Security Council.

37. "Statement at the Security Council on Terrorism," by the permanent representative of Spain to the UN on behalf on the EU, January 18, 2002.

38. "Draft Declaration of the European Council on the Contribution of CFSP, Including ESDP," Seville European Council, June 21–22, 2002; available online at http://www.europarl.eu.int/meetdocs/delegations/kaza/20020703/014%20A%20EN.pdf.

39. See European Council, "Plan of Action of the Extraordinary European Council," SN140/01, September 21, 2001; available online at http://europa.eu.int/comm/justice_home/news/terrorism/documents/concl_council_21sep_en.pdf; and Justice and Home Affairs Council, "Measures Designed to Improve Cooperation with the United States, Conclusions Adopted by the Council (JHA)," Brussels (SN 3926/6/01 REV 6), September 20, 2001.

40. In 2001, EUROPOL also signed agreements with Estonia, Hungary, Iceland, Norway, Poland, and Slovenia.

41. The purpose of the agreement is to "establish and maintain cooperation between the Parties in combating serious forms of organized international crime within the field of competence of each Party." See "Co-operation Agreement between INTERPOL and EUROPOL," The Hague, November 5, 2001. Available online at http://www.interpol.com/Public/ICPO/LegalMaterials/cooperation/agreements/Europol2001.asp.

42. "NATO's Response to Terrorism," statement issued at the Ministerial Meeting of the North Atlantic Council, Brussels, December 6, 2001. Available online at http://www.nato.int/docu/pr/2001/p01-159e.htm.

43. Joint Press Statement by the NATO Secretary-General and the EU Presidency, December 6, 2001. Available online at http://www.nato.int/docu/pr/2001/p01-167e.htm.

44. "Speech by NATO Secretary-General Lord Robertson at the Conference on 'International Security and the Fight Against Terrorism,'" Vienna, June 14, 2002; available online at http://www.nato.int/docu/speech/2002/s020614a.htm.

45. In September 2002, Russia and the EADRCC conducted an exercise called Bogorodsk 2002, which simulated a terrorist attack on a chemical production facility involving mass civilian casualties and involved OCHA and the Organisation for the Prohibition of Chemical Weapons (OPCW).

46. "Speech by NATO Secretary-General," June 14, 2002. Also see "Prague Summit Declaration: Issued by the Heads of State and Government Participating in the Meeting of the North Atlantic Council," Prague, November 21, 2002; available online at http://www.nato.int/docu/pr/2002/p02-127e.htm.

47. Samuel Bacharach and Edward Lawler, *Power and Politics in Organizations* (San Francisco: Jossey-Bass, 1980), 205, quoted in Christer Jönsson, "Interorganization Theory and International Organization," *International Studies Quarterly* 30 (1986): 41.

48. Howard Aldrich, "The Origins and Persistence of Social Networks: A Comment," in Peter Marsden and Nan Lin, eds., *Social Structures and Network Analysis* (London: Sage, 1982), 282, quoted in Jönsson, "Interorganization Theory," 42.

49. Stephen Krasner, "Structural Causes and Regime Consequences: Regimes as Intervening Variable," *International Organization* 36 (1982): 185.

50. See *Report of the Secretary-General on the Work of the Organization* (A/57/1), August 28, 2002, 9–10.

51. As far as the fight against terrorism is concerned, see the sparse section dedicated to "Information Received from International Organizations" in two successive reports of the secretary-general on *Measures to Eliminate International Terrorism,* (A/55/179), July 26, 2000, and (A/56/160), July 3, 2001.

52. Eighteen regional organizations were represented, which included the EU (which was represented by the Council and the Commission), NATO, and the OSCE. See "Meeting Between United Nations, Regional Organizations to Be Convened at Headquarters, 30 April–2 May," UN Press Release PI/1418, April 30, 2002.

53. *Report of the Policy Working Group on the United Nations and Terrorism* (S/2002/875), August 6, 2002, 3.

54. Ibid., 6.

55. In his opening remarks at the symposium entitled Combating International Terrorism: The Contribution of the United Nations, Foreign Minister Benita Ferrero-Waldner of Austria stated that "the relevance of ODCCP and its vast expertise for the fight against international terrorism has yet to be explored and defined." ODCCP, Vienna, 3–4 June 2002.

56. In January 2002, the General Assembly invited the secretary-general to consider "in consultation with Member States and the Commission on Crime Prevention and Criminal Justice, the ways in which the Centre could contribute to the efforts of the UN system against terrorism." See "Strengthening the UN Crime Prevention and Criminal Justice Programme, in Particular Its Technical Cooperation Capacity," General Assembly resolution A/RES/56/123, January 23, 2002.

57. In a draft document of the Vienna Action Plan issued in June 2001, the "Action against Terrorism" section gives the Terrorism Prevention Branch (TPB) a key role in fostering cooperation with other relevant organizations. In the final document, the TPB has been replaced by the CICP. See "Revised Draft Plans of Action for the Implementation of the Vienna Declaration on Crime and Justice" (ECOSOC document E/CN.15/2001/14), June 25, 2001.

58. "Joint Press Statement by the NATO Secretary General and the EU Presidency," NATO-EU Ministerial Meeting, Reykjavik, May 14, 2002; available online at http://www.nato.int/docu/pr/2002/p02-060e.htm.

59. Neither the *Report of the UN Secretary-General on Cooperation between the United Nations and the Organization of African Unity* (A/57/351), August 26, 2002, nor the *Report of the UN Secretary-General on Cooperation between the United Nations and the League of Arab States* (A/57/386), September 6, 2002, addresses the issue of terrorism.

60. ASEAN was, however, involved in the process leading to the adoption at the fourth Asia-Europe Meeting (ASEM), held in Copenhagen in September 2002, of the "ASEM Copenhagen Declaration on Cooperation against International Terrorism." The declaration lists short-term, medium-term, and long-term activities aimed at enhancing ASEM cooperation on terrorism and transnational organized crime. Available online at http://www.europa.eu.int/comm/external_relations/asem/asem_summits/asem4/1.htm.

61. See in particular Robert Axelrod, *The Evolution of Cooperation* (New York: Basic Books, 1984); and Kenneth Oye, ed., *Cooperation under Anarchy* (Princeton, N.J.: Princeton University Press, 1986).

62. Robert Axelrod and Robert Keohane, "Achieving Cooperation under Anarchy: Strategies and Institutions," in Oye, ed., *Cooperation under Anarchy*, 226.

63. Kenneth Oye, "Explaining Cooperation under Anarchy: Hypotheses and Strategies," in Oye, ed., *Cooperation under Anarchy*, 13, 18, and 19.

64. Robert Keohane and Lisa Martin, "The Promise of Institutionalist Theory," *International Security* 20, no. 1 (Summer 1995): 42. Also see Kenneth Abbott and Duncan Snidal, "Why States Act through Formal International Organizations," *Journal of Conflict Resolution* 42, no. 1 (1998): 3–32; and Lisa Martin and Beth Simmons, "Theories and Empirical Studies of International Institutions," *International Organization* 52, no. 4 (Autumn 1998): 729–757. For a counterargument, see John Mearsheimer, "The False Promise of International Institutions," *International Security* 19, no. 3 (Winter 1994/95): 5–49; and Joseph Grieco, "Anarchy and the Limits of Cooperation: A Realist Critique of the Newest Liberal Institutionalism," *International Organization* 42, no. 3 (Summer 1988): 485–508.

65. Oye, "Explaining Cooperation under Anarchy," 11.

66. See Michael Barnett and Martha Finnemore, "The Politics, Power, and Pathologies of International Organizations," *International Organization* 53, no. 4 (Autumn 1999): 699–732.

67. See "Prague Summit Declaration."

68. On NATO and organization theory, see Robert Rauchhaus, "Marching NATO

Eastward: Can IR Theory Keep Pace?"; and Ernst Hass, "Organisation Theory: Remedy for Europe's Organizational Cacophony?" in Robert Rauchhaus, ed., *Explaining NATO Enlargement* (London: Frank Cass, 2001), 3–20 and 83–90.

69. Barnett and Finnemore, "The Politics, Power, and Pathologies of International Organizations," 706.

70. See Philip Gordon, "Reforging the Atlantic Alliance," *The National Interest* 69 (Fall 2002): 91–97; and Dick Leurdijk, "NATO's Shifting Priorities: From Peace Support Operations to Counter-Terrorism," in Tardy, ed., *Peace Operations after 11 September,* forthcoming.

71. Jönsson, "Interorganization Theory," 42–43.

72. Howard Aldrich and David Whetten, "Organization-Sets, Action-Sets, and Networks: Making the Most of Simplicity," *Handbook of Organizational Design* (Oxford: Oxford University Press, 1981), 390, quoted in Jönsson, "Interorganization Theory," 42. On the need to have a "command and coordination structure," see Bruce Hoffman and Jennifer Morrison-Taw, "A Strategic Framework for Countering Terrorism," in Fernando Reinares, ed., *European Democracies against Terrorism: Governmental Policies and Intergovernmental Cooperation* (Brookfield, Vt.: Ashgate Publishing Company, 1999), 9.

73. See Daniel Drezner, "Bargaining, Enforcement, and Multilateral Sanctions: When Is Cooperation Counterproductive?" *International Organization* 54 (Winter 2000): 73–102.

74. See Commission on Crime Prevention and Criminal Justice, *Report on the Eleventh Session, (April 16–25, 2002).* Also see "Role of Vienna-Based UN Centre for International Crime Prevention in Fighting Terrorism Could Be Strengthened" (UNIS/CP/399), November 16, 2001.

75. See Monica Den Boer, "The Fight against Terrorism in the Second and Third Pillars of the Maastricht Treaty: Complement or Overlap?" in Reinares, ed., *European Democracies against Terrorism,* 211–226.

76. Paul Wilkinson, "International Cooperation against Terrorism," in Paul Wilkinson, ed., *Terrorism Versus Democracy: The Liberal State Response* (London: Frank Cass, 2000), 196. On the EU, also see Malcolm Anderson, "Counterterrorism as an Objective of European Police Cooperation," in Reinares, ed., *European Democracies against Terrorism,* 227–243.

77. "Secretary-General, Addressing Council meeting on Counter-Terrorism, Says United Nations Stands 'Four-Square' Against Scourge," UN Press Release SG/SM/8105, January 18, 2002.

78. *Report of the Policy Working Group on the United Nations and Terrorism,* 8 and 13.

79. See Fernando Reinares, "Introduction," in Reinares, ed., *European Democracies against Terrorism,* x; and Malcolm Anderson, "Counterterrorism as an Objective of European Police Cooperation," in ibid., 227–243.

80. See "Assembly's Legal Committee Is Told Fight against Terrorism Should Go to Root Causes, Not Contravene Human Rights, Democratic Values," UN Press Release GA/L/3210, October 3, 2002.

81. See Michael Radu, "E-Notes: The Futile Search for 'Root Causes' of Terrorism," Foreign Policy Research Institute, April 23, 2002. Available online at http://www.fpri.org/enotes/americawar.20020423.radu.futilesearchforrootcauses.html.

82. Wilkinson, "International Cooperation against Terrorism," 197.

83. "Address by H. E. Amre Moussa, Secretary-General of the League of Arab States, on 'International Security and the Fight against Terrorism,'" Vienna, June 14, 2002. On the divergence on the meaning of international security, also see Mustapha Al Sayyid, "Mixed Message: The Arab and Muslim Response to 'Terrorism,'" *The Washington Quarterly* 25, no. 2 (Spring 2002): 177–190.

84. See "Prague Summit Declaration."

85. On the other side, the centrality of the United States led to some form of cooperation involving institutions: between EUROPOL and the United States (agreement signed on December 11, 2001); between INTERPOL and the FBI (through the INTERPOL Task Force created after September 11); and between the ASEAN and the United States (agreement signed on August 1, 2002). But in each case, IOs have preferred direct cooperation with the state that was directly concerned rather than a more general interinstitutional cooperation.

86. Wilkinson, "International Cooperation against Terrorism," 200 and 201.

87. Barnett and Finnemore, "The Politics, Power, and Pathologies of International Organizations," 711.

Part III

The World Organization Responds to Terrorism

7

The Role of the Security Council

Chantal de Jonge Oudraat

International terrorism has been a concern of UN member states since the late 1960s. It was placed on the Security Council's agenda in the early 1990s. On January 31, 1992, at the council's first-ever meeting of heads of state and government, the members of the council "expressed their deep concern over acts of international terrorism and emphasized the need for the international community to deal effectively with all such acts."[1] In March 1992, the council backed up this rhetorical commitment with action and adopted mandatory sanctions against Libya, which was accused of involvement in the terrorist bombing of two commercial airliners. This was a first. The Security Council would impose sanctions to fight terrorism on two other occasions in the 1990s—in 1996 against the Sudan and in 1999 against the Taliban regime in Afghanistan.

Although every permanent member of the Security Council has been the object of terrorist attacks, the United States has been the driving force behind the council's increasingly activist stance on terrorism. Washington became particularly active after the 1998 bombings of its embassies in East Africa. In a speech to the General Assembly in 1998, President Bill Clinton placed the fight against terrorism "at the top of the U.S. agenda."[2] Secretary of State Madeleine Albright maintained that terrorism is "the biggest threat to our country and the world as we enter the 21st century."[3] In 1999, the Security Council recognized international terrorism as a threat to international peace and security and strongly condemned all such acts in resolution 1269.[4]

The greater attention paid by Washington and the Security Council to the issue of terrorism was motivated by new developments in international terrorist activities. Five trends stood out. First, an increasing proportion of terrorist attacks were aimed at U.S. facilities or citizens. According to some calculations, attacks on U.S. targets increased from about 20 percent of the total attacks in 1993–1995 to almost 50 percent of the total in 2000.[5]

Second, the average number of casualties per incident increased. U.S. State Department statistics show that there was a fourfold increase in the number of casualties per attack in the latter half of the 1990s.[6]

Third, terrorist groups seemed to be operating as part of a global network. The 1998 attacks in East Africa underscored the global reach of the Al Qaeda network, which was estimated to have 4,000–5,000 well-trained fighters scattered around the world. Compared to the 500 members of the Abu Nidal organization, the 200–400 activists of the Irish Republican Army (IRA) and the Basque Fatherland and Liberty (ETA), and the 50–75 hard-core members of the Red Brigades, Al Qaeda was a significantly larger and qualitatively different type of terrorist organization.[7]

Fourth, fears that terrorists might one day use chemical, biological, or nuclear weapons were increasing. The 1995 sarin nerve gas attack in the Tokyo subway by Aum Shinrikyo made such fears less of a theoretical proposition.[8] The possibility of terrorists obtaining biological, chemical, or nuclear weapons—either by buying or stealing or through collusion with states developing weapons of mass destruction (WMD)—was a growing concern.[9]

Fifth, the United States was, and is, particularly concerned by the role certain states play in supporting and sponsoring terrorism. State support enhances the reach and power of terrorist groups. It might also provide them with WMD.[10] States could use terrorist groups as proxies in their own fights.[11]

The terrorist attacks on September 11, 2001, have made terrorism a top priority for the Security Council. Within hours of the attacks, the council president, French ambassador Jean-David Levitte, circulated a draft resolution strongly condemning the attacks and paving the way for military action. On September 12, resolution 1368 was adopted unanimously. Two weeks later, the council adopted another unprecedented decision—resolution 1373—obligating all member states to take far-reaching domestic legislative and executive action in order to forestall future terrorist activities.[12]

The U.S. permanent representative to the council, John Negroponte, called the United Nations "a unique partner in troubled times" and described resolution 1373 as the UN's "single most powerful response" in the war on terrorism.[13] Many others echoed these sentiments and have praised the world organization for its swift and energetic response.

This chapter analyzes the Security Council's actions with regard to terrorism since the early 1990s. First, I assess the efficacy of economic sanctions regimes imposed in the 1990s. Second, I examine the responses of the Security Council to the September 11 attacks. Third, I conclude by outlining the remaining policy challenges and developing some policy recommendations for UN member states, in particular for the United States.

I develop five main arguments. First, contrary to what many may think, terrorism has been on the agenda of the UN Security Council for many years—well before September 2001.

Second, Washington has been the driving force behind the council's increasingly activist stance on terrorism. However, the United States could not have succeeded in this campaign without the active agreement of the other permanent members of the council. They too saw terrorism as a growing national and international security threat.

Third, the sanctions regimes of the 1990s have had some effect on the global terrorist threat. They were important in stigmatizing terrorism as an illegitimate activity that needed to be countered through international action. The sanctions regimes made support of terrorist activities more costly, and the state sponsors of terrorists were responsive. Sanctions regimes changed the declaratory positions of state sponsors of terrorism. That said, sanctions regimes have had little effect on non-state terrorist actors—including terrorist organizations themselves. State sponsors of terrorism continue to provide some—albeit more limited—support to these groups. In addition, the funding of terrorist groups has become more diversified and hence more difficult to control.

Fourth, the response of the Security Council after September 11 legitimized unilateral military action by states in response to terrorist threats. Even so, it is in the interest of the U.S. and other permanent members of the Security Council to restrain themselves in exercising this right; weakening the prohibition on the use of force is not in their long-term interests.

Fifth, the Security Council took unprecedented action following the terrorist attacks. It ordered every member state to take a wide array of measures that would forestall terrorist activities. It asserted itself as the global instrument for collective action. That said, implementation of these measures is likely to be problematic. It will require huge resources and pose difficult political questions in cases of noncompliance. Now that bold Security Council resolutions have been passed, the danger is that member states will fail to follow through effectively, thereby undermining the council's authority and weakening the United Nations.

The 1990s: Brandishing Economic Sanctions

Two terrorist attacks in the late 1980s—against Pan Am flight 103 over Lockerbie, Scotland, in December 1988 and against Union des Transports Aériens (UTA) flight 772 in September 1989 over Niger—prompted France, the United Kingdom, and the United States to involve the Security Council in the fight against terrorism. Economic sanctions became the main policy instrument. In the 1990s the council imposed sanctions against Libya, the Sudan, and the Taliban regime in Afghanistan.

Libya

The downing of the Pan Am flight cost the lives of all 259 people on board as well as 11 people on the ground. The UTA bombing killed 171 people. In both cases, initial investigations indicated Libyan involvement in the attacks.

Although France, Britain, and the U.S. were deeply concerned by these specific attacks, they also had broader concerns—namely, state support for terrorist groups.[14] The UK, in particular, was agitated by Libya's support for the Irish Republican Army.

The three Western governments had two main demands. First, they demanded that the Libyan government cooperate with the criminal investigations into the bombings of the Pan Am and UTA flights and surrender those charged with the bombings. Second, they demanded a more general renunciation of terrorism by Libya, in particular that it stop training terrorists and providing military aid to terrorist groups abroad.

The Security Council in its January 1992 resolution 731 put the Libyan government on notice.[15] Washington also made it known that, failing a swift Libyan response, it would seek the imposition of mandatory sanctions—an instrument the council was more willing to impose since the end of the Cold War.[16]

In response to these pressures and several council-directed initiatives by UN Secretary-General Boutros Boutros-Ghali, the Libyan government offered to surrender the UTA suspects to a French court and those responsible for the Pan Am explosion to an international court. However, Washington insisted that the suspects of the Pan Am bombing be turned over to either a U.S. or British court.

France, the UK, and the U.S. introduced a Security Council resolution in March 1992 that declared Tripoli's failure to respond positively to the earlier requests a "threat to international peace and security." It invoked Chapter VII of the UN Charter and imposed economic sanctions. All flights to and from Libya were prohibited. Resolution 748 also imposed an arms embargo and required reductions in personnel at Libyan diplomatic missions abroad. Finally, it imposed travel restrictions on Libyan nationals suspected of terrorist activities.[17]

Six years of deadlock followed. A strengthened sanctions package in resolution 883 was adopted in November 1993 but seemed only to harden positions.[18] The families of those who perished in Scotland became a powerful lobbying group in the United States, demanding even tougher sanctions on Libya.[19]

Libya made some conciliatory gestures. In 1996, it gave the chief French investigator in the UTA bombing access to Libyan officials and government documents. The French judge subsequently charged six people, including Muammar el-Qaddafi's brother-in-law, with involvement in the attack.[20]

It took until 1998 for the Libyan issue to be resolved. Faced with a crumbling sanctions regime—including weakening support from European allies and the announcement in June 1998 by the members of the Organization of African Unity (OAU) that they would no longer comply with the sanctions regime if no solution was found by the end of the year—Washington softened its stance. Together with London, it developed a proposal to have the two Libyan suspects tried under Scottish law in a court in the Netherlands. The Security Council adopted the plan and decided that sanctions would be suspended once the two suspects arrived in the Netherlands. If Libya did not comply, additional sanctions would be imposed according to resolution 1192 (1998). Tripoli accepted the plan early in 1999. The two Libyan suspects arrived in the Netherlands on April 5, 1999, and sanctions were suspended three days later.[21]

The sanctions regime on Libya was a success in that ultimately the suspects were handed over.[22] This case also vindicates the idea that the threat of sanctions is often more effective than their actual imposition. Indeed, it was the threat of sanctions that led Qaddafi almost immediately to make a major concession—namely, acceptance of the principle that the suspects should stand trial. He also agreed early on to have them judged in a court monitored by the Arab League or the United Nations.[23] However, Washington stuck to its initial position and continued to insist that a trial be held in a U.S. or British court.

The intransigent position of the United States was influenced by domestic politics as well as by broader objectives—such as crippling Libya's program of weapons of mass destruction and weakening its support for terrorist groups. This necessitated continuing the imposition of sanctions. These broader security objectives were largely achieved by the late 1990s. In 1996, the U.S. State Department stated that Libya's support for terrorism had been sharply reduced.[24] Continuing UN sanctions hence became increasingly difficult to justify.

The Sudan

Mandatory UN economic sanctions were imposed on the Sudan in April 1996 by resolution 1054 after it refused to extradite three suspects in the assassination attempt on the Egyptian president, Hosni Mubarak, in Addis Ababa, Ethiopia, on June 26, 1995.[25] These Chapter VII sanctions required member states to reduce the number of Sudanese diplomatic personnel and restrict the movement of those who remained abroad. It also restricted the travel of Sudanese government officials, including military personnel. Finally, it required international organizations to stop convening conferences in the country.

Khartoum's continued denial of any knowledge of the suspects and any support to terrorist groups led the council to adopt an air embargo against the Sudan in resolution 1070 (1996). This ban never took effect, however. Many states—including Egypt—opposed the ban because of its potential humanitarian consequences.[26] Indeed, the humanitarian impact of sanctions in Iraq and Haiti had made the Security Council more hesitant about imposing economic sanctions in general.[27] In addition, Sudan's involvement in the assassination attempt was more contentious. Finally, although Khartoum denied involvement in the assassination attempt, it did inform the Security Council in May 1996 that it had requested a number of Egyptians, Palestinians, and "Arab Afghans"—including Osama bin Laden—to leave the country.[28]

Sanctions were more symbolic than real in the Sudan. The Security Council did not set up a sanctions committee to monitor implementation. Washington's interest in this sanctions regime was not driven by the particulars of the case—the apprehension and extradition of the three suspects in the assassination attempt of Mubarak—but by the more general message that support of terrorist activities was not acceptable. This message was received to some extent; the Sudanese government did expel a number of foreigners, and it imposed more stringent visa requirements. Even so, the United States argued that several terrorist groups continued to use the Sudan as a safe haven—including Osama bin Laden's associates. In August 1998 and following lethal attacks on its embassies in Nairobi and Dar es Salaam, the United States bombed a pharmaceutical plant in north Khartoum, which was financed by bin Laden and suspected of developing chemical weapons.[29]

In return for cooperation in the war against terrorism after September 2001, Security Council resolution 1372 lifted the sanctions against the Sudan on September 28, 2001.[30] Sanctions seem to have had some effect on the country's behavior. That said, the threat of U.S. military force also gave the Sudan a powerful incentive to show continuing good behavior, particularly after 1998.

The Taliban

On August 7, 1998, two bombs exploded simultaneously in the U.S. embassies in Nairobi, Kenya, and Dar es Salaam, Tanzania. The explosions killed 263 people (including twelve Americans) and injured over 5,000 people (including fifteen Americans). The Security Council strongly condemned the attacks in resolution 1189 and called upon all member states to cooperate with the investigations. U.S. investigations quickly pointed to the involvement of Osama bin Laden who, in 1996, had found refuge in Afghanistan.

On August 20, 1998, Washington launched retaliatory cruise missile strikes against those who were believed to be involved in the attacks. It leveled a pharmaceutical plant in the Sudan that had been financed by bin Laden and was suspected of developing chemical weapons. The U.S. also destroyed a number of installations in eastern Afghanistan—mostly terrorist training camps financed by bin Laden and run by Al Qaeda.[31]

The raids provoked an outcry both within and outside the United States.[32] That said, criminal investigations into the embassy bombings revealed increasing evidence of Osama bin Laden's involvement. Pressured by Washington, the Security Council imposed mandatory aviation and financial sanctions against the Taliban regime in Afghanistan through resolution 1267 in October 1999.[33] The resolution invoked Chapter VII of the Charter and demanded that the Taliban stop its support for international terrorists and extradite bin Laden. The United States had indicted bin Laden on November 4, 1998, for his involvement in the bombing of the U.S. embassies in Africa.

In December 2000, the Security Council strengthened the sanctions package and required all member states to close all Taliban offices in their countries and to freeze the financial assets of bin Laden and his associates. It also imposed an arms embargo on the Taliban in resolution 1333.[34] Russia, which was concerned about the spread of Islamic extremism, strongly supported the latter measure and also supported the Northern Alliance's fight against the Taliban. Faced with poor implementation of the sanctions regime, the council created a monitoring mechanism in July 2001 in resolution 1363.

The increasingly broad scope of the regime had no noticeable effect on the Taliban, which refused to hand over bin Laden. Even the prospect of war—which grew in the wake of the attacks of September 11—failed to make the Taliban budge. After the U.S.-led military campaign of late 2001 led to the fall of the Taliban, the council lifted sanctions on Afghan airlines, but it retained sanctions on the Taliban, bin Laden, and his Al Qaeda associates.[35]

Sanctions were not successful against the Taliban. They had limited funds abroad, and the extent of Taliban-controlled air traffic was negligible. Economically, the Taliban was not operating in the global economy. Its international economic dealings were in the black market—much of its money came from the illegal opium and heroin trade. Moreover, Afghanistan was already awash in weapons, and the arms embargo did little to change that. All of this made the Taliban relatively immune to outside pressure.

The Effectiveness of Sanctions in the Fight against Terrorism

The sanctions regimes of the 1990s helped to consolidate a growing international consensus that saw terrorism as an illegitimate activity that needed to be countered through collective international actions. Sanctions therefore helped to change the public attitudes of states toward terrorism—particularly in those states sponsoring terrorism.[36]

The great powers also hoped that sanctions would have a deterrent effect. Washington viewed the Security Council actions in the 1990s against Libya, the Sudan, and the Taliban not only as punitive measures but also as warnings. The U.S. government stated that "this type of concerted multilateral response to terrorism serves as an important deterrent to states considering support for terrorist acts or groups."[37]

After the September 11 attacks, the Security Council imposed a blanket mandatory sanctions regime on all terrorists. Resolution 1373 would not have been adopted were it not for the precedents set with the sanctions regimes in the 1990s.

Sanctions are an important component of attempts to curb terrorist activities, but they are not—by themselves—the solution. Sanctions regimes suffer from chronic implementation problems.[38] Moreover, sanctions have little effect on the behavior of groups—such as the Taliban and Al Qaeda—that situate themselves outside the international system and reject its institutions and norms. Sanctions can make terrorist operations more costly, but they are certainly no panacea. Finally, by designating terrorist activities "threats to international peace and security," these sanctions regimes paved the way for a military approach to terrorism.

2001 and Beyond: Militarizing and Globalizing International Responses

The Security Council took swift and unprecedented action in the wake of the events of September 11. Two resolutions were particularly important. Resolution 1368 of September 12 legitimized militarized action against terrorism. Resolution 1373 of September 28, 2001, broadened the scope of international responses.

Militarizing Responses

The first anniversary of the September 11, 2001, attacks and the Bush administration's apparent determination to strike Iraq reignited a debate in international policy circles over the use of force. During the 1990s, this debate focused on military intervention for humanitarian purposes; in the summer and fall of 2002, it shifted to the use of force in response to terrorist attacks and against producers of WMD.[39]

At the heart of these debates lies the question of whether force can be used lawfully in situations other than those foreseen by the UN Charter.[40] Most legal scholars and most governments argue that the world organization's constitution contains a general prohibition on the use of force. This prohibition is embodied in Article 2.4: "All Members shall refrain in their international relations from the threat or use of force against the territorial integrity or political independence of any state, or in any other manner inconsistent with the Purposes of the United Nations."

Scholars and governments generally maintain that the Charter allows only two exceptions to this rule. One is for self-defense in response to an armed attack (Article 51).[41] The other is when the use of force is authorized by the Security Council in order to maintain or restore international peace and security (Article 42).[42]

Some scholars maintain that Article 2.4 does not contain a general and comprehensive prohibition on the use of force. They argue that it merely regulates the conditions under which force is prohibited but leaves room for exceptions—only two of which are mentioned in Articles 51 and 42. They maintain that the Charter permits the use of force in other circumstances. State practice—despite declaratory policies to the contrary—seems to substantiate this view. Over the years, governments and scholars have argued that force can be lawfully used to protect and rescue one's nationals abroad, free people from colonial domination, protect people from gross violations of human rights, and fight terrorism.

Israel has often resorted to the use of force to fight terrorism. The United States has also used force in its fight against terrorism. Since 1945, it has done so four times.[43]

- Against Libya in 1986, in retaliation for the latter's involvement in the bombing of La Belle Discothèque, a nightclub in Berlin regularly frequented by U.S. servicemen
- Against Iraq in 1993, in retaliation for its attempt to assassinate former U.S. president George H. W. Bush and the emir of Kuwait
- Against Afghanistan and the Sudan in 1998, in retaliation for the bombings of the U.S. embassies in Kenya and Tanzania
- Against Afghanistan in 2001, in retaliation for the September 11 attacks in the United States

In all these cases, the United States invoked the right to self-defense, which is recognized in the Charter as an inalienable right of states. However, it is generally accepted that this right is not open ended. In particular, it ceases to operate when the Security Council takes action.

Four questions are critical in judging the lawfulness of self-defense actions: Was there an armed attack? Was the response necessary? Was the response proportionate? Was the response timely?

In the 1970s and 1980s, the lack of a common analytical framework—that is, the absence of any widely shared answers to these questions—led to vastly diverging and often critical opinions about the legality of military strikes in response to terrorist acts.[44] Such strikes often led to condemnations in the General Assembly.[45]

Attempts within the world organization to come to a consensus on this issue have made little progress. Agreement was impeded mainly because of differences of opinion about the use of violence by national liberation and self-determination movements. Recognizing the depth of these ideological divides, member states agreed to disagree on the big picture and settled instead on a piecemeal approach to the problem. The General Assembly developed several conventions that addressed specific terrorist acts—such as the hijacking of aircraft, the kidnapping of diplomats, and the taking of hostages. The General Assembly favored a domestic law enforcement approach that obligated states to either prosecute or extradite those accused of terrorist acts.

The changing nature of terrorism in the 1990s—in particular, its more global reach—exposed this approach as less than effective. The increased lethality of terrorist acts also quelled long-standing disagreements about definitions and ideology. As terrorism became increasingly seen as a threat to international peace and security, states started to favor a more muscular approach that allowed for the use of economic sanctions and military force. The Security Council's resolutions in the 1990s, and especially resolution 1368, codified this approach. For the first time, and unanimously, it recognized the right of states to individual and collective self-defense in response to terrorist acts. The relevant part of the resolution reads as follows:

[The Security Council], [r]ecognizing the inherent right of individual or collective self-defense in accordance with the Charter,

1. Unequivocally condemns in the strongest terms the horrifying terrorist attacks which took place on 11 September 2001 in New York, Washington (D.C.) and Pennsylvania and regards such acts, like any act of international terrorism, as a threat to international peace and security.

The Security Council regarded the attacks of September 11 as threats to international peace and security, but it did not call for collective action. By invoking a state's right to self-defense, it handed over this responsibility to individual states. Resolution 1368 therefore became a very important instrument—if not a blank check—legitimizing the unilateral use of force in re-

sponse to terrorist acts. Russian President Vladimir Putin invoked the resolution and its right to individual and collective self-defense one year later when
he justified Russia's right to military intervention against Chechen rebels operating in Georgia.[46]

The broader implications of this resolution on the legality of the use of
force have received little attention. Taken together with the debate in the 1990s
on humanitarian intervention, it is clear that the prohibition on the use of
force is evolving. This is not necessarily a bad thing when there is a clear international consensus on when, why, and whether to intervene militarily. Unfor-
tunately, there is no such consensus at present.

Globalizing the Fight against Terrorism:
Resolution 1373 and the CTC

Two weeks after the September 11 attacks, the United States introduced a resolution in the Security Council that strengthened and broadened the fight
against terrorism. Resolution 1373 obligated all member states to take a wide
range of measures to prevent future terrorist activities. It required states to
change and/or adopt domestic legislation to implement the resolution. In
particular, it directed states to criminalize terrorist acts, including the support and financing of such acts; deny safe haven to terrorists and prohibit any
other support for terrorists, such as the provision of arms; and cooperate with
other states in the implementation of these measures.

Many of the specific measures in the resolution were present in two important conventions negotiated in the late 1990s—the 1997 Convention for
the Suppression of Terrorist Bombings, which entered into force in May 2001,
and the 1999 Convention on the Suppression of Financing of Terrorism, which
prior to September 11 had not yet entered into force.[47] Many states had not
signed or ratified these conventions.[48] The United States, for example, had
ratified neither. Even so, resolution 1373 made many of the provisions of these
conventions binding on all states.

To monitor implementation, the resolution established the Counter-
Terrorism Committee (CTC). Jeremy Greenstock, the United Kingdom's permanent representative, who was elected by the council as its first chairman,
emphasized the technical nature of the CTC.[49] Political assessment of compliance problems would remain in the hands of the council. In his words, the
functions of the CTC "were to monitor, to be analytical and to report facts to
the Security Council for consideration." He said, "[I]t is not the primary purpose of the Counter-Terrorism Committee to get into the politics of what is
happening in the short-term."[50] The committee was created "to help the world

system to upgrade its capability, to deny space, money, support, haven to terrorism, and to establish a network of information-sharing and co-operative executive action."[51]

The CTC initiated a multistage program. In the first stage, it reviewed existing legislative and executive measures in member states to combat terrorism. Resolution 1373 ordered states to provide the CTC with reports by December 27, 2001.[52] The second stage focused on institutional mechanisms and assistance.

By January 2002, the CTC had received some 117 reports from states—by all historical standards, a remarkable response. By December 2002, this number had increased to 175. By this time, the committee had requested follow-up reports and engaged many countries in dialogue about them.[53]

An initial reading pointed to several problems.[54] First, the resolution laid down very general prohibitions that were often difficult to implement in ways that respected basic human rights.[55] Second, many states dealt with terrorist activities in their own territories, yet many were silent with respect to terrorist acts carried out by their nationals elsewhere. Third, states often had different interpretations of key terms. For example, the financing of terrorist activities and groups was frequently equated with money-laundering and was dealt with within that legislative context. However, money used to finance terrorism is not necessarily generated by illegal business transactions—on the contrary, much of this money is legal and has been acquired by legitimate means. Similarly, there was frequent confusion about the meaning of freezing, seizing, confiscating, or suspending accounts. Fourth, information on international cooperation was sketchy. It focused mainly on formal judicial issues, particularly on extradition. Fifth, it was clear that many states lacked the legislative and administrative capacity to implement the resolution. Even so, few states requested assistance from the United Nations.

Some of these problems were not new and had surfaced in the implementation of earlier sanctions regimes in the 1990s.[56] For example, criminalizing the financing of terrorism was easier said than done. In their review of the UN sanctions regimes in the 1990s, David Cortright and George Lopez estimated that only twelve countries had laws that enabled them to enforce financial sanctions.[57] The UN group monitoring sanctions on the Taliban and Al Qaeda reported in September 2002 that Al Qaeda continued to have access to considerable financial and other economic resources. It noted that while $112 million were frozen in the first three months after the September 2001 attacks, only $10 million had been blocked in the following eight months. It concluded "Al Qaeda is by all accounts 'fit and well' and poised to strike again at its leisure."[58]

The safe haven provisions of resolution 1373 were similarly hampered by implementation problems. Border controls were and are weak in many countries. Indeed, many countries do not have control over large swaths of land that are nominally theirs. Many countries often do not have enough capacity to effectively police the territories that are under their control.

To deal with these legislative and administrative capacity gaps, serious resources are needed. The CTC, with a staff of a dozen and no independent budget, is waging a heroic but losing battle. Without sufficient resources, it will not be able to provide the assistance that is needed. Initial ideas to set up an assistance trust fund were vetoed by the United States, which preferred to have monies for assistance provided through bilateral channels.[59]

Beyond these practical implementation problems, there are two larger political problems that impede implementation of the resolution. First, despite a general declaratory consensus on the importance of outlawing terror, states continue to have widely divergent views on the exact nature of these threats and who should be labeled a "terrorist"—as opposed to a "freedom fighter." Second, states disagree on what to do with states that do not comply with resolution 1373. The CTC has wisely declined to get involved in making judgments about political compliance. In paragraph 8 of resolution 1373, the council "expresses its determination to take all necessary steps in order to ensure the full implementation of this resolution, in accordance with its responsibilities under the Charter." However, these steps are not spelled out. In theory, the Security Council has an entire range of coercive instruments at its disposal to deal with noncompliance. In practice, there is a risk that the assessment of compliance and the response to noncompliance will be taken by individual states without reference to the council.[60] Washington's letter to the Security Council detailing its action against Al Qaeda and the Taliban hinted that action might be taken against other targets.[61] Similarly, in its September 2002 letter to the Security Council and other international organizations, Russia claimed that Georgia was not complying with resolution 1373 and that Moscow could therefore invoke its right to individual self-defense. In a televised statement on the first anniversary of September 11, Putin warned Georgia "that Russia would defend itself in line with the United Nations Charter and its resolutions if the Georgian government fails to end rebel raids into Chechnya across the border."[62]

In sum, by directing member states to take similar legislative and administrative measures to combat terrorism at home and abroad, resolution 1373 has made the fight against terrorism a global one. The scope of the proposed measures is enormous and the declaratory resolve of the Security Council is unprecedented. That said, implementation risks being marred by huge technical and political problems and will thus likely be incomplete. The technical assistance that the CTC is able to provide is minimal given its lack of resources. Most will thus have to come through bilateral channels. It will hence be ad hoc and selective. Similarly, reactions to noncompliance will be idiosyncratic; they will be based on political expediency and the capacities of those who can organize responses.

Policy Challenges and Recommendations

After September 2001, the members of the Security Council adopted a set of comprehensive measures to combat terrorism. They did so under Chapter VII, thereby making these measures mandatory for all member states. While the resolve of the council is to be applauded, five sets of problems remain to be addressed.

First, although a consensus exists at the declaratory level on the importance of outlawing terror, states continue to have widely divergent views on the exact nature of these threats. They also have different ideas about the most appropriate responses.

The United States should take the lead in forging a consensus on the nature of the terrorist threat and appropriate policy responses. Sustained attention to the concerns of other states, consultation, and genuine efforts to come to a multilateral understanding will help convince other states that Washington is concerned not only about its own national interests but also about those of the larger community of states as well.

Second, the long-term implications of the council's actions with respect to the use of force are problematic. Resolution 1368 legitimizes the unilateral use of force against terrorist attacks. The U.S. appears to think of this resolution as a blank check. In its letter to the Security Council informing it of its action against Al Qaeda and the Taliban—as it was required to do by Article 51 of the UN Charter—the U.S. hinted that action might be taken against other targets: "[O]ur inquiry is in its early stages. We may find that our self-defense requires further actions with respect to other organizations and other states."[63] Secretary-General Kofi Annan and many diplomats at the United Nations were naturally concerned by this statement. Indeed, in the absence of any international agreement on a definition of terrorism, the possibilities for abuse are obvious and dangerous. In addition, U.S. officials have argued that terrorist threats require preemptive and possibly covert military actions.[64] This further complicates the issue of using military force for self-defense.[65]

The United States should take the lead in defining criteria for the use of force in self-defense, and it should engage the members of the Security Council in a discussion of this issue. When are terrorist acts the equivalent of armed attacks? Do imminent threats of attack always justify a military response? What constitutes an appropriate response? Washington should be careful in its handling of this issue: weakening the existing norm on the prohibition of the use of force is neither in its, nor in anyone else's, long-term interests.

Third, who will have the authority to determine if Security Council resolutions are being violated and who will have the authority to determine what the appropriate response to noncompliance will be? The United States and Russia believe that the authority to determine noncompliance with council resolutions belongs largely—but not exclusively—with the Security Council itself. They have argued that noncompliance with resolution 1373 would allow them to exercise their right to self-defense. In his letter to the Security Council and the OSCE, Russian president Vladimir Putin railed against the "glaring violation by Tbilisi of counter terrorist resolution 1373 of the UN Security Council." He stated: "[I]n this situation we must ensure that Georgia fully complies with its obligations to the international community." He concluded by saying, "[I]n this connection Russia may be forced to use the inalienable right to individual or collective defense in accordance with the Charter, stipulated in resolution 1368 of the UN Security Council."[66]

Unilateral responses to noncompliance with council resolutions are highly problematic. They set dangerous precedents. In the fall of 2002, as a prelude to agreeing on resolution 1441 on Iraq, the United States and the other members of the Security Council engaged in a constructive discussion. This was a good start. However, the issue came up again in early 2003 when the U.S. and the UK withdrew the draft resolution rather than having it vetoed. This problematic issue will continue to come up as the campaign against terrorism unfolds. Washington should not dodge these debates when they materialize; debate will not necessarily constrain its policy options. On the contrary, such debates can provide greater support and legitimacy for U.S. actions.

Fourth, implementation of the UN's counterterrorist measures will continue to be difficult. The financial and safe haven measures of resolution 1373 require monitoring and enforcement capabilities at the national level that most countries do not possess and that may be too expensive to acquire. The Security Council's response has been inadequate. Without ample resources, the CTC is able to provide only minimal technical assistance. Thus, most of this assistance will have to come through bilateral channels. It will hence be ad hoc and selective.

To minimize this problem, the CTC should be given more financial support. The council should also push for the establishment of a UN mechanism that could help finance programs in states without adequate counterterrorism capacity. Ultimately, if council members are serious in their determination to fight terrorism, they should provide the resources that will help states implement counterterrorist measures. Transforming the CTC into a CTO—that is, a Counter-Terrorism Organization, an independent UN agency—that can address this type of technical and implementation issues should be considered.[67]

Fifth, the fight against terrorism is a long-term fight against the root causes of terrorism. This involves broader societal problems—poverty, disease, social disorder, the lack of democracy, and poor governance. The UN has a limited but promising track record in dealing with these problems. Its capacities in these areas should be enhanced. Investing in social and development programs will ultimately have significant payoffs in the campaign against terrorism. Terrorism is not just a military problem; it will require a wide range of policy responses. The United Nations can make important contributions in many of these areas.

The United States, as the largest and most powerful state in the world, has a special responsibility—and a special interest—in making the Security Council an effective instrument in the fight against terrorism. The world organization has great political and operational value in the campaign against terrorism, and the Security Council has been extremely responsive to U.S. demands and concerns since the end of the Cold War. The story of the UN's involvement in the fight against terrorism attests to this. The UN could do more, however. Whether it does will depend to a large degree on the United States.

Notes

1. See *Note by the President of the Security Council* (S/23500), January 31, 1992.
2. See Barbara Crosette, "Clinton Urges World Action on Terror," *New York Times*, September 22, 1998, 1.
3. Quoted in John Carey, "Missile Defense vs. Terror: New Terrorism Has Many Faces, Including Ballistic," *Defense News*, August 31–September 6, 1998, 27.
4. See "Responsibility of the Security Council in the Maintenance of International Peace and Security," Security Council resolution 1269, October 19, 1999.
5. See Audrey Kurth Cronin, "Rethinking Sovereignty: American Strategy in the Age of Terrorism," *Survival* 44, no. 2 (Summer 2002): 123.
6. Ibid., and note 22 on 136. See also Bruce Hoffman, "Terrorism Trends and Prospects," in Ian O. Lesser, Bruce Hoffman, John Arquilla, David Ronfeldt, Michele Zanini, and Brian Michael Jenkins, *Countering the New Terrorism* (Santa Monica, Calif.: RAND, 1999), 7–38.
7. Hoffman, "Terrorism Trends and Prospects," 10.
8. The attack killed a dozen people and wounded 3,796 others. See ibid., 18.
9. Proliferation concerns were on the rise in the 1990s. At its historic 1992 meeting, the Security Council declared that "the proliferation of all weapons of mass destruction

constitutes a threat to international peace and security" and promised to take appropriate action "to prevent the spread of technology related to the research for or production
of such weapons." See *Note by the President of the Security Council,* January 31, 1992. See
also "High-Level Meeting of the Security Council: Combating Terrorism," Security
Council resolution 1456, January 20, 2003.

10. Cuba, Iran, Iraq, Libya, North Korea, the Sudan, and Syria have all been
designated by the U.S. government as states that sponsor terrorism. All of these states
have been suspected of wanting to acquire weapons of mass destruction. Iran, North
Korea, and Iraq have been of particular concern. Prior to the decision of the Security
Council to insist upon the return of UN arms inspectors to Iraq in resolution 1441, the
arms inspectors had been denied access to Iraq since December 1998. Most Western
experts were convinced that Iraq was hiding chemical and biological weapons. For
details, see press statement of John Chipman, director, International Institute for
Strategic Studies, "Iraq's Weapons of Mass Destruction: A Net Assessment," September
9, 2002 (available online at http://www.telenoticies.com/especials/iraq/docs/IISS-Iraq-
nuclear2002.pdf); *A Decade of Deception and Defiance: Saddam Hussein's Defiance of the
United Nations* (Washington, D.C.: The White House, September 12, 2002). See also
Chantal de Jonge Oudraat, "UNSCOM: Between Iraq and a Hard Place," *European
Journal of International Law* 13, no. 1 (February 2002): 139–152.

11. This would be a potentially attractive option for Saddam Hussein. However,
despite persistent rumors after the September 11, 2001, attacks, no links between Al
Qaeda and Iraq were found. See *A Decade of Deception and Defiance.* In February 2003,
the United States presented information to the Security Council that tried to link
Iraq and Al Qaeda. See the briefing of the U.S. Secretary of State Colin Powell to the
Security Council on February 5, 2003; available online at http://www.un.int/usa/
03clp0205.htm.

12. See also "Threats to International Peace and Security Caused by Terrorist Acts,"
Security Council resolution 1377, November 12, 2001, which directs the CTC to work
with regional and subregional organizations.

13. See "Negroponte Discusses Post-9/11 U.N. Agenda during House Appropriations
Subcommittee Hearing," March 26, 2002. Available online at http://www.unausa.org/
newindex.asp?place=http://www.unausa.org/policy/newsactionalerts/info/dc032602.asp.

14. U.S.-Libyan relations had been strained since the early 1970s. In December 1979,
the U.S. government declared Libya "a state sponsor of terrorism" and imposed a
tougher set of unilateral economic sanctions on Libya over time. Relations with Libya
came to a head in 1986, when U.S. officials became convinced of Libya's involvement in
the April 4 bombing of a nightclub in Berlin; the attack killed two U.S. soldiers and
wounded seventy-nine American servicemen. In retaliation, the U.S. sent some 100
aircraft to Libya and bombed several military and terrorist-associated sites in and
around Tripoli and Benghazi on April 14. The U.S. attack led to much physical destruction and collateral damage, including the destruction of residential quarters of the
Libyan leader Muammar Qaddafi and the death of thirty-six civilians. It was the first
time that the U.S. had retaliated militarily to a terrorist attack. Internationally, the strike
provoked an outcry. A General Assembly resolution condemned the attack (See

"Declaration of the Assembly of Heads of State and Government of the Organization of African Unity on the Aerial and Naval Military Attack Against the Socialist People's Libyan Arab Jamahiriya by the Present United States Administration in April 1986," General Assembly resolution A/Res./41/38, November 20, 1986). A similar Security Council resolution was defeated in the council when the U.S., the UK, and France vetoed the resolution. It is generally accepted that the 1988 Pan Am attack was a retaliation for the U.S. attack on Libya in 1986.

15. For more details on this case, see David Cortright and George A. Lopez, *The Sanctions Decade: Assessing UN Strategies in the 1990s* (Boulder: Lynne Rienner, 2000), 107–121.

16. In 1990, the Security Council imposed economic sanctions on Iraq. The former republics of Yugoslavia were hit with an arms embargo in 1991, and economic sanctions for the Former Republic of Yugoslavia were considered. The council also considered imposing an arms embargo on Somalia.

17. The resolution also established a Sanctions Committee tasked with monitoring implementation of the resolution. Five members of the council abstained: Cape Verde, China, India, Morocco, and Zimbabwe.

18. This resolution strengthened the aviation sanctions and banned the import of some oil-transporting equipment, but it did not impose a full-fledged oil embargo. The resolution also ordered UN member states to freeze specified Libyan government assets. Finally, the resolution stipulated that these new sanctions would be suspended when Libya extradited the two suspects of the Pan Am bombing for trial in a British or American court.

19. This lobby group also wanted sanctions imposed on Iran, which was also believed to be involved in the attack on the Pan Am flight. In July 1996, the U.S. Congress responded to these pressures by adopting the Iran and Libya Sanctions Act. This act imposed secondary sanctions on companies that continued to do business with Libya. It would become a powerful irritant in U.S.–European relations.

20. France did not insist on extradition until after the trial. The six suspects were tried in absentia and found guilty of the bombing in 1999.

21. See "Statement of the President of the Council," (PRST/1999/10), April 8, 1999. Sanctions were not formally lifted. The United States argued that sanctions should be lifted only after the settlement of the compensation issue. Libya paid compensation to the families of the victims of the UTA attack, but negotiations for compensation of the families of the victims of the Pan Am flight are ongoing. Since Libya continued to be designated by the United States as a state sponsor of terrorism, unilateral U.S. economic sanctions remained in place.

22. In January 2001, the court found one of the suspects guilty; the other was acquitted.

23. Qaddafi was worried that a direct linkage to him and his government could threaten his regime. Hence, he refused to turn the suspects over to a U.S. or British court. Qaddafi's worries were not unreasonable, given the initial demands of the three permanent members of the council and the 1986 U.S. attack on Libya. *New York Times*

correspondent Judith Miller reported that Qaddafi accepted the plan only after receiving assurances from the United States that the trial would not be used to undermine his rule. See Gideon Rose, "The United States and Libya," in Richard N. Haass, ed., *Transatlantic Tensions: The United States, Europe and Problem Countries* (Washington, D.C.: Brookings Institution Press, 1999), 141.

24. See *Patterns of Global Terrorism 1996*, U.S. State Department Annual Report, April 1997. See also subsequent editions of this U.S. State Department publication.

25. See also the earlier Security Council resolution requesting the Sudan to cooperate: "Resolution Condemning Assassination Attempt against President Mubarak of Egypt and Calling upon the Government of Sudan to Comply with OAU Requests," Security Council resolution 1044, January 31, 1996.

26. Egypt was also worried that the Sudan might retaliate with countermeasures. See Cortright and Lopez, *The Sanctions Decade*, 123–124.

27. Because of possible unintended consequences, the council decided against an arms embargo. The Sudan was in the midst of a civil war, and an arms embargo would have seriously jeopardized the chances of the Christian south.

28. See *Report of the Secretary-General Pursuant to Security Council Resolution 1070 (1996)* (S/1996/940), November 14, 1996. The Sudan was put on the U.S. list of state sponsors of terrorism in 1993. In the early and mid-1990s, many renowned terrorists resided in Khartoum, including Carlos (the Jackal), Osama bin Laden, and Abu Nidal.

29. At the same time, the United States bombed Al Qaeda training camps in Afghanistan. The attacks were justified by the United States as a measure taken in self-defense under Article 51 of the UN Charter. Many condemned the attacks. The bombing of the plant in northern Khartoum was particularly criticized. As it turned out, the plant was producing regular pharmaceutical products, not chemical weapons. It even had a UN contract. Similarly, the United States had not been able to make a convincing case of ties to bin Laden. Even those who supported the U.S. action politically—such as the UK—would not publicly endorse the legal basis of the attacks, which is the expansive U.S. doctrine of self-defense.

30. The United States abstained. The Sudan continues to be on the U.S. list of state sponsors of terrorism. See U.S. State Department, *Patterns of Global Terrorism 2001* (Washington, D.C.: U.S. Department of State, 2001).

31. The United States had considered bin Laden a serious threat since the 1993 World Trade Center bombing.

32. People questioned both the political and legal justifications of this action.

33. See "Resolution on the Situation in Afghanistan," Security Council resolution 1267, October 15, 1999. As in the other two cases, unilateral U.S. sanctions were already in place.

34. See "Resolution on the Situation in Afghanistan," Security Council resolution 1333, December 19, 2000.

35. See "Resolution on the Situation in Afghanistan," Security Council resolution 1388, January 15, 2002; "Resolution on the Situation in Afghanistan," Security Council resolution 1390, January 16, 2002; and "Threats to International Peace and Security Caused by Terrorist Acts," Security Council resolution 1455, January 17, 2003.

36. In 2001, the U.S. State Department noted the continuation of a slow trend away from state sponsorship of terrorism. That said, it continued to designate Cuba, Iran, Iraq, Libya, North Korea, Syria, and the Sudan as state supporters of terrorism. See U.S. State Department, *Patterns of Global Terrorism 2001*.

37. See *Measures to Eliminate Terrorism: Report of the Secretary-General* (A/48/267/ Add.1), September 21, 1993, paragraph 6.

38. See Chantal de Jonge Oudraat, "Making Economic Sanctions Work," *Survival* 42, no. 3 (Autumn 2000): 105–127.

39. Although terrorism and the proliferation of WMD have potential horrifying connections, they are two distinct problems. However, in the debate over the use of force the two became increasingly intertwined.

40. See Chantal de Jonge Oudraat, "Intervention in Internal Conflicts: Legal and Political Conundrums," Working Paper No. 15, August 2000, Carnegie Endowment for International Peace, Washington, D.C.

41. Article 51 states: "Nothing in the present Charter shall impair the inherent right of individual or collective self-defence if an armed attack occurs against a Member of the United Nations, until the Security Council has taken measures necessary to maintain international peace and security. Measures taken by Members in the exercise of this right of self-defence shall be immediately reported to the Security Council and shall not in any way affect the authority and responsibility of the Security Council under the present Charter to take any time such action as it deems necessary in order to maintain or restore international peace and security."

42. The cases foreseen in Articles 53.1 and 107 that permit action against World War II enemy states have become obsolete.

43. One could add the 2003 Iraq war to this list. Indeed, in the run-up to the war, some U.S. officials pointed to links between the regime of Saddam Hussein and Al Qaeda and justified a military intervention against Iraq as an anticipatory (preemptive or preventive) act of self-defense. That said, the primary official justification for the war against Iraq was based on the alleged continued Iraqi possession of weapons of mass destruction and noncompliance by the Iraqi regime with Security Council resolutions.

44. For further discussion of these legal issues, see Anthony Clark Arend and Robert J. Beck, *International Law and the Use of Force* (London/New York: Routledge, 1993).

45. This issue generally did not come up in the Security Council. U.S. veto power would have prevented that from happening.

46. See "Russia Writes U.N., OSCE Invoking Right to Self-Defense," *UNWire*, September 12, 2002. Available online at http://www.unwire.org/UNWire/20020912/ 28865_story.asp.

47. This convention entered into force in April 2002.

48. Only two countries had signed and ratified both conventions—Cuba and the United Kingdom.

49. In April 2003, Ambassador Inocencio Arias of Spain took over the chairmanship of the committee.

50. See Press Briefing by the Chairman of the CTC, October 19, 2001; available online at http://www.un.org/Docs/sc/committees/1373, click on "Open Briefings."

51. Ibid.

52. The CTC had provided states with specific guidelines for the submission of reports. Available online at http://www.un.org/Docs/sc/committees/1373/reports.html.

53. In January 2003, reports had been received from all but thirteen states. These states were given a deadline of March 31, 2003, to comply. See "High-Level Meeting of the Security Council: Combating Terrorism," Security Council resolution 1456, January 20, 2003; and "Ministerial-Level Security Council Meeting Calls for Urgent Action to Prevent, Suppress All Support for Terrorism," Security Council Press Release SC/7638, January 20, 2003. By early April only three states—São Tomé and Principe, Swaziland, and Vanuatu—had not filed any reports as required by resolution 1373. See "Terrorism: British Envoy Reviews U.N. Progress," *UNWire*, April 7, 2003.

54. See "Recurrent Issues: Briefing for Member States on 4 April 2002," by Walter Gehr, available online at http://www.un.org/Docs/sc/committees/1373/rc.htm. See also the summary records of the special Security Council CTC meeting with international, regional, and subregional organizations on March 6, 2003; available online at http://www.un.org/Docs/sc/committees/1373.

55. See, for example, the address to the CTC by UN High Commissioner for Human Rights Sergio Vieira de Mello, October 21, 2002; available online at http://www.un.org/Docs/sc/committees/1373.

56. See de Jonge Oudraat, "Making Economic Sanctions Work."

57. See Cortright and Lopez, *The Sanctions Decade,* 234.

58. Cited in "Terrorism: Efforts to Freeze Al-Qaeda's Funds Stalled, U.N. Report Says," *UNWire*, September 3, 2002. Available online at http://www.unfoundation.org/unwire/util/display_stories.asp?objid=28644.

59. In January 2003, France took up this issue again and proposed setting up a cooperation and assistance fund. See "Ministerial-Level Security Council Meeting Calls for Urgent Action."

60. In this regard, the explicit link in the preamble of resolution 1373 with resolution 1368—which allows for the unilateral use of force—might be read as allowing states to resort to individual and collective self-defense when they find states in noncompliance with this particular Security Council resolution.

61. See "Letter from the United States to the President of the UN Security Council" (A/2001/946), October 7, 2001.

62. See Misha Dzhindzhikhashvili, "Tbilisi Weighs Putin's Warning," *Moscow Times,* September 13, 2002, 3.

63. See "Letter from the U.S. to the President of the UN Security Council."

64. See "The National Security Strategy of the United States of America," September 2002, The White House, Washington, D.C., 15. Available online at http://www.whitehouse.gov/nsc/nss.pdf. The Pentagon is actively drafting guidelines for covert missions against terrorists in weak and failed states and in countries where the

local authorities would object to American action. See "U.S. Moves Commandos to Base in East Africa," *New York Times,* September 18, 2002, A14.

65. Preemptive actions are difficult to launch in a multilateral context. Preemptive actions require doctrines that support offensive wars. They also require good intelligence—a commodity difficult to generate and protect in any multilateral setting, let alone the United Nations. Even for a war-fighting organization such as NATO, the issue of preemption is difficult. NATO Secretary General Lord Robertson has stated his opposition to preemptive missions. See Thomas E. Ricks and Vernon Loeb, "Bush Developing Military Policy of Striking First: New Doctrine Addresses Terrorism," *Washington Post,* June 10, 2002, A1. On the issue of intelligence, see also de Jonge Oudraat, "UNSCOM: Between Iraq and a Hard Place."

66. See the Russian letter to the Security Council and the OSCE on September 11, 2002. Putin also stated: "I want to stress that we are not considering actions that would undermine the sovereignty and territorial integrity of the country in question or a change of its political regime."

67. The decision to establish such an organization would be a General Assembly decision. It alone has the power of the purse.

8

Using the General Assembly

M. J. Peterson

The General Assembly has addressed international terrorism in two ways: by developing a normative framework that defines terrorism as a common problem and by encouraging concerted government action to develop more particular international and national legal rules for dealing with terrorists. This chapter examines how these efforts by the assembly have influenced government behavior over the last three decades. Assessing the assembly's efforts requires an understanding of the general institutional characteristics of the General Assembly, the specifics of its debates on terrorism, and the politics surrounding the various streams of debate.

Norms and Cooperation:
The Business of the General Assembly

Institutional characteristics circumscribe the measures the General Assembly can take in its efforts to counter international terrorism. It cannot act as a direct coordinator of action against terrorism because it lacks authority to command governments and other influential actors to take or avoid particular actions. Moreover, the General Assembly oversees no administrative structure capable of implementing its decisions and it lacks the resources needed to provide material rewards for good behavior or material punishments of bad behavior. Given these constraints and the fact that it is the only intergovernmental body dealing with broad political issues in which nearly all states of the world are represented and have equal votes, it is able to serve as a developer of normative discourse and an encourager of cooperative action. As Inis Claude has pointed out,[1] the General Assembly functions as an organ for collective legitimization or collective delegitimization of normative prescriptions that guide the activity of member governments in some general-issue areas, and it influences the statements, policies, or behavior of individual governments and other actors in particular situations. This collective legitimation most often proceeds at the level of generally applicable norms. Related efforts to influence particular governments' behavior through resolutions praising or condemning their actions or inactions occur, but their impact is often minor or very slow in developing and depends on existence of a strong consensus on the norms applicable to the situation at hand.

Like all deliberative bodies, the General Assembly provides members with a tribune for raising matters they regard as important, a forum for exchanging views, and an arena for contending over which problems should be viewed as common challenges and the preferable, or at least acceptable, ways of addressing them. The majoritarian voting rules[2] permit coalitions of some states to claim that they are speaking for all. However, most resolutions are recommendations,[3] and all member governments realize that a resolution's political and moral weight increases as the size of the supporting majority increases. This leads them to seek unanimity, consensus, or adoption without a vote whenever possible, even at the expense of watering down portions of their proposals to attract greater support. However, there are limits to how far majoritarian coalitions will go to secure additional support. They sometimes prefer adoption by a majority vote, particularly when they anticipate that opposition will be scattered or expressed primarily through abstention rather than negative votes.

Consensus has been regarded as both the basis and the bane of assembly influence in world politics. A real consensus overcomes some of the problems inherent in the General Assembly's lack of capacity to implement decisions or impose sanctions by engaging the efforts of the member states. Yet when pursued in the face of strong disagreements among governments, consensus can be achieved only by papering them over, which produces vacuous pronouncements that different member governments can interpret in divergent ways.[4] Even when disagreement is less strong, a particular consensus may express a least-common-denominator outcome—a weak statement that hardly seems worth the diplomatic energies expended to develop it. However even a least-common-denominator understanding is useful for identifying the state of current opinion about some issue or situation. Over time the General Assembly is also a good register of shifts in the terms of consensus; new resolutions may indicate convergence on the identification of new problems or programs of action or indicate deepening disagreement as tensions among governments' divergent positions increase and can no longer be hidden behind bland phrases. These institutional characteristics have encouraged the assembly to deal with terrorism as a general problem rather than focus on responses to particular terrorist incidents.

General Assembly Discussions on Terrorism

Although assembly resolutions have commented on particular terrorist incidents, member governments have not sought to use the General Assembly as a forum for close coordination of action by invoking the "Uniting for Peace" procedures. Despite grumbling about the permanent five's tendency to leave even the other ten members of the Security Council out of key discussions, the assembly majority has deferred to the Security Council's more immediate competence on this matter.

The General Assembly's efforts to develop a normative framework have proceeded primarily in three streams of resolutions addressing terrorism as a general problem. Resolutions commenting on particular events reveal how this general normative framework is understood and applied by governments at any particular moment and thereby help illuminate the evolution of governments' views on terrorism. The assembly's related efforts to encourage concerted international action against terrorists have taken three forms: it has convened two ad hoc committees on terrorism, composed of delegates of member states, to work out more specific measures; it has encouraged UN specialized agencies with competence in fields likely to be affected by terrorist activity to address the issue; and it has urged governments to perfect the international and domestic laws against terrorist activity and cooperate more closely with one another in suppressing terrorism.

The General Assembly first defined international terrorism as a general problem in 1972; it returned to the subject sporadically in the mid-1980s and has addressed it fairly continuously since adopting the Declaration on Measures to Eliminate International Terrorism by resolution 49/60 in December 1994.[5] The particular suggestions for dealing with terrorism included in these resolutions have shifted over time as the assembly's broad conception of the problem has changed. The evolving contours of the assembly's collective conception of terrorism can be traced through the titles and preambles of the resolutions containing general prescriptive statements. Preambular paragraphs identify the broad considerations guiding adoption of a resolution, trace the assembly's prior consideration of the issue addressed when a new resolution builds on earlier ones, and remind member states of the more general international norms informing the assembly's approach.

The titles and preambles reveal that the General Assembly's approach to the problem of terrorism underwent a marked change in the early 1990s. From 1972 through 1989, consideration of terrorism as a general problem was assigned primarily to the Sixth Committee (Legal) under an agenda item title beginning "measures to prevent international terrorism," and this phrase was

used in resolution titles as well. However the preambles devoted more attention to distinguishing justifiable armed struggle from terrorism than they did
to suggesting measures for reducing the incidence of terrorism. The operative
paragraphs provided no more guidance; rather, they reflected sharp disagreements among governments about whether terrorism should be prevented by
cooperation to suppress terrorist activity or removal of the "root causes" said
to inspire terrorism. The issue was still assigned to the Sixth Committee in
the 1990s, but the resolutions adopted in that decade were quite different in
character. In 1991, by consensus, the first resolution on the general problem of
terrorism that was adopted renamed the agenda item, and hence the resulting
resolutions, "measures to eliminate international terrorism." The new name
reflected wider agreement that the existence of root causes did not justify
terrorist acts; the effort to ensure that justifiable armed struggles were not
labeled "terrorism" shifted from differentiating among the goals of armed
struggle to differentiating among the means employed. Even the many member governments that continued to stress the need to remove root causes agreed
that a greater measure of cooperative action against anyone engaging in terrorist acts was needed in the meantime. In 1993, an additional stream of resolutions on "human rights and terrorism" addressing the situations of both
victims and those accused of engaging in terrorist activity emerged from the
Third Committee (Social, Humanitarian, and Cultural). Elements of this
stream were incorporated into the "measures to eliminate" series when it was
given its current form in resolution 49/60 (1994).

   The different normative concerns animating the streams are indicated in
the mix of multilateral treaties, international declarations, and earlier General Assembly resolutions cited in their respective preambles. Resolution 3034
(1972), the first of the "measures to prevent" stream, invoked the 1970 Declaration on Principles of International Law Concerning Friendly Relations and
Cooperation among States in Accordance with the Charter of the United Nations.[6] This lays out a vision of how states should conduct relations with each
other and affirms the illegitimacy of colonialism, racist rule, and foreign intervention in states' affairs. Resolution 48/122 (1993), the first in the "human
rights and terrorism" stream, invoked the UN Charter, the Universal Declaration of Human Rights, the two international covenants on human rights, and
the 1993 Vienna Declaration and Programme of Action of the World Conference on Human Rights.[7] Resolution 49/60 (1994) captured both sets of concerns by invoking "the principles and purposes of the UN Charter," the
Declaration on Principles of International Law concerning Friendly Relations
and Cooperation among States in Accordance with the Charter of the United
Nations, the Declaration on Strengthening of International Security,[8] the

Definition of Aggression,[9] the Declaration on the Enhancement of the Effectiveness of the Principle of Refraining from the Threat or Use of Force in International Relations,[10] the Vienna Declaration and Programme of Action, and both international covenants on human rights.

Until 1999, successive resolutions in each stream could be traced not only by their titles but also by the previous resolutions recalled in their preambles. Since then, recitals of individual General Assembly resolutions have been replaced by reference to "previous resolutions" having the same title. The common titles and specific invocations allow us to trace the following sequences of related resolutions on terrorism:

- "Measures to Prevent Terrorism"
  resolutions 3034 (XXVII) (1972), 31/102 (1976), 32/147 (1977), 34/145 (1979), 36/109 (1981), 38/130 (1983), 40/61 (1985), 42/159 (1987), 44/29 (1989), and 46/51 (1991)
- "Human Rights and Terrorism"
  resolutions 48/122 (1993), 49/185 (1994), 50/186 (1995), 52/133 (1997), 54/164 (1999), and 56/160 (2001)
- "Measures to Eliminate Terrorism"
  resolutions 49/60 (1994), 50/53 (1995), 51/210 (1996), 52/165 (1997), 55/158 (2000), 56/88 (2001), 56/88 (2001), and 57/27 (2002)

Inspiration and Content of the Three Streams

When the problem of terrorism was first brought before it in 1972, the General Assembly was a well-established body with a long enough agenda that it had little time to anticipate problems and address them before they emerged. As with most new items, international terrorism was added to the agenda when it began inspiring widespread concern among member states. On the topic of terrorism, the General Assembly, like most deliberative bodies at any level of governance, functioned primarily as a reactive body and took up the matter only when a significant portion of the membership was ready to regard it as a "problem."

The one constant feature in the General Assembly's discussion of terrorism as a general problem has been the member states' inability to agree on common definitions of the terms "terrorism," "terrorist acts," and "international terrorism." Even the central statement in the current "measures to eliminate" stream, the Declaration on Measures to Eliminate International Terrorism adopted in resolution 49/60, does not go beyond categorizing terrorism as criminal activity in its three definitional provisions:

1. The States Members of the United Nations solemnly reaffirm their unequivocal condemnation of all acts, methods, and practices of terrorism,
   as criminal and unjustifiable, wherever and by whomever committed, including those which jeopardize the friendly relations among States and
   peoples and threaten the territorial integrity and security of States;
2. Acts, methods, and practices of terrorism constitute a grave violation of
   the purposes and principles of the United Nations, which may pose a
   threat to international peace and security, jeopardize friendly relations
   among States, hinder international cooperation and aim at the destruction of human rights, fundamental freedoms and the democratic basis
   of society;
3. Criminal acts intended or calculated to provoke a state of terror in the
   general public, a group of persons or particular persons for political
   purposes are in any circumstance unjustifiable, whatever the considerations of a political, ideological, racial, ethnic, religious or any other
   nature that may be invoked to justify them.[11]

This inability to agree on a definition is not a new phenomenon. The League
of Nations produced a draft treaty defining terrorism as "all criminal acts
directed against a State and intended or calculated to create a state of terror in
the minds of particular persons or a group of persons or the general public."
However, it never received enough ratifications to enter into force. Definitions offered in General Assembly resolutions continue to offer variations of
the phrasing used in 1937, though they have dropped the qualification that
the terrorist actions must be directed against a state.[12]

Contemporary efforts to define the term "terrorism" are hobbled by the
same problem that stymied the League's efforts: how to formulate the term
without criminalizing all armed resistance to oppressive regimes. This dilemma
has not kept the General Assembly from discussing terrorism, but it has in-
flected the direction of discussion as governments contend with how to distinguish legitimate armed struggle from terrorism and how much emphasis
to place on identifying root causes of grievances that lead individuals and
groups to adopt terrorist methods.

The General Assembly first addressed terrorism as a distinct problem in
September 1972 on the initiative of Secretary-General Kurt Waldheim, who
proposed that it consider the problem in the wake of several major incidents,
most notably the attack on Lod Airport in Israel and the capture and killing
of Israeli athletes at the 1972 Summer Olympics in Munich. Waldheim proposed that the General Assembly create an ad hoc committee to explore practical ways of improving national and international efforts to identify,

apprehend, and punish those involved in terrorist activities. However, the assembly's discussion was quickly redirected by a coalition of Third World states, the Soviet bloc, and China toward affirming the rights of national liberation movements fighting against colonial or (white) racist regimes and other forms of external domination, condemning such regimes for their repression of national liberation movements, and emphasizing that the surest way to end terrorism is to eliminate these forms of domination that provoked it. This redirection of attention was signaled by a change in the title of the agenda item and the resolution. Waldheim's proposal was labeled "measures to prevent terrorism and other forms of violence which endanger or take innocent human lives or jeopardize fundamental freedoms." When the matter was assigned to the Sixth Committee for discussion, Third World preferences for a wider discussion were reflected in the new title "measures to prevent international terrorism which endangers or takes innocent human lives or jeopardizes fundamental freedoms and study of the underlying causes of those forms of terrorism and acts of violence which lie in misery, frustration, grievance and despair, and which cause some people to sacrifice human lives, including their own, in an attempt to effect radical changes."

The ad hoc committee on international terrorism established by resolution 3034 was charged with examining both practical measures for suppression and identification of the causes of terrorism. However, the text of the resolution itself was tilted so heavily toward emphasizing the putative causes that it was adopted by a vote of 76 to 35 with 17 abstentions.[13] Continuing disagreement over how the discussion should develop in the ad hoc committee led the assembly to defer consideration of the issue in 1973, 1974, and 1975. Resolutions 31/102 of 1976 and 32/147 of 1977, renewing the ad hoc committee's mandate, and resolution 34/164, accepting its report, maintained the strong emphasis on distinguishing national liberation movements from terrorists but incorporated clearer condemnations of violent acts and sufficient attention to action against the perpetrators to win support from the more moderate Third World states and abstentions from some Western ones. Thus the first was adopted by a vote of 100 to 9 with 27 abstentions, the second by a vote of 91 to 9 with 28 abstentions, and the third by a vote of 118 to 0 with 22 abstentions.[14]

As the Cold War reintensified in the early 1980s, the Soviets and some of the more radical leftist Third World governments raised the issue of "state terrorism," defined largely as use of force by the U.S., Israel, and South Africa against leftist revolutionary movements, Palestinians, and anti-apartheid activists, respectively. However the notion got a mixed reception among the members of the Non-Aligned Movement (NAM). Cuban and other delegates of governments strongly sympathetic with Soviet views eagerly adopted it. Yugoslav delegates indicated that they accepted the concept of "state terrorism"—which they defined as "all forms of violent behavior by States," including "aggression, various types of force, reprisals, the use of subversive agents and the occupation of the territory of other States"—but believed that "state terrorism" should be considered separately rather than incorporated into resolutions addressing terrorism by individuals and groups.[15] The less pro-Moscow elements of the NAM also evinced little enthusiasm for the concept. In 1984, when international and domestic criticism of Reagan administration policies in Central America was at its height, the Soviets did succeed in winning sufficient support for discussing "state terrorism" in the First Committee (Disarmament and International Security). By accommodating a wide range of other opinions they also gained broad support for a resolution titled "Inadmissibility of the policy of state terrorism and any actions by States aimed at undermining the socio-political system in other sovereign States," which was adopted by a vote of 117 to 0 with abstentions from 30 Western and moderate Latin American governments.[16] Yet the resolution can be viewed as part of the more general Third World emphasis on limiting the use of armed force in interstate relations rather than as a statement on terrorism. Though the title referred to "state terrorism," the Western Europeans' preferred formulation of "policies and practices of terrorism in relations between States" was used in the body of the text. By the time members of the NAM were finished making suggestions, the resolution as a whole was far more reminiscent of resolutions calling on states to refrain from threatening or using force in relations with other states or against those struggling for self-determination and to respect the rights of peoples to choose their own socio-economic systems than of any of the resolutions on terrorism.

Another difference with other resolutions on terrorism was that resolution 39/159 did not include a provision placing the matter on the agenda of a future General Assembly session, a sure sign that most delegations had little interest in continuing the discussion. A Cuban-led effort to include reference to "state terrorism" in the Sixth Committee draft of what became resolution 40/61 in 1985 also failed after sharp procedural maneuvering. Though only Cuba voted against adoption of the final text, explanations of vote by delegates from Algeria, Burkina Faso, Iran, Iraq, Mongolia, Syria, and the USSR included regrets that these references had been dropped.[17] While East-West polemics about "state terrorism" faded with the Cold War itself, the term continued to be invoked in criticisms of U.S., Israeli, and South African policies in the 1990s.

One part of this discussion—concern with government support for, assistance to, or connivance with terrorist activity—was incorporated into the main discussions through use of the term "state-sponsored terrorism." Governments used this phrase both to describe a possible situation of cooperating with or winking at terrorists and to accuse other governments of instigating, supporting, encouraging, or allowing their territory to be used as a haven by terrorists. Unlike "state terrorism," the term "state-sponsored terrorism" has been an omnidirectional accusation: leveled by the U.S. and other governments against governments in Africa and the Middle East; by Cuba, Iraq, Libya, and others against the U.S. government; and by several Third World governments against immediate or regional neighbors. The concern with government use of or connivance with terrorists is fully consistent with the assembly's evolving normative framework because the "measures to eliminate" stream has consistently called upon governments to refrain from aiding, supporting, or tolerating terrorists operating from their territory.

This shift of attention from "state terrorism" (which covers activities that can be condemned by reference to international law on the use of armed force between states) to "state-sponsored terrorism" also reflects the shift in emphasis marking the ongoing effort to distinguish between terrorism and justifiable armed resistance. Resolutions adopted in the 1970s affirmed that persons and groups resisting colonial rule, racist rule, or foreign occupation should not be regarded as terrorists no matter how they wage their armed struggle. Resolution 40/61 adopted in 1985 also included "mass and flagrant violations of human rights" among the "root causes" of terrorism, suggesting that many governments would not regard persons engaged in armed struggle against brutally oppressive regimes as terrorists.[18] Though the formulation was general, prior Vietnamese intervention to remove the embarrassingly brutal Khmer Rouge regime in Cambodia allowed the coalition of left-wing nonaligned, Soviet-bloc, and other Leninist governments to focus their condemnations on military governments facing leftist revolts and use the longer list of justified combatants as another base for polemics.

The end of the Cold War created circumstances conducive to reconsidering the problem of international terrorism. The superpowers began disengaging from conflicts in the Third World and either participating in or refraining from hindering efforts to negotiate settlement of several long-running civil wars. In this new context, the General Assembly was able to reach consensus on the terms of a statement about the problem of terrorism for the first time when it adopted resolution 46/51 in December 1991. Particularly noteworthy was the new formulation for distinguishing terrorists from righteous resisters of oppression, which defined the latter as those who "struggle legitimately" to end colonial or racist rule or foreign domination.[19] This indicated that more of the NAM were coming around to the view that even persons or groups having morally justified ends need to employ morally justifiable means and exercise certain restraints in the conduct of their armed resistance.[20]

Hopes that the end of the Cold War would mean a lessening of terrorist activity were dashed. New and continuing ethnic conflicts turned violent, and the conscious targeting of civilians became more frequent. While the Middle East continued to be home to the largest number of individuals said to be involved in terrorist actions and the locale of the largest number of incidents said to be terrorist acts, conflicts in Africa and the former Soviet Union were marked by similar activity. Yet the General Assembly discussions took on new flavor as the individuals involved in or affected by terrorism became a more significant element of discussion.

Concern for those harmed by terrorist acts has been given greatest expression in the "human rights and terrorism" stream of resolutions drafted in the Third Committee. Though delegates in this committee are primarily diplomatic generalists, they have drawn heavily on discussions among criminologists and human rights advocates, who took advantage of a more favorable climate for raising their concerns when the Cold War ended. Recent UN congresses on the Prevention of Crime and the Treatment of Offenders, the UN Committee on Crime Prevention and Control, and the UN Human Rights Commission and its Sub-commission on the Promotion and Protection of Human Rights have been the major sources of inspiration for Third Committee deliberations. This stream of assembly resolutions started as an expression of concern for the situation of victims and for the due process rights of individuals accused of engaging in terrorist activity. They now reflect more fully the normative dilemmas raised by urging governments to take swift and effective action against perpetrators of terrorist acts while avoiding erosion of international human rights and due process standards. Particularly since September 2001, the normative balance has shifted, and human rights advocates have expressed concern about leading governments' tendencies to subordinate human rights issues to cooperation against terrorists.[21]

The "measures to eliminate" stream of resolutions is more government centered and, like the earlier "measures to prevent" stream, lays out a normative framework encouraging governments to treat terrorism as a form of criminal activity, to suppress it using police methods, and to cooperate with one another in suppressing it. The General Assembly has given less explicit attention to identifying the underlying causes of terrorism, though invocation of the Declaration on the Occasion of the Fiftieth Anniversary of the United Nations[22] and the UN Millennium Declaration[23] in the preambles of more recent resolutions on terrorism include references to visions of a more just, equitable, and ecologically sustainable world. This stream also sidesteps the stalemate over defining the term "terrorism" by characterizing particular acts widely regarded as likely to be committed or attempted by terrorists as "unlawful" and urging cooperation against those who commit such acts.

Like the "measures to prevent" stream, the "measures to eliminate" stream is the province of the international lawyers on national delegations constituting the Sixth Committee. They are strongly attuned to the substantive and procedural values at stake in distinguishing legitimate armed resistance from terrorism and in encouraging governments to treat terrorism as a form of illegal activity to be handled through cooperative law enforcement rather than used as a justification for threats or uses of armed force against other states.

Though references to "state terrorism" continue to be heard in debates, the term does not appear in the "measures to eliminate" resolutions. The resolutions address the primary concerns expressed in the 1980s discussions of "state terrorism" by drawing instead on the general international law regarding threat or use of armed force by states against other states to emphasize two principles. The first affirms the duty of states to refrain from organizing, instigating, assisting, or participating in terrorist acts against other states; the second affirms that terrorist acts may not be used as an excuse for threats or uses of force against other states.

This is where the assembly's approach to terrorism diverges most clearly from the Security Council's. Assembly resolutions emphasize treating terrorism as a form of transnational crime to be suppressed through policing while council resolutions treat terrorism as a security question. It is clear that greater adherence to the duty to avoid aiding or harboring terrorists would reduce the excuses available for responding to terrorism by threatening or using force against a state. However, it is not obvious that avoiding threats or uses of force would assure fewer violations of the duty to avoid aiding or harboring, and many governments—not just the United States—refuse to close off the possibility of using military force against terrorists or states appearing to harbor them.

The "measures to eliminate" stream continues to emphasize the need to develop national and international legal rules adequate to suppressing terrorism. The assembly sought to foster this work more directly by establishing a new ad hoc committee on international terrorism in 1996. The committee has been encouraged to identify and help close gaps in the set of global multilateral treaties addressing cooperation against terrorist activity. The more ambitious proposals to develop a single comprehensive treaty have again foundered on disagreements over definition of the terms "terrorist" and "terrorism." The related notion of holding a high-level conference on the causes of terrorism has also failed to win sufficient support for preparations to begin. The new ad hoc committee did help draft the 1997 Convention on Terrorist Bombings and the 1999 Convention for Suppressing the Financing of Terrorism. The current "measures to eliminate" stream also routinely calls on governments to provide the UN secretary-general with information regarding their adherence to the multilateral treaties on terrorism and the state of their national law on suppressing and punishing terrorism. This information guides the ad hoc committee's efforts to encourage national action against terrorism. In general, however, this committee has been overshadowed by the Security Council's Counter-Terrorism Committee (CTC).

The General Assembly has also endorsed a number of norms that more clearly distinguish terrorists from other persons fleeing their homelands that have significant implications for national efforts to prosecute suspected terrorists. The first emphasizes that terrorist acts should not be treated as "political offenses." This norm diverges from the rule found in most treaties and national laws on extradition, which permits states to refuse to extradite persons whose alleged crimes were committed in the course of an organized political struggle against the authorities of the requesting state. The second emphasizes that terrorists should not be given asylum or be allowed to invoke refugee status to escape prosecution and punishment. The resolutions have, however, maintained the traditional rule of *non-refoulement* (non-return) to a state where the person might be persecuted for political affiliation, race, ethnicity, gender, or other characteristics.[24]

While General Assembly resolutions and UN websites shy away from suggesting that the list is definitive by saying that there may be other relevant treaties, repeated calls for governments to accede to a set list of twelve global treaties give them central place in anti-terrorist cooperation.[25] These treaties all define actions that should be treated as crimes to be prosecuted rather than as political acts deserving respect. Shifting views about the modes of legitimate armed struggle are reflected in these definitional provisions. The earlier treaties incorporated "saving clauses" that defined a range of circumstances and always included the commission of acts in the course of resistance to colonial, racist, or foreign domination, in which circumstances the action should not be regarded as a criminal act. The treaties drawn up after 1985 limit or omit these saving clauses and are more sweeping in their formulation of the bases for states to claim jurisdiction over the act. All of the treaties dealing with ships or aircraft specify that they do not apply to acts aboard planes or ships used for military, patrol, and police purposes. Persons aboard such craft are typically members of armed forces or state agencies covered by military or police discipline, and their plane or ship is considered to be "noncivilian" within the established rules of aviation and maritime law. As is usual in criminal law, both older and newer conventions also include abetting, aiding, and attempting the act within the category of criminal activity.

Together, the current multilateral agreements define the following ten acts as crimes:

- Any act on board an aircraft flying over the high seas that may or does endanger the safety of the aircraft or good order and discipline on board[26]
- Hijacking aircraft by direct seizure or by forcing the pilots to divert to a different destination[27]
- Interfering with safe flight by violence against persons; onboard acts damaging the aircraft; placement of explosive devices or other substances on board; destruction or damage to an aircraft on the ground that makes it incapable of flight; destroying, damaging, or interfering with air navigation facilities; or communication of false information that endangers the safety of aircraft in flight[28]
- Seizing control of, attacking, destroying, or damaging severely enough to endanger the safety of offshore platforms[29]
- Seizing control of a ship on the high seas[30]
- "Intentional commission" of murder, kidnapping, or assault on heads of state or government, ministers of foreign affairs, or representatives of a government or an intergovernmental organization entitled to diplomatic immunity who are outside their own country at the time of the act or an attack on their official premises, private accommodation, or means of transport that is likely to endanger them[31]
- Unlawful receipt, possession, transfer, or disposal of those isotopes of uranium and plutonium most useful for making weapons[32]
- Seizing and holding any person to compel a government, an international intergovernmental organization, a natural or juridical person, or a group of persons to do or abstain from doing any act[33]
- Violence against persons, facilities, or aircraft in airports serving international civil aviation that causes death or serious injury and destruction of or serious damage to airport facilities or aircraft not in service that disrupts operations at such an airport[34]
- Intentionally destroying or damaging buildings open to the public or other public spaces with the intention of causing death or injury to occupants[35]
- Knowingly providing funds directly or indirectly to persons or groups engaging in terrorism or assisting them through money-laundering[36]

As some commentators have noted,[37] most of these conventions establish norms against attacking civilians, taking hostages, or killing prisoners that parallel the law of warfare most recently codified in the 1949 Geneva conventions and 1977 additional protocols. The treaty norms also reflect the widespread understanding that terrorists typically seek to accomplish their goals not by attacking the actor or actors they hope to influence but by attacking some third party in the expectation that this will create pressures on the target actor to accede to their demands.

The jurisdictional clauses of the conventions establish rules for cooperation against perpetrators of terrorism by defining the circumstances in which individual states can assert jurisdiction over a particular terrorist incident, outlining certain procedural safeguards for the accused, and obligating states where accused perpetrators are located to try them or to extradite them to another state having jurisdiction that is willing to try them. The precise formulations of these clauses have shifted over time as governments have become willing to make clearer commitments. The conventions often reflect contemporaneous General Assembly resolutions fairly closely because delegates involved in the negotiations take cues from changes in the latter's formulations.

The conventions focus primarily on post-attack responses of locating and trying accused perpetrators. The General Assembly has also encouraged governments to take preventive action by endorsing a variety of measures intended to reduce the likelihood of terrorist activity. One line of possible measures that includes adopting administrative routines or other policies meant to inhibit terrorism is identified in the conventions on Physical Safety of Nuclear Materials, Marking of Plastic Explosives,[38] and Suppression of Financing. The first outlines standards for physical custody of nuclear materials in transit and permits governments to disallow an international transfer if those standards cannot be met. The second specifies that governments should require producers to add stipulated chemicals to plastic explosives so they are easier to detect and to ban manufacture or possession of "unmarked" plastic explosives. The last deals with cutting off the financial resources flowing directly or through intermediaries to terrorists or terrorist groups.

The assembly's Ad Hoc Committee on Terrorism also serves a reminding and prodding function via the reporting mechanism first established in resolution 51/210 in 1996. This asks governments to list the global, regional, and bilateral treaties on suppression of terrorist activity to which they are parties, to note terrorist incidents and the prosecutions and convictions of persons for terrorist activity they have undertaken, and to provide information about their national laws and regulations on suppression of terrorism. Government responses have been scattered, but the reporting system does create the possibility that the ad hoc committee could function as a prod toward greater co-operation against terrorism.[39] However, it became somewhat overshadowed by the 2001 Security Council's resolution 1373 establishment of a similar system of reporting to its Counter-Terrorism Committee.

Impact of the General Assembly's Resolutions on Government Behavior

It is difficult to assess the extent to which General Assembly endorsement has encouraged governments to take action against terrorism because numerous factors come into play. A closer look at government behavior suggests that major terrorist incidents, particularly those hitting close to home, have far greater impact on governments' willingness to pay attention than do General Assembly resolutions. It is also clear that government attention waxes and wanes, but how closely these variations are tied to the actual incidence of terrorist activity is hard to assess because determining the precise extent of terrorist activity is difficult.

There is considerable room to argue about the number of terrorist acts in any year, not least because any count depends heavily on the forms of violence included within the term "terrorism." The U.S. State Department has been reporting on incidents of "international terrorism" (acts affecting or involving nationals of more than one state or accomplished by persons outside

Table 8.1. Incidents of International Terrorism, 1968–2001

Year	Number of Incidents	Year	Number of Incidents
1968	170	1985	635
1969	190	1986	612
1970	300	1987	665
1971	250	1988	605
1972	525	1989	375
1973	325	1990	437
1974	425	1991	565
1975	360	1992	363
1976	457	1993	431
1977	419	1994	322
1978	530	1995	440
1979	434	1996	296
1980	499	1997	304
1981	489	1998	274
1982	487	1999	395
1983	497	2000	426
1984	565	2001	348

Source: U.S. State Department, *Patterns of Global Terrorism 1992* (Washington, D.C.: U.S. Department of State, 1992), 57; *1995,* 71; and *2001,* 171.

their own state) since 1968, one of the lengthier data-gathering efforts on the issue of terrorism. Its definitions and counting rules are open to challenge— and defined clearly enough to permit challenge—but they have been fairly consistent through time. The most serious inconsistency involves incidents involving Palestinians as both perpetrators and victims, which were shifted from the "international" to the "domestic" category in 1984, without complete retrospective standardization of the data. Even with these caveats, the data series in Table 8.1 provides a reasonably accurate view of the changing prevalence and forms of terrorist activity. A different count indicating that there were 5,431 terrorist incidents leaving 4,684 persons dead during the 1980s and 3,824 incidents leaving 2,468 dead in the 1990s is consistent with the State Department data on trends in the number of incidents.[40]

There is still much truth to the jaded maxim that one person's (or government's) terrorist is another's freedom fighter. The sharpest and most publicized disagreement about who is or is not a terrorist today arises out of the Palestinian-Israeli conflict. The Council of the League of Arab States continues to exclude all acts by those exercising "the legitimate right of peoples to struggle against occupation" from its definition of "terrorism."[41] This allows Arab League members to believe they are not contradicting themselves when they vote in favor of statements such as General Assembly resolution ES-10/2 (1997) on "Illegal Israeli actions in occupied East Jerusalem and the rest of the occupied Palestinian territory," which blames Israel for all the tensions and violent action in the region while also stipulating that the assembly "[reject] terrorism in all its forms and manifestations, in accordance with all relevant United Nations resolutions and declarations."[42] Meanwhile, the Israeli government regards Palestinian suicide bombers as terrorists and uses military as well as police measures in response.

Students of "low-level conflict" contend that terrorism is a weapon of the extremely weak and excluded that is used by individuals or groups who have no other way to secure political leverage. Supporters of a particular group engaged in armed struggle that involves repeated attacks on civilians use similar arguments when explaining their position.[43] Though they are plausible on some occasions, such claims of thorough exclusion and lack of alternative modes for acquiring political leverage are becoming more problematic with the increased prevalence of fully or partly democratic governance around the world. Though they define it in many ways, advocates of democracy all agree that it involves "substituting the counting of hands for the cracking of heads"[44] in political decision-making. Where this is true, those trying to affect an ongoing political process in their own country or put pressure on the government of another by causing death, severe injury, or severe psychic pain to ordinary people are unlikely to gain wide support.

Whatever the political circumstances, General Assembly resolutions on terrorism explicitly—and the multilateral conventions on unlawful acts implicitly—urge states to refrain from threats of or the use of armed force against other states in response to terrorist incidents. Consistent with the long debates over state use of armed force during the Cold War era, the General Assembly's formulation of this norm always includes the phrase "uses or threats of armed force contrary to the UN Charter." This phrase allows governments that decide to use military measures against terrorists to claim that their response is consistent with the Charter and hence permissible. Other governments' reception of such claims depends heavily on the circumstances. After both its 1986 bombing raid against Tripoli and Benghazi, Libya, and its 1998 missile attack on a factory in the Sudan, the U.S. government was severely criticized,[45] even though the governments of both Libya and the Sudan were at odds with many neighbors, were correctly suspected of tolerating or abetting activity covered by the multilateral conventions, and were under Security Council sanctions for failure to hand over persons suspected of terrorism to governments wishing to try them.[46] International acceptance of the U.S. government's claim that using armed force against the Taliban in Afghanistan was an act of self-defense was much broader and was explicitly endorsed by the Security Council in resolutions 1368 and 1373 following the September 11 attacks. The Taliban was a special case, however. Only two other governments maintained formal diplomatic relations with the Taliban regime in September and October 2001, its delegates had not been accepted as representatives of Afghanistan at the UN, every neighboring state was financing at least one opposition group, and in resolution 1297 in 1999 the Security Council had imposed sanctions against it for continuing to allow Al Qaeda to use camps in Afghanistan. In contrast, even U.S. Defense Department hawks realized that making such a claim about Iraq in 2002–2003 would win no support. Though they continued to include accusations regarding links to Al Qaeda, they emphasized the urgent necessity of keeping Saddam Hussein from increasing or using his arsenals of weapons of mass destruction.

One preliminary indication of governments' readiness to clamp down on terrorists is ratification of or accession to the multilateral conventions criminalizing violent actions or outlining preventive measures. Ratification of multilateral conventions is often a drawn-out process, but striking incidents of the problem addressed in a convention often hasten the process. Tables 8.2 and 8.3 indicate that the pace of ratification had picked up *before* September 11, providing additional evidence that the problem of international terrorism was already on governments' agendas.

Ratification is a promise to act in particular ways, but it does not necessarily mean that promises will be acted upon when the need arises. In many

Table 8.2. Multilateral Conventions Concluded in the 1960s and 1970s

O indicates year opened for signature, ratification, and accession. The first number indicates the states ratifying in each year; the second indicates the total number of states that were parties at the end of that year.

Year	Offenses on Aircraft	Hijacking Aircraft	Safety of Aviation	Protected Persons	Taking Hostages	Nuclear Material
1963	O	—	—	—	—	—
1964	1; 1	—	—	—	—	—
1965	1; 2	—	—	—	—	—
1966	0; 2	—	—	—	—	—
1967	3; 5	—	—	—	—	—
1968	2; 7	—	—	—	—	—
1969	12; 19	—	—	—	—	—
1970	17; 36	O	—	—	—	—
1971	13; 49	18; 18	O	—	—	—
1972	14; 63	24; 42	16; 16	—	—	—
1973	4; 67	16; 58	27; 43	O	—	—
1974	7; 74	7; 65	13; 56	1; 1	—	—
1975	7; 81	4; 69	5; 61	10; 11	—	—
1976	2; 83	3; 72	7; 68	7; 18	—	—
1977	6; 89	8; 80	8; 76	11; 29	—	—
1978	5; 94	15; 95	16; 92	8; 37	—	—
1979	9; 103	9; 104	9; 101	3; 40	O	O
1980	2; 105	2; 106	3; 104	9; 49	4; 4	1; 1
1981	2; 107	3; 109	3; 107	2; 51	13; 17	1; 2
1982	2; 109	2; 111	5; 112	3; 54	2; 19	2; 4
1983	7; 116	6; 117	6; 118	2; 56	3; 22	2; 6
1984	3; 119	6; 123	6; 124	2; 58	3; 25	2; 8
1985	2; 121	2; 125	3; 127	5; 63	3; 28	5; 13
1986	2; 123	3; 128	3; 130	2; 65	7; 35	4; 17
1987	3; 126	5; 133	6; 136	3; 68	10; 45	2; 19
1988	4; 130	2; 135	1; 137	3; 71	7; 52	3; 22
1989	6; 136	5; 140	4; 141	2; 73	4; 56	3; 25
1990	1; 137	0; 140	0; 141	2; 75	6; 62	0; 25
1991	5; 142	5; 145	5; 146	2; 77	5; 67	12; 37
1992	2; 144	2; 147	2; 148	4; 81	2; 69	3; 40
1993	3; 147	2; 149	2; 150	4; 85	4; 73	9; 49
1994	4; 151	4; 153	4; 154	3; 88	2; 75	2; 51
1995	6; 157	4; 157	5; 159	1; 89	0; 75	1; 52
1996	4; 161	4; 161	4; 163	2; 91	2; 77	4; 56
1997	3; 164	2; 163	3; 166	4; 95	2; 79	2; 58
1998	3; 167	5; 168	3; 169	4; 99	2; 81	4; 62
1999	2; 169	2; 170	3; 172	2; 101	2; 83	1; 63
2000	2; 171	3; 173	2; 174	4; 105	8; 91	4; 67
2001	2; 173	2; 175	3; 177	8; 113	9; 100	1; 68
2002	1; 174	1; 176	1; 178	9; 122	8; 108	12; 80

Notes: This table uses the date of initial Yugoslav ratification rather than the 2001 reratification by Serbia and Montenegro.

Sources: Convention on Offenses and Certain Other Acts Committed on Board Aircraft, available online at http://untreaty.un.org/English/Terrorism/Conv1.pdf; Convention for the Suppression of Unlawful Seizure of Aircraft, available online at http://untreaty.un.org/English/Terrorism/Conv2.pdf; Convention for the Suppression of Unlawful Acts against the Safety of Civil Aviation, available online at http://untreaty.un.org/English/Terrorism/Conv3.pdf; Convention on the Prevention and Punishment of Crimes against Internationally Protected Persons, Including Diplomatic Agents, available online at http://untreaty.un.org/English/Terrorism/Conv4.pdf; International Convention against the Taking of Hostages, available online at http://untreaty.un.org/English/Terrorism/Conv5.pdf; Convention on the Physical Protection of Nuclear Material, available online at http://www.iaea.org/worldatom/Documents/Legal/cppn.shtml.

Table 8.3. Multilateral Conventions Concluded since 1980

O indicates year opened for signature, ratification, and accession. The first number indicates the states ratifying in each year; the second indicates the total number of states that were parties at the end of that year.

Year	Safety of Airports	Attacks on Shipping	Attacks on Platforms	Marking of Plastic Explosives	Terrorist Bombings	Financing Terrorism
1988	O 1; 1	O	O	—	—	—
1989	13; 14	5; 5	—	—	—	—
1990	14; 28	4; 9	—	—	—	—
1991	7; 35	6; 15	—	O	—	—
1992	5; 40	1; 16	15; 15	3; 3	—	—
1993	6; 46	7; 23	6; 21	2; 5	—	—
1994	7; 53	7; 30	4; 25	5; 10	—	—
1995	9; 62	2; 32	3; 28	6; 16	—	—
1996	10; 72	1; 33	3; 31	10; 26	—	—
1997	5; 77	0; 33	0; 31	8; 34	O	—
1998	11; 88	5; 38	3; 34	10; 44	1; 1	—
1999	9; 97	5; 43	4; 38	11; 55	7; 8	O
2000	9; 106	9; 52	8; 46	10; 65	9; 17	2; 2
2001	5; 111	8; 60	5; 51	8; 73	28; 45	14; 16
2002	14; 125	6; 66	6; 57	7; 80	31; 76	27; 43

Note: This table uses the date of initial Yugoslav ratification rather than the 2001 reratification by Serbia and Montenegro.

Sources: Protocol for the Suppression of Unlawful Acts of Violence at Airports Serving International Civil Aviation, available online at http://www.icao.int/icao/en/leb/Via.htm; International Convention for the Suppression of Acts against the Safety of Maritime Navigation, 1988, available online at http://www.imo.org/includes/blastDataOnly.asp/data_id%3D5510/end2001.pdf; Attacks on Platforms, available online at http://www.imo.org/includes/blastDataOnly.asp/data_id%3D5510/end2001.pdf; Convention on Marking of Plastic Explosives for the Purpose of Detection, done at Montreal on January 3, 1991, available online at http://www.icao.int/icao/en/leb/MEX.htm; International Convention for the Suppression of Terrorist Bombings, available online at http://untreaty.un.org/English/Terrorism/Conv11.pdf; International Convention for the Suppression of the Financing of Terrorism, available online at http://untreaty.un.org/English/Terrorism/Conv12.pdf.

countries, action needs to be preceded by legislation or decrees that incorporate treaty provisions into national law. The General Assembly resolutions on elimination of terrorism have asked governments to report changes in national legislation regarding terrorist acts, and most governments do report at least some elaboration of national law. Many governments also need to develop the administrative capacity to carry out their newly accepted obligations. The UN has begun to address this need in modest ways. In 1999, a separate Terrorism Branch was established within the Office for International Crime Control. It has undertaken a number of activities, including organization of workshops for national law enforcement agencies and development of guides to "best practices" in the field.[47] News reports indicate a stepping up of cooperation in information-sharing and investigation focused on suspected

Al Qaeda cells but continued unevenness in efforts directed at other groups. Some studies of cooperative police work against transnational criminal organizations have concluded that the criminals are far ahead of the police in networking and using contemporary communications technologies. Criminals and terrorists can also operate more quickly than police because they are unconstrained by the need to respect national sovereignty or the rights of accused persons.

Concluding Observations

The resolutions addressing terrorism as a general problem put forward what the General Assembly is most suited to provide: formulations of norms enjoying the widest support among member governments at the time that they are adopted and indications of the breadth of that support through votes and statements in debate. The guidelines about dealing with international terrorism that have been adopted thus far show a preference for treating terrorist activity as a problem of individual and collaborative law enforcement rather than as an excuse for threats or uses of armed force. The General Assembly has not defined the term "terrorism," preferring a more oblique approach of identifying certain acts as "criminal" whatever the motivation for or the circumstances of their commission. The assembly has also suggested some practical measures that would make terrorist operations more difficult. Resolutions also reveal continued concern that the "terrorist" label not be extended to those engaged in what the General Assembly's majority regards as justified acts of political resistance and reminders that both victims and accused perpetrators have rights that deserve respect.

Expressions of concern about conditions encouraging resort to terrorism have grown less prominent in the texts of resolutions adopted in the 1990s, but they persist and continue to appear in assembly discussions in three ways. The first concerns the general debates on terrorism-related resolutions in the Third and Sixth Committees and the ongoing Third World efforts to have the General Assembly convene a high-level UN conference on terrorism that would include identifying and addressing underlying causes. The second consists of statements about particular situations that include reference to reasons members of one population or another have been driven to adopt armed resistance and expressing sympathy with their motives though sometimes deploring their choice of means. The third arises in resolutions on other issues. Some, such as the Millennium Declaration, express visions of a better world in which violent conflict of all sorts would be largely eliminated. Others, such as resolutions on nuclear disarmament or international trade, suggest that failure to make progress on disarmament[48] or to create a more equitable international economic system creates conditions conducive to terrorism. However some governments, including the U.S., are quite reluctant to discuss root causes, much less accept resolutions about them, and the assembly majority has not pressed forward in the face of this reluctance.

The General Assembly's efforts to promote coordinated action, whether in the form of elaborating an international legal framework that promotes cooperation against terrorism or in the form of urging governments to work together, have had more mixed results. Here, too, the possibilities of assembly action are defined by the attitudes of the member states. What is notable about the current "measures to eliminate" stream is the breadth of consensus at the verbal level about taking additional measures against perpetrators of particular actions and closing off some of the legal loopholes that let such perpetrators avoid prosecution and punishment by slipping through the cracks created by uneven national responses. Even the Sudan and Libya have become less active supporters of terrorism and have joined in the general condemnation of more recent terrorist acts.

There is a long tradition among international lawyers and other reformers of attributing to the General Assembly strong legal as well as moral authority. They argue that through frequent recitation and invocation, some resolutions have acquired the status of binding legal rules. They note that the 1950 "Uniting for Peace" resolution 377 has been used to justify an active role in crisis management or conflict resolution through convening conferences or special sessions on particular situations, such as the 1980 session on Afghanistan or the 1982 session on the Middle East.[49] They observe that the assembly's power to create subsidiary bodies under Article 22 of the Charter could be used to establish quasi-judicial bodies to deal with terrorist activity. They also note that the assembly has put pressure on particular governments through refusals to accept delegation credentials, effectively preventing those governments from participating in most UN activities because other organizations of the system often follow the assembly's lead on such matters.

All of these observations suggest possibilities for moving the General Assembly beyond being a forum for mutual exhortation and the formulation of norms toward concrete cooperation. Yet whether these possibilities are ever realized depends on the attitudes and reactions of governments. Member states occasionally opt for ostracism rather than continued engagement with a particular government, but ostracism by the assembly in itself has not altered a determined government's conduct. The additional prods of unilateral pressures by powerful countries, collective sanctions mandated by the Security Council, and (most notably in the case of South Africa under apartheid) transnational social movements have been needed to bring about significant changes of policy. Though most of the world's governments have agreed to establish an International Criminal Court (ICC), its jurisdiction does not currently extend to terrorist activities. Additionally, its establishment followed the more traditional process of convening a UN conference to develop a multilateral treaty, and that treaty gives the ICC a more solid basis in international law than it would have if established by a General Assembly resolution.

The politics of consensus still plays out in complex ways—sometimes serving to obscure continued disagreement by carefully written phrases and sometimes indicating real agreement. Yet the scope of actual agreement regarding international terrorism has expanded considerably in the last decade. The "least common denominator" is more clearly opposed to acts which attempt to express grievances through armed attacks on ordinary civilians and daily life than it was in 1990, and governments are more determined to prevent terrorists from enjoying the rights of asylum written into extradition and refugee law for those who engage in violent political struggle against their own governments.[50] However, real limits remain on what governments want to do and real dilemmas exist about how to react to particular situations. Governments are not yet ready to adopt the strong forms of multilateral coordination in treating terrorism as a form of transnational crime that some of the lawyers' suggestions would require.

Notes

1. Inis L. Claude, Jr., "Collective Legitimization as a Political Function of the United Nations," *International Organization* 20, no. 3 (Summer 1966): 367–379.

2. Most resolutions can be adopted by 50 percent plus one of the delegations present and voting, and those on "important questions" can be adopted by two-thirds of those present and voting.

3. The General Assembly decides matters of internal UN organization.

4. A particularly trenchant expression of this view is Julius Stone, *Conflict through Consensus* (Baltimore: Johns Hopkins University Press, 1977).

5. Text in *Yearbook of the United Nations, 1994* (Lake Success, N.Y.: Department of Public Information, United Nations, 1995), 1294–1295. The *Yearbook of the United Nations* will hereafter be referred to by title and year.

6. General Assembly resolution 2625 (XXV). Text in *Yearbook of the United Nations, 1970,* 788–792.

7. See *Report of the World Conference on Human Rights: Report of the Secretary-General* (A/CONF.157/24), Part 1, Chapter III, October 13, 1993 or *Situation of Human Rights in Sudan,* A/48/601, November 18, 1993.

8. General Assembly resolution 2734 (XXV). Text in *Yearbook of the United Nations, 1970,* 105–107.

9. General Assembly resolution 3314 (XXIX). Text in *Yearbook of the United Nations, 1974*, 846–848.

10. General Assembly resolution 42/22. Text in *Yearbook of the United Nations, 1987*, 1055–1057.

11. Text in *Yearbook of the United Nations, 1994*, 1294.

12. For example, operative paragraph 2 of General Assembly resolution 56/88, adopted in December 2001. Available online at http://www.un.org/documents/resga.htm.

13. Text in *Yearbook of the United Nations, 1972*, 650. Vote reported on 647.

14. *Yearbook of the United Nations, 1976*, 834; *1977*, 971; and *1979*, 1149.

15. Remarks of Yugoslav delegate in *General Assembly Official Records*, 36th Session, Sixth Committee, 69th meeting, December 3, 1981, paragraph 8.

16. General Assembly resolution 39/159. Vote reported and text given in *Yearbook of the United Nations, 1984*, 121–22.

17. Sixth Committee Debate, *General Assembly Official Records*, 40th Session, Sixth Committee, 55th meeting, December 6, 1985.

18. Text in *Yearbook of the United Nations, 1985*, 168.

19. Text in *Yearbook of the United Nations, 1991*, 823–825.

20. See, for example, Nicholas P. Kuttrie, *Rebels with a Cause* (Boulder: Westview Press, 2000).

21. This was most clearly manifest in the failure of efforts by UN High Commissioner for Human Rights Mary Robinson to get human rights experts included in the Security Council's Counter-Terrorism Committee and has been the subject of much journalistic commentary.

22. General Assembly resolution 50/6. Text in *Yearbook of the United Nations, 1995*, 289–292.

23. "United Nations Millennium Declaration," General Assembly resolution 55/2, September 8, 2000. Available online at http://www.un.org/documents/resga.htm.

24. General Assembly resolution 51/210. Text in *Yearbook of the United Nations, 1996*, 1209.

25. Such as General Assembly resolution 46/41, third preambular paragraph; General Assembly resolution 51/210, paragraph 6; and General Assembly resolution 55/158 (December 12, 2000), paragraph 7. Texts of the first two in *Yearbook of the United Nations, 1991*, 824; and *1996*, 1209. Text of the third is available online at http://www.un.org/documents/resga.htm.

26. Convention on Offenses and Certain Other Acts Committed on Board Aircraft, 1963, Article 1. In *United Nations Treaty Series* (New York: United Nations), 704, 219.

27. Convention for the Suppression of Unlawful Seizure of Aircraft (Hijacking), 1971, Articles 1 and 3. In *International Legal Materials* 10 (1971): 133.

28. Convention for the Suppression of Unlawful Acts against the Safety of Civil Aviation, 1971, Articles 1 and 3. In *International Legal Materials* 10 (1971): 1151.

29. Protocol for the Suppression of Acts against the Safety of Fixed Platforms to the International Convention for the Suppression of Acts against the Safety of Maritime Navigation, 1988, Article 1. In *International Legal Materials* 27 (1988): 685.

30. International Convention for the Suppression of Acts against the Safety of Maritime Navigation, 1988, Article 3. In *International Legal Materials* 27 (1988): 672.

31. Convention on the Prevention and Punishment of Crimes against Internationally Protected Persons, including Diplomatic Agents, 1973, Articles 1 and 2. In *Yearbook of the United Nations, 1973* (General Assembly resolution 3166), 775.

32. International Convention on the Physical Protection of Nuclear Material, 1980, Article 7. In *International Legal Materials* 18 (1980): 419–433.

33. International Convention against the Taking of Hostages, 1979, Article 1. In *Yearbook of the United Nations, 1979* (General Assembly resolution 34/146, December 17, 1979), 1144.

34. Protocol for the Suppression of Unlawful Acts of Violence at Airports Serving International Civil Aviation supplementary to the 1971 Convention for the Suppression of Acts against the Safety of Civil Aviation, 1988, Articles II and III. Available online at http://www.icao.int/icao/en/leb/Via.htm.

35. International Convention for the Suppression of Terrorist Bombings, 1997, Article 2. In *Yearbook of the United Nations, 1997*, 1348.

36. International Convention for the Suppression of the Financing of Terrorism, 1999, Article 2. In *Yearbook of the United Nations, 1999*, 1233.

37. Kuttrie, *Rebels with a Cause*; Alex Peter Schmid and Ronald D. Crelinsten, eds., *Western Response to Terrorism* (London and Portland, Ore.: Frank Cass, 1993).

38. "Marking of Plastic Explosives," *International Legal Materials* 30 (1991): 726–732.

39. José Alvarez suggested this possibility. The large literature on reporting requirements established by treaty, which carry greater legal obligation than a resolution urging members to report to a General Assembly subsidiary body, indicates that only a minority of such systems have significant prodding effects. See, for example, Anne F. Bayefsky, ed., *The UN Human Rights Treaty System in the 21st Century* (The Hague: Kluwer Law International, 2000); and David G. Victor, Kal Raustiala, and Eugene B. Skolnikoff, eds., *The Implementation and Effectiveness of International Environmental Commitments* (Cambridge, Mass.: MIT Press, 1998).

40. Noted in Barry Gewen, "Thinking the Unthinkable," *New York Times Book Review*, September 15, 2002, 12.

41. Council of the League of Arab States, statement on terrorism, October 1998. Circulated as UN Doc. S/1998/800.

42. General Assembly resolution ES-10/2 (April 22, 1997), paragraph 12. Text in *Yearbook of the United Nations, 1997*, 397.

43. As did anonymous supporters in spring 2002 who posted signs around downtown Northampton, Massachusetts, reading "Don't approve of suicide bombings? Then arm the Palestinians properly!"

44. A phrase often used by Professor Don McKee at Uppsala College (East Orange, N.J.) in the late 1960s without naming an author or claiming it as his own.

45. General Assembly discussions noted in *Yearbook of the United Nations, 1998*, 1219. The Sudanese even circulated copies of U.S. criticisms of the attack to other member governments.

46. Sanctions imposed on Libya by Security Council resolution 748 (1992) for harboring persons suspected of involvement in the aircraft explosion over Lockerbie, Scotland, and on the Sudan by Security Council resolution 1054 (1996) for harboring persons involved in an attempt to assassinate President Hosni Mubarak of Egypt in Ethiopia.

47. The office's website, http://www.odccp.org/terrorism, accessed on September 7, 2002.

48. See, for example, General Assembly resolution 56/24T of 2002. Available online at http://www.un.org/documents/resga.htm.

49. See Peter J. van Krieken, ed., *Refugee Law in Context—the Exclusion Clause* (The Hague: Kluwer Law International, 1999).

9

The Political Economy of Terrorism

Mónica Serrano

What has the United Nations done for the war against terrorism? There are twelve existing UN conventions on terrorism which, most would agree, have been better at identifying particular forms of terrorist action to be out-lawed than at producing a definition of terrorism per se.[1] Indeed, while progress has been made on a number of practical fronts since the first convention in 1963, the lack of multilateral consensus among member states on the issue of definition exposes the depth of the problem posed by terrorism for the UN, one that is more than a matter of asking certain member states to sign up to a condemnation of themselves. Even so, an appreciation that terrorist acts em-body a threat to order in many states has gradually fostered an international consensus that recognizes the need to tackle the problem. The UN has thus proceeded, perhaps more productively, to declare measures against terrorism while avoiding becoming embroiled in a definition of what terrorism *is* be-yond an arbitrary set of violently unlawful acts.[2]

This prudently pragmatic prevarication became untenable after Septem-ber 11, 2001. What could be the relevance of the UN to the United States if its conventions did not amount to a norm upon which to base action against terrorism? As early as 1970, there was an international convention on the un-lawful seizure of aircraft. After September 11, that was small comfort. Indeed, with the U.S. declaration of "war" against terrorist groups "of global reach," it was now the creation of a principle upon which to base a response to terrorist activity that would be more practical.

If the UN had avoided committing itself to a definition of terrorism, it was because of a desire to avoid becoming mired in deeper disagreements about the justice of political causes and the conditions beneath the resort to tactics of terror. In some parts of the world in the late twentieth century, notions of liberation struggles and freedom fighters still enjoyed a fading, but residual, currency.[3] September 11 marks a global watershed here, too. In the aftermath of the terrorist attacks, any declaration of principle about terrorism cannot contain a lurking subtext of sympathy for the goals, as distinct from the methods, of terrorist groups.

So in the twenty-first century, who is a terrorist? Does the UN have anything to say? Surprisingly, it does. The UN's contribution to the U.S. war is to be found in the implications of its last convention on terrorism in 1999 and in the Convention on Transnational Organized Crime of 2000. After eleven conventions on terrorist *acts,* "on specific activities that are capable of being outlawed," the UN's International Convention for the Suppression of the Financing of Terrorism was the first to try to get at a *source* of terrorism. This convention marks an important shift in the direction of a definition of "terrorist" with which the U.S. appears satisfied; namely, that a terrorist is by definition a criminal.[4]

The eleven previous conventions brought terrorist actions under the purview of international criminal law. The twelfth brings the financing of those actions—laundered money and illegally acquired assets and funds—into the sphere of that law. Implicitly, this convention separates terrorism from politics and replaces it with a sanctionable action—financial transactions by identified criminal groups. In the words of the Special Recommendation of the Financial Action Task Force late in 2001: "Each country should criminalize the financing of terrorism, terrorist acts and terrorist organizations."[5] Terrorists are no longer to be allowed the refuge of ambiguity that historically attended their status as would-be combatants. The circle was closed with the targeting of transnationally organized criminals as a top security threat—in other words, as part of a spectrum including terrorism.

The blanket criminalizing of terrorism, however, raises some vexing questions. Far from pulling the plug on terrorism as such, recent UN conventions may have merely ended a debate that failed to deliver what the post–September 11 climate demanded—a right answer. This chapter explores the evolution of the criminalization of the financing of terrorism and sketches a more appropriate response than that approach to fighting terrorism has offered and argues that one has to look less at finances and more at an economy of an entirely different kind, the informal economy of popular support if international efforts are to be successful.

Crime and Terrorism

The Convention for the Suppression of the Financing of Terrorism does correspond to a new global reality, one which it was time to take stock of after September 11. There is no doubt that the identities of terrorists, guerrillas, drug traffickers, and arms smugglers have become more slippery and that international measures are needed to act against them in concert. Guerrilla and terrorist organizations have been tapping into the parallel world of transnational organized crime, where with the right black-market connections easy money is to be had in significant quantities, for some time. Similarly, organized criminals such as drug trafficker Pablo Escobar resorted to traditional terrorist tactics against the state in the 1980s in Colombia. The experience of Italy demonstrates the many ways in which transnational organized criminals have used terrorist tactics to pursue their economic interests and protect themselves from law enforcement. The circularity of terrorists becoming organized criminals and organized criminals becoming terrorists and the apparent identity mutation across these two groups attracted attention in the armed conflicts and civil wars of the late twentieth century, from Africa to the former Yugoslavia.

Developments in these regions have implied a serious erosion of the old internal logic of political violence and the subordination of political motivations to an "econocentered" dynamic of violent exchanges.[6] From Peru to Afghanistan, the grid of connections between terrorism and criminal networks has become highly crisscrossed. The Kosovo Liberation Army (KLA/UCK), for example, is formally committed to satisfying the political aspirations of ethnic Albanians in Kosovo and Macedonia. It is also, however, deeply involved in organized crime, and while the proceeds of its criminal activities are partly used to finance the "political struggle," it has become increasingly difficult for outside actors to disentangle criminal from political agendas.

Not surprisingly, underworld techniques, as well as investments in the legal economy by criminals, have been identified as unequivocal threats to the legal economy. At the same time, since drug-trafficking is the largest source of illicit capital around the world, it seems likely that if terrorists want money—and want to hide its tracks—they will go to the drug barons and their bankers.[7]

This assumption has mobilized the highest-level follow-up to the UN convention, the recommendations of the Financial Action Task Force (FATF), which cooperates with the UN, the Egmont Group of Financial Intelligence Units, the G-20, and international financial institutions (IFIs). The proposed measures from the FATF are designed to "deny terrorists and their supporters access to the international financial system."[8] Thus, the FATF recommends that the assets of terrorists be frozen and confiscated, that suspicious transactions related to terrorism be reported, and the like. These measures expand the FATF's mission beyond money-laundering, thereby mandating it to closely monitor the financial service industry and corporate institutions, including remittance systems and wire transfers.

Such proposals have attracted criticism, particularly from Washington, where the American Bankers Association and the securities industry, along with representatives of almost every U.S. financial institution, have claimed that they will be costly and unworkable and will disrupt legitimate financial relationships and activity.[9]

Pragmatic criticisms of measures such as those of the FATF may at first seem compelling, but in the end, they are actually quite weak. Certainly one can ask how security dealers, money brokers, futures traders, and even credit-card dealers are supposed to know one shady client from another. One can also question the track record of the financial and accounting world in re-porting suspicious transactions to outside authorities. But, rather in the man-ner of the arguments about the disruptive costs of cross-border inspection, a pragmatic reductio ad absurdum is vulnerable to the countercharge, "Do you just want to sit there and do nothing about organized crime/terrorism?" If a regulatory system is said to be incapable of working, the pragmatic solution may be to throw more resources at it. But since insurance companies, stock-brokers, and bureaux de change in countries (including the U.S.) are not yet required by law to report on suspicious transactions, why should the answer be to give up on regulation rather than fix the law?[10]

The more fundamental weakness of pragmatic criticisms, however, is that they accede to the premises of the financial regulatory approach to terrorism. The debate becomes one about the balance between the optimum level of regulation sought by government and the minimum level sought—with some notable exceptions—by the industry. Both sides have evidence which they can air in the media. On the one hand, for example, David Aufhauser, head of the U.S. Joint Agency Committee on Terrorist Financing, has been reported as saying that "action against terrorist financing was the most reliable way of thwarting terrorist activity. The global effort to halt the financial flows upon which Al Qaeda operatives have depended has led to $113 million of funds being frozen globally so far."[11] And on the other, a report has emerged claim-ing that asset seizures have stalled because "terrorists" have moved their assets out of accounts into gold and diamonds—and that some of the $113–125 mil-lion seized has in any case belonged to companies and individuals with names that are easy to misspell and even to people who are now deceased.[12]

Bandying about figures like this, the low-intensity media war colludes in disseminating the reassuring impression that through their finances, we do indeed know who the terrorists are. Again in Aufhauser's words, "[A]udit trails do not lie—they are diaries of terror." Yes, the financial industry may moan about the inconvenience it is being put to and gloat when the federal govern-ment makes a mistake. But the industry cannot contest the key point: that terrorism is now a vein in the circulatory system of the international financial system which, given enough cooperation and resources, one could isolate. It is one thing to say that the industry lacks incentives to track illicit transactions and quite another to concede that the industry is incapable of knowing what comes in and goes out of its house.

So the regulatory case gets the upper hand. Follow the money and find the terrorists. Through their transactions we shall know them.

Terrorism on the Cheap

Given the new synergies between organized crime and terrorism, the regulatory campaign is right as far as it goes. If the money flows can be traced, they should be—as much money-laundering as possible should be prohibited. The point of a *principled* criticism of this approach to terrorism is not about the moral right to act against terrorism but rather about the image of the terrorist on which the financial approach is based. Where the previous UN conventions at least focused upon terrorist acts, and thus kept in mind that terrorism is about violent action, the financial categorization of terrorism has the unfortunate effect of conflating it with economic crime. To hunt terrorists through the warrens of company accounts as if they were organized criminals may seem appealing—it may even promise more tangible results than hunting them through mountain caves. However, it is a sleight of hand. Even though they now share cooperative business practices with organized criminals, terrorists are not primarily motivated by financial profit. No war against them will be won by seizing their assets.

As Dimitri Vlassis has pointed out, this was in fact the conclusion reached during the negotiation process leading to the UN Convention against Transnational Organized Crime.[13] Although terrorism was initially considered a necessary feature, it was eventually dropped, while the pursuit of "financial and other material benefit" was clearly deemed intrinsic to the definition of "transnational organized crime." Not only is it the case that transnational organized criminal activities such as trafficking in drugs, laundering money, and smuggling migrants follow the logic of profitability and economic gain, but these activities (particularly drug-trafficking) also require a never-ending search for ways to increase profits because of the costs of buying into the legitimate apparatus of the state, from paying for lawyers and police protection to paying for political campaigns and parties. Drug-trafficking, one might say, pays its dues, whereas terrorism owes no dues to legitimate states.[14]

Transnational criminal organizations favor the status quo and are notoriously withdrawn from politics except when it comes to financing those political groups that allow them to further their economic agendas. This accounts for the instability of their political loyalties. One day they may be in cahoots with guerrillas, the next day in business with paramilitary organizations. And conversely, guerrilla movements such as the Fuerzas Armadas Revolucionarias de Colombia (FARC), and indeed the Irish Republican Army (IRA) in Colombia, which go beyond dirtying their hands to fully participating in the profiteering of criminal business enterprises from kidnapping to drug-running, make themselves vulnerable to "legitimate" criminalization (that is, crime for profit rather than crime based on ideology). At the same time, the debate set off by the U.S. inclusion of the FARC on the roster of global terrorism is a reminder of the deleterious effects such criminalization may bring to ongoing peace processes.

The notion of the pure, innocent "freedom fighter" may belong to the past, but to swing to the opposite extreme and label all ideologically motivated terrorists as "criminals"—involved not for "the cause" but for the assets— seriously misses the point. In the case of Al Qaeda, that point has been well captured by Lawrence Freedman's notion of asymmetrical violence.[15] The extreme weakness of Al Qaeda in conventional military and strategic terms was more than compensated for by its reliance on terrorist tactics. And, if we pursue the financial approach to its truly logical conclusion, terrorist action is cheap. While estimates for the direct costs of the September 11 attacks vary, the lowest come in at around $100,000. For this outlay, the "profit" to Al Qaeda was U.S. costs of at least a million times higher.

In this respect, terrorism such as Al Qaeda's is more of a throwback to the ideological motivations and asymmetrical actions of a pre-criminal (that is, purely ideological) guerrilla movement like the Sendero Luminoso in the 1970s in Peru. The solution, now as then, is to cut off its support base.[16] But to find that base, one has to look less at its finances and more at the informal economy of popular support.

Terrorism and Charity

The Sendero Luminoso, one of the most terroristic of guerrilla movements, was supported by Peruvian campesinos because it offered to free them from police and army oppression. The movement was squarely in line with the political history of terrorism that starts with the Jacobins in revolutionary France in 1793–1794, whose Reign of Terror—or, as others might say, its permanent revolution—was possible only after the law of the maximum had been passed, guaranteeing affordable bread to their class of supporters in the Parisian sections. While we still tend to think of such political terrorism as a phenomenon that consumes itself as well as others in violence, it is salutary to recall this aspect of the origin of terrorism, namely, that it promises some kind of "gift"—such as security, autonomy, or employment opportunities—to potential supporters. In return for the "gift," the populace is expected to reciprocate. Hence, such "gifts" are not free. But at the same time, the terrorist-populace interaction tries to base itself upon the illusion of freedom. It is not a relationship that can afford to be openly one of exploitation or expropriation. It is indeed when the terrorist-guerrilla movement does try to tax its own base that that base evaporates. One of the fundamental questions in the political terrorist tradition is not Who benefits? but Who gives? The answer is both the terrorists and the populace that supports them. Based upon a myth of mutual assistance, terrorism in fact is organized as if it were a charitable aid institution.

In this light, the suggestion that the diaries of terrorists such as Mohammed Atta are audit trails is grotesquely wrong-headed. The actual diaries of such psychopaths speak of sacrifice—a far cry from the emerging countermythology of the terrorist as a profit-driven criminal. Deeply repellent as it may be to the secular-materialist West, we cannot ignore the symbolic logic at work in a terrorism for which "liberation" is a promised good and sacrifice a positive appeal. Even in terrorist movements without a dimension of religious fanaticism, recruitment could not happen without this discourse in which intangible rewards are promised to those willing to sacrifice themselves in action.

The deep financial logic of terrorism, then, is to be found in the symbolic structures of philanthropy. Consequently, we should be looking at the role of donations in funding terrorism more than to money-laundering in the quest to close terrorism at its source. Tom Naylor in particular has drawn attention to this neglected field of "underground politics and covert foreign aid."[17] From the support of private individuals and diasporas motivated by ideological, religious, and ethnic solidarity to the support of public sponsors and aid agencies, the picture that emerges is potentially far more troubling than the image of terrorists who are criminal profit seekers from beginning to end.

We can catch the distinction at stake here by contrasting the challenges money-laundering and donations pose to bodies such as the FATF. Money-laundering poses difficulties pertaining to transparency. How, in a legal economy that cannot stop the entry of illegal income into its financial stream, do we identify the trail of illegally earned money? Some have argued that the movement of assets of criminals becomes apparent only when it heads out of the legal economy back into reinvestments in criminal activity. In other words, while illegally earned income is in the legal economy, it may in fact pose little or no threat to a financial structure in spite of its potentially corrupting effect on business ethics.

To assess the actual threat posed by the presence of illegally earned money in the legitimate economy, Michael Levi and Tom Naylor prompt us to look at a number of variables: the actual amount of illegally earned income; alterations in the ratio of legal to illegal income; the actual distribution (i.e., the concentration as opposed to dispersion) of illegal income; the profits generated from illegal income; and, most important, the manner in which criminals decide to enter the legal economy. These analysts seek to instill caution rather than alarm because the impact is different.[18]

Donations, on the other hand, are potentially more visible. They are indeed the object of fund-raising campaigns by terrorists. The problem they pose is that as freely given gifts, they are a legal source of finance. In the most spectacular cases, such as the $3 billion given by the end of the 1980s by the U.S. government to the Mujahideen, donations are openly made, thereby appearing to be legitimate.[19] Indeed, legitimacy is the currency of donations, whether they go to "charities" in Northern Ireland, Israel, Somalia, or Afghanistan. Much as is the case with political parties, then, the challenge is to decide when a donor, who by definition considers a free gift to be legitimate, is in fact doing something illegitimate.

Put another way, the challenge of donations is the problem of double standards. How many Saudi Arabian businessmen viewed Osama bin Laden as a legitimate fund-raiser in the 1990s in the same way that U.S. conservatives viewed the contras in the 1980s? Who is to legislate between the 5–7 percent levy by the Palestinian Liberation Organization (PLO) on the salaries of Palestinians employed in the Gulf states and the tax-deductible benefits to those who donate to the Institute for the Jewish Idea, whose mantra is "a Jewish state can never make the Arab equal?"[20] The problem has less to do with money and more with a prior decision about who is and who is not a terrorist. That decision—hide as it may beneath the paraphernalia of a financial regulatory approach to the problem—is political.

What of aid agencies who contribute to development programs in places such as Colombia or Chiapas in Mexico, whose funds may be cooped by insurgent movements? The uncomfortable prospect arises of taking away funds from terrorists with the International Convention for the Suppression of the Financing of Terrorism while giving with the other hand through sponsored aid. Such foreign aid may now indeed be one of the "gifts" which terrorist movements may be able to promise their popular constituencies. Not only are these movements particularly adept at presenting themselves as charitable fronts, it is also in their nature to consider themselves as genuine charities.

Attacks upon terrorism have hardly begun to be pointed in the direction of donations and aid. Yet armed with demands for both transparency and legitimacy, the Western war on terrorism ought to demolish the myth that terrorist movements are charitable (and tax-deductible) organizations. How it might achieve that is largely a matter of education. Terrorist movements are nothing without their donor constituencies, both at home and abroad. The donors are also the vulnerable flank of terrorism. Take away its legitimate power to attract donors and a terrorist movement will quickly degenerate into a rent-seeking outfit that betrays its own symbolic logic of generous philanthropy.

Yet for every case of donor "re-education," there will be myriad other cases of fresh donors to provide resources for terrorism. Nowhere is this more evident today than in the dispersed world of Islamic conflict and terroristic struggle, from Bosnia and Kosovo to Kashmir and Chechnya, where donations will continue to be both legitimate and a legitimate cause for concern.

The Capitals of Terrorism

As the combination of financial backtracking and intelligence work (especially in Pakistan) has finally begun to deliver the Al Qaeda quartermasters and treasurers behind September 11, it has become abundantly clear that—even if the actual operation was cheap to fund—the web of terrorist finance was wide indeed. Jonathan Winer has collated evidence of movements of Al Qaeda funds to banking institutions in Albania, Australia, the Bahamas, Belgium, Canada, the Cayman Islands, Cyprus, France, Germany, Indonesia, Iraq, the UK, and the U.S., among others.[21]

This combination of the cheapness of terrorist action itself—Winer's estimate for the total terrorist expenditure for their September 11 success is $500,000—and the ramifications of the financial web makes for a difficult enforcement equation. The consensus emerging from analysts is that while detection of terrorist finance may indeed be possible, it is a retrospective business that is possible only after the event of the terrorist strike.[22] Financial detective work does not tell us who the terrorists are; the terrorists do.

But retrospective tracking is still worthwhile. It is, for instance, a crucial lead to find that the financial institutions most pivotal in the planning of the September 2001 attacks were those of the United Arab Emirates, as it happens, the Middle East's most sophisticated financial service sector.[23] It is success stories like this which lend both weight to the case for the sweeping regulatory initiatives after September 11 and momentum to their enforcement.

Just as one should not doubt that terrorists do at some point need to lay their hands on cash or commodities for arms, one should not doubt either that the regulatory measures now being advanced by both the UN and U.S. serve a laudable aim. If the assets that could be used for terrorist purposes could really be seized, as the convention envisages, who would quarrel with that? Once again, however, the regulatory impulse with which the FATF is running raises questions even as it provides answers. The specific point at issue is the paradigm within which these measures are being enacted. The post–September 11 anti-terrorist strategy, which focuses on financial regulation and law enforcement, occurs within a paradigm designed to target money-laundering.

There is a pragmatic debate about the successes and failures of the anti-money-laundering regime. On the plus side, the FATF can point to an impressive diffusion of anti-money-laundering laws in many previously suspect jurisdictions in the world. Its impetus is also clear in the European Union's (EU) Second Money Laundering Directive of 2001. On the negative side, as Winer has emphasized, Dubai was in fact already a partner in the anti-money-laundering regime before Al Qaeda made use of its banking services.[24]

Pragmatically, then, we return to the old debate—if it did not work once, does that mean that it will not work at all? If we allow that debate to run its course, however, we may turn to a deeper one: the financial regulatory perspective ultimately treats terrorist finance as a problem to be subsumed within the anti-money-laundering paradigm. But is it?

Two arguments need to be made here. The first is about where the anti-money-laundering paradigm really leads. Far from leading to the terrorists, there is a strong case for saying that it leads instead to the banks. What is really at issue in anti-money-laundering initiatives is the inability of international, suprastate financial institutions to monitor and audit electronic currency transactions by clients who are often anonymous. The burden of the paradigm thus really falls on globalized financial service institutions, and it is not difficult to predict the pitfall of waiting for the unlikely marriage of public regulatory and private self-regulatory regimes. Indeed, the evidence against the paradigm comes from just those cases where attempts are made to work with it—as in the Wolfsberg Principles, a late-1990s initiative from twelve of the world's largest international banks that launched Global Anti-Money-Laundering Guidelines for Private Banking, to which no single institution in China, Russia, Latin America, the Middle East, or Africa has yet signed up.[25] Nonetheless, in the post-Enron era, the jury is clearly more undecided than ever about the issue of corporate accountability. It will be an irony of history, though, if the war on terrorism is the catalyst for the trial.

If regulating the money of terrorists ends by targeting banks, what of the capital of the terrorists themselves? What tools does the anti-money-laundering paradigm have to use against terrorist capital? The second argument is controversial. We need to keep in mind two interrelated but distinct forms of terrorist capital: the "real" money of transferable assets and the symbolic capital of terrorist action itself. The latter is no less valuable because it is symbolic. There is an understandable taboo against hinting at this after September 11, but the destruction of the Twin Towers in New York was a "sublimely" profitable terrorist action. In the strict meaning of that word from the history of aesthetics, the sublime designates an event calculated to inspire terror. However, the amount of destruction and the motivation behind such actions is actually beyond calculation.[26]

To the extent that the anti-money-laundering paradigm proceeds as if costs and benefits are the chips of the game, what it may really tell us is less about terrorism than about the deep repugnance of the liberal Western mind toward the symbolic logic of acts of terror. Better to proceed as if one is confronting a phenomenon that one can regulate—that is, the manipulation of "real" money for criminal purposes. After all, criminals are part of a global economic order; are not even terrorist actors?

The Political Economy of the War on Terrorism

For all the grand synthetic connotations of "the war on terrorism" as a slogan, the "axis of evil" will sooner or later fragment into distinct categories of threat. If declaring a "war" against Al Qaeda was an unnecessary concession to the enemy—granting it precisely the combatant status hitherto denied terrorists—conflating many different battles into one megawar will prove impossible to sustain.[27] The war against terrorism will bifurcate.

Two fronts have already opened—terrorist organizations and state sponsors of terrorism. How linked are they? Certainly a state with stockpiles of biological and chemical weapons may be a bridgehead to terrorist organizations. But what is the nature of the link between the state and criminal and terrorist organizations in the first acknowledged case of an attempt to sell nuclear weapons-grade enriched uranium in Russia?[28] Where does the line between states and such terrorist groups as Egypt's Islamic Jihad or Algeria's fundamentalists begin and end?

Already one can draw two very distinct pictures of the threat, one in which terrorist groups are perceived as random and unpredictable and another in which they are portrayed as somewhat interconnected. In the first, we are confronted by many groups and movements, each with its own grievances and resentments, histories and "struggles"—a sea of underworld organizations so seething that we shall not know where the next terrorist strike is coming from until it hits us. In the second picture, we have an archipelago of interlinked bases of terrorism, some of which are clearly distinguishable landmasses and some of which are smaller islands. The ocean is uncharted; the islands appear to be mappable.

There are some good reasons why the second picture has prevailed. On the one hand, the image of the seething sea is too disconcerting. It is almost a counsel to passivity, to sitting back and waiting. The image of chains of islands, on the other hand, offers the prospect of striking back, of indeed breaking the chain.

The problem with the chain, however, is that there is more and more of it to unlink. Why should anti-terrorist action be taken at one point rather than another? Instead of scoring victories against terrorists, one is left to fight endlessly against "terrorism." If Colombia's FARC is on the chain, for example, why is a war not going on against it along with the wars against the Euskadi ta Askatasuna (ETA, or Basque Fatherland and Liberty), the IRA, Hezbollah, and so on?[29]

Despite a plausible pragmatic answer that "we'll get to them in time," the chain image and its attendant theory of superconspiracies have gathered momentum. It promises a response mechanism as far-reaching as the image of the enemy it evokes. "War" is only a segment of this response mechanism. Indeed, war is as much a metaphor as an actual threat against terrorism, in that any action that can be taken against terrorism can be claimed as part of the war effort. No global action against terrorism has been proposed other than that of suppressing terrorist finances; this action is war too.

The key advantage of targeting financial resources is that it promises to be as global as "terrorism." It is a striking coincidence that the aftermath of September 11 also seems to have dealt a temporary blow to the anti-globalization movement. On the one hand, terrorist operations are deemed to be nothing without terrorist financial organizations; on the other hand, state sponsors can be cast as terrorist banks as well as donors and can be "regulated" as such— financial sanctions were, after all, first devised for "pariah" states.

The Convention on the Suppression of Terrorist Finance, then, is a normative declaration of war, as befits the UN's role as an international norm-setter. But such declarations do not come in isolation. Putting to one side the overwhelming impact and aftermath of September 2001, one can trace a very precise genealogy for the "follow the money" paradigm. From the suppression of terrorist finance, one can trace a line to the crusade against money-laundering and from there to the crusade against drug-trafficking. Under the cover of the war on terrorism, that is, we are still talking about the repercussions of the war on drugs.

This is apparent at many levels, from the rhetorical to the institutional. From a book on *Terrorism, Drugs and Crime in Europe* comes the following:

"The problem is so urgent that it should be regarded as a world war."[30] Not, the author hastens to add, "a conventional war," but a war nonetheless in which civilization is at stake. The origin of an institution such as the FATF, created in 1989 in recognition of the threat posed by drug-trafficking revenues and drug-money-laundering, is also curious.[31] In 1998, the Basel Declaration was signed by over eighty countries, which committed themselves to identifying sources of drug money and cooperating with international judicial inquiries into illegal drug-related activities. One could invoke many international conventions against illicit and psychotropic drugs, illicit payments, and transnational organized crime to make the point that the war on terrorism is several wars rolled into one.

This is where pragmatic criticisms really cast doubt on the effectiveness of the financial regulatory approach. Overall drug revenues have continued to rise even as international measures have been taken against them. It is not so much that the anti-money-laundering regime is either wrong in principle or impossible in practice—although when transfers of electronic funds run into trillions of dollars, the task is close to the impossible—as much as that "following the money" is not the way to wage war on drugs.[32] Politics are.

But politics take us back to multiple double standards. Where financial regulatory approaches promise across-the-board impartiality (all money-launderers are equally at risk of detection), political attempts to deal with both drug-traffickers and terrorists will necessarily fall short of a uniform standard. The expediency of political decision makers will dictate whether the opium trade in Afghanistan is serving to consolidate the local bases of the new regime by providing a livelihood for large numbers of people, whether the heroin trade in Pakistan could be disrupted without risking a loss of leverage over the Pakistani intelligence service, or whether some Latin American producer and transit countries should be decertified and others not.

Expediency is understandable in practice but hard to justify. It requires higher levels of justification than most morally questionable acts, and none has come more readily to hand than the equation of drug-trafficking with certain insurgency movements such as the FARC. If some instances of criminality are worse than others and if certain guerrilla and terrorist movements are criminalized, then some sense of a standard will be restored, at least in theory.

In theory, the war on terrorism will be conducted along the lines of the war on drug-trafficking. Just as the latter mutated into a war against insurgents engaged in criminal activity, so the war against terrorism will delegitimize the terrorists by redefining them as economic criminals. At some point, if this logic is to hold, the war on terrorism should visit supervillains such as the terrorist-guerrilla-criminal FARC.

But there is one last hurdle. If the FARC has used drug money for insurgency and terror, isn't it the best policy to cut off the money rather than to merely track it? In theory, that is what the prohibition of drugs aims to do. In practice, prohibition is the single biggest factor driving up the total value of drugs being traded; it has created ever-widening price differentials between production costs and street values.[33] If drug money, which is the most criminal of all sources of terrorist finance, is the target, then the political economy of the war on terrorism ought to address the fact that drug traffickers and drug-related insurgent groups and terrorists benefit when prohibition is applied. If we could really take away the drug money—rather than chase its trail—then we might begin to get an idea of whether insurgent and terrorist groups are in it because of the money or because of their stated ideological goals.[34]

Concluding Remarks

The war on terrorism that the Bush administration declared in late 2001 has thus targeted the proceeds of terrorists. While the logic of drying up the means of terrorist networks may appear at first sight to be impeccable, it does not consider the ends of terrorism.

The new anti-money-laundering offensive makes sense as a strategy of war against a specific enemy: the criminal as rational actor, motivated by cost-benefit calculations and profit maximization. It also makes sense if the industrialized countries have been flooded with narcotics and drug-related money and if this has posed a major threat to their security. When one puts the two assumptions together, the subsequent strategy certainly looks rational: it seeks to strike at the heart of the operation and remove the profits as a powerful deterrent to crime; draining the capital thereby reduces the capacity for future crimes. This leads to the winner's prize: confidence that such an approach helps safeguard the legitimate economy.[35] More than merely rational, this is also a "good news" policy. That it did not work well in the war on drugs was secondary. Notwithstanding the apparent lack of impact of the follow-the-money strategy on the operation of illegal markets, the proceeds-of-crime approach became one of the two main pillars of the Bush administration's response to September 11.

The rationality of the policy was never stronger than one of internal consistency, of fidelity to flawed assumptions. The fact was that the policy did not work where it should have, in the profitable and illicit drug marketplace, was irrelevant. The magnetic pull of the policy was such that Al Qaeda would be recast as a supremely powerful hierarchical organization controlled by a small group of masterminds with control over vast sums of money generated by crime. In the process, other perspectives got squeezed out of the frame, including explanations such as the structural legacies left by the end of the Cold War in Afghanistan. These included the boom in the opium economy, the boom in the arms trade, and the boom in Islamic charities (which was first encouraged by the U.S. to help finance the war effort against the Soviet occupation).

There is little doubt that Osama bin Laden and the Al Qaeda network found in this "well-oiled" (but actually chaotic) economic structure a useful niche from which to eviscerate what little remained of the state and use the remaining shell as cover for a dreadful terrorist campaign.[36] The dreadfulness of terrorism is not in dispute. But neither should be its primitiveness. Rather than sit at the center of a global web of electronic money flows, bin Laden was ready to sit it out in a cave. Rather than being moved by profit, those of his lieutenants who were in on the plan were moved by a hatred so pathologically rooted as to leave most Western analysts grasping for explanations. Looked at dispassionately, the anachronistic and pathological members of Al Qaeda were simply not of the stature to be enemies of the lone superpower, let alone winners. The psychological function of the anti-money-laundering policy, which has been diffused through the media, is that it gives the U.S. and the Western mind a more readily understood enemy.

Wishful thinking, however, is a dangerous course in security matters. On the one hand, voluntary economic contributions to the "cause" are unlikely to be dried up by a proceeds-of-crime approach. Even if a moratorium on charity for terrorism could be imposed, the actual amounts of money required for terrorist acts are—to repeat one of the surprising and crucial features of September 11—fractional. On the other hand, the collateral damage done by the progressive escalation of the follow-the-money information requirements of global financial systems could turn out to be significant.

Critics of the anti-money-laundering approach often appear to be either out of the loop or counselors of inaction or both. To some extent, the coordination of any anti-terrorism policy is such a cumbersome and crisis-led business that it is unrealistic to expect a switch to a new approach rather than a reliance on established paradigms. With all of its problems and failures, the anti-money-laundering paradigm is now a powerful precedent in its own right, which gives it enough force to work some of the time. And where this policy works some of the time in removing capital from the hands of violent organizations, thus weakening their capacity to commit future terrorist acts, this will be good "local news." However, anti-money-laundering techniques should be just one component of police and intelligence work. Gathering information is not spectacular work, but in the long run it is essential, while policing includes frustrating plots, deactivating bombs, and arresting and trying by due process those responsible for terrorist acts. These measures may well be cast as a widening of the war on terrorism. Even if they entail dilemmas from the budgetary to the political, they are to be preferred to single-focus initiatives which, as with the analogous case of military-punitive responses, tend to carry with them unintended and perverse consequences.

Unworthy though they are, groups such as Al Qaeda are ideological enemies. There is a cost in not accepting this, a particularly poignant one, for the ideological war is surely winnable by the West. Not territory, but hearts and minds are the new stakes of war in the post–Cold War, globalized world. This is all the more the case when many of the decisive actors live beyond U.S. borders. In the war on global terror, the most important dimensions of response may not be primarily military or financial. Instead, the war on global terror may well turn on the capacity of industrialized countries to live up to ideals of equal justice under the rule of law that have long been a source of inspiration for others elsewhere in the world.[37] The key is legitimacy—ambiguous, unequal, now more contested than ever after the war in Iraq but also a defendable asset.

Notes

1. See Adam Roberts, "Terrorism and International Order," in Lawrence Freedman, Christopher Hill, Adam Roberts, R. J. Vincent, Paul Wilkinson, and Philip Windsor, *Terrorism and International Order* (London: Routledge and Kegan Paul/Royal Institute of International Affairs, 1986), 9–10; and International Institute for Strategic Studies, "Defining Terrorism Focusing on the Targets," *Strategic Comments* 7, no. 9 (November 2001).

2. Roberts, "Terrorism and International Order," 12–13.

3. The experience of the 1977 European Convention for the Suppression of Terrorism is a case in point. By adhering to this convention, signatories agreed that for extradition purposes certain offenses such as kidnapping, hijacking, hostage-taking, and bombing would not be regarded as political. Against this, though, the convention was considerably weakened by additional articles protecting the accused from prejudicial prosecution and granting states power to judge certain offenses political after all. See Richard Clutterbuck, *Terrorism, Drugs and Crime in Europe After 1992* (London: Routledge, 1990), 123. See also Philip Windsor, "The Middle East and Terrorism," in Freedman et al., *Terrorism and International Order,* 27–28, for the argument that the deeply embedded terrorist tradition in the Middle East, where terrorism "acquired an international dimension, was indeed based in international politics, from the beginning."

4. The September attacks created the conditions for the implementation of this convention. After September 11, the pressures exerted by both Security Council resolution 1373 and the Counter-Terrorism Committee set up by that resolution helped increase the number of ratifications. In June 2003, the treaty was signed by 132 states, of which 84 had become party to its terms.

5. "Special Recommendations on Terrorist Financing," from the summary of the Financial Action Task Force (FATF) Extraordinary Plenary Meeting on the Financing of Terrorism, held in Washington, D.C. on October 29–30, 2001. Available online at http://www1.oecd.org/fatf/SrecsTF_en.htm.

6. See David E. Apter, "Political Violence in Analytical Perspective," in David Apter, ed., *The Legitimization of Violence* (New York: New York University Press, 1997), 18; Mats Berdal and David M. Malone, eds., *Greed and Grievance: Economic Agendas in Civil Wars* (Boulder: Lynne Rienner, 2000).

7. Based on IMF figures, Guilhem Fabre has calculated the value of global illicit funds as between $800 million and $2 trillion, or 2–5 percent of the world GDP. The global drug trade, estimated at around $400–500 billion, has been considered a major component of this illicit money flow. However, the figures quantifying global drug money have been challenged by experts that include Peter Reuter and Tom Naylor. Reuter's sophisticated attempt to construct global expenditure on drugs as the sum of national estimates soon ran into difficulties. Not only are most national expenditure data unreliable, but even in the largest and most monitored market, the U.S., estimates oscillate widely between $40 and $100 billion. In light of this, Reuter asserts that it is difficult to justify a global total of more than $150 billion. See Guilhem Fabre, "Prospering in Crime: Money Laundering and Financial Crisis," paper presented at the International Conference on Drug Control Policies, México D.F., Secretaría de Relaciones Exteriores, October 28–29, 2002; Peter Reuter, ed., *Transnational Organized Crime: Summary of a Workshop* (Washington, D.C.: National Press Academy, 1999), 25; Michael Levi, "Money Laundering and its Regulation," *Annals of the American Academy of Political and Social Science* (special issue on the International Aspects of Drug Policy), no. 582 (2002): 184. For a critical interpretation of the figures provided by the UN International Drug Control Programme, see T. R. Naylor, *Wages of Crime: Black Markets, Illegal Finance and the Underworld Economy* (Ithaca, N.Y.: Cornell University Press, 2002), 33.

8. In autumn 2001, the Financial Action Task Force issued eight special recommendations to be considered in conjunction with its previous forty recommendations on money-laundering. The new recommendations include reporting suspicious transactions related to terrorism; strengthening international cooperation and assistance with investigations relating to the financing of terrorism; licensing and registering alternate remittance systems; enhancing scrutiny and monitoring in all financial institutions, including money remitters and wire transfers; and properly regulating entities (that is, charities) that can be abused for the financing of terrorism. See FATF, "Special Recommendations on Terrorist Financing." Available online at http://www1.oecd.org/fatf/SrecsTF_en.htm.

9. See Edward Alden, "Finance Sector Hits at Moves to Curb Terror Funds," *Financial Times,* July 2, 2002.

10. Significant amounts of assets have been moved through unregulated bureaux de change. Some observers estimate that 65 percent of the 4 billion pounds leaving Britain through bureaux de change originates in "illegal" sources, and research found that one

outlet laundered 70 million pounds between 1994 and 1996. See Claire Hu, "Bureaux de Change Could Be the Conduit for Crime," *The Guardian,* October 1, 2001; and "Terrorist Finance: Follow the Money," *The Economist,* May 30, 2002.

11. Quoted by Mark Huband, "Funding of Terror Network 'Now Less Efficient,'" *Financial Times,* September 10, 2002.

12. Al Qaeda appears to have derived important lessons from Washington's decision to freeze $254 million of Taliban funds back in 1998. These actions were taken in response to the bombings of the U.S. embassies in Africa. Indeed, in anticipation of similar measures in the aftermath of the planned attacks, Al Qaeda appears to have sought to protect its money by investing in gemstones, diamonds in particular (a commodity that is easily concealed and easily smuggled). Al Qaeda may have struck cash-for-diamond deals worth over $20 million in the months prior to September 11. Information leaked by European governments, the Belgian government in particular, revealed that Aziz Nassour employed couriers to exchange $300,000 for diamonds every week between December 2000 and September 2001. This suggests that Al Qaeda was able to continue its operations despite the international agreement to freeze bank accounts and assets with suspected links to the terrorist group. Douglas Farah, "Al Qaeda Cash Tied to Diamond Trade," *The Washington Post,* November 2, 2001; Amelia Hill, "Bin Laden's $20m African 'Blood Diamond Deals,'" *The Observer,* October 20, 2002; and Hu, "Terrorist Finance: Follow the Money."

13. See Dimitri Vlassis, "The UN Convention against Transnational Organized Crime," in Mats R. Berdal and Mónica Serrano, eds., *Transnational Organized Crime and International Security: Business As Usual?* (Boulder: Lynne Rienner Publishers, 2002), 86–88.

14. The distinction between money-laundering and the financing of terrorism has also been underlined in the context of sessions held by the Counter-Terrorism Committee. In a briefing for member states, Walter Gehr highlighted the differences between these two phenomena, which may indeed be interrelated but whose crimes are not identical. Money-laundering is the movement and the processing of the proceeds of criminal acts to disguise their illegal origin and nature. The difference between money-laundering and the financing of terrorism is that monies that fund terrorist activities are not necessarily illegal. As allegations about the fortune of Osama bin Laden suggest, "[A]ssets and profits acquired by legitimate means and even declared to tax authorities can be used to finance terrorist acts too." Al Qaeda and Osama bin Laden's financial operations have revealed the presence of both legal and illegal means. According to the State Department, bin Laden, one of the fifty-two children of Saudi Arabia's most successful building magnate, may have inherited $300 million. Other sources claim that these assets were frozen in the mid-1990s when bin Laden's Saudi citizenship was revoked. They highlight his capacity to orchestrate financial operations to evade these and other controls by setting up companies that are used as business fronts to both move money and generate profits to fund subsequent activities. According to intelligence sources, companies set up in Spain first served to fund the development of a Spanish cell and then through subsequent profits (worth around $2 million) to again

divert funds concealed as donations (of about $605,000). Al Qaeda has thus benefited from donations from wealthy families in the Middle East and charitable organizations and may also have benefited by the taxes imposed by the Taliban on the Afghan opium trade. See Walter Gehr, "Recurrent Issues: Briefing to Member States, 4 April 2002"; available online at http://www.un.org/docs/sc/committees/1373/rc.htm. See also *New York Times*, September 21, 2002; "The Spider in the Web," *The Economist*, September 20, 2001; available online at http://www.economist.com/ displaystory.cfm?story_id=788472.

15. See Lawrence Freedman, "The Third World War?" *Survival* 43, no. 4 (Winter 2001): 61–88. For the argument on "asymmetric violence," see 64–67.

16. Hassan Salameh, a captured Hamas bomber, revealed that the average budget for suicide bombings is about $1,500. "Follow the Money," *The Economist*, June 1, 2002 (U.S. edition).

17. Naylor, *Wages of Crime*, 49.

18. Michael Levi and Tom Naylor, "Organised Crime, the Organisation of Crime, and the Organisation of Business," London, Department of Trade and Industry, Department of Science and Technology Foresight Directorate Crime Prevention Panel, 2000, 7–8. Available online at http://www.cf.ac.uk/socsi/whoswho/levi-orgcrime.pdf.

19. Naylor, *Wages of Crime*, 52.

20. Ibid., 78, 83, and 122.

21. For this and the following, see Jonathan M. Winer, "Combating Global Conflict By Promoting Financial Transparency: The Utility of a Global White List," paper prepared for the Program on Economic Agendas and Civil Wars, Bellagio, Italy, May 20–24, 2002.

22. Investigators and FBI reports have shown that the hijackers had access to a total of $500,000 to $600,000. Investigations based on the thirty-five bank accounts opened by the hijackers in the U.S. provided some of the most concrete evidence, which helped uncover the extent of closely coordinated action among four groups of hijackers. James Rise, "Sept. 11 Hijackers Easily Misled U.S. Banks," *International Herald Tribune*, July 11, 2002.

23. Saudi Arabia, like many other countries, including the U.S., presents an odd mixture of financial services. At one end of the spectrum is a highly developed and (in principle) regulated financial system; at the other, the trust-based networks that move large flows of money and have remained beyond the confines of regulation. The remittance system has also gained salience in the Americas, where it links legal and illegal workers in the U.S. with their communities throughout Latin America.

24. Moreover, by the end of August 2001, a UN report offered little hope about the prospects of this financial "war." By the end of November 2002, only $121 million had been confiscated and Al Qaeda had shown its ability to divert resources to nontraditional financial channels, including small valuable commodities and informal banking networks. "La ONU afirma que ha fracaso el bloqueo de las cuentas de Al Qaeda," *El País*, August 30, 2002; and "Sólo se han intervenido 120 millones a grupos terroristas," *El País*, November 27, 2002.

25. Winer, "Combating Global Conflict."

26. This view of terrorism closely resembles the "terrorism for terrorism's sake" depicted by Philip Windsor. He sees this manifestation of extreme violence as an "autonomous activity" which is removed from a particular context or reality and inspired by a "desire for revenge" and a "psychotic determination to make a mark in the world" that is triggered in turn by a pattern of "outrage and reprisal." The carrier of such aggression does not (and cannot) aspire to become a political actor or a political interlocutor. In consequence, argues Ludolfio Paramio, such "fundamentalist" terrorism should be confronted in itself rather than as the symptom of a deeper problem. See Windsor, "The Middle East and Terrorism," in Freedman et al., *Terrorism and International Order*, 30–31; R. J. Vincent, "Concluding Observations," in Freedman et al., *Terrorism and International Order*, 103; and Ludolfio Paramio, "Falsos Consuelos," *El País*, October 6, 2001.

27. For a more nuanced approach to the language of war and to the utility of military means, see Michael Howard, "'9-11' and After: A British View," *Naval War College Review* (Autumn 2002): 10–21; and Joseph D. McNamara, "The Defensive Front Line," *Regulation Magazine* 24, no. 4 (Winter 2001): 61–63.

28. See "Russia Says It Foiled Illegal Sale of Weapons-Grade Uranium," *New York Times*, December 7, 2001. See also Alex P. Schmid, "The Links between Transnational Organized Crime and Terrorist Crimes," *Transnational Organized Crime* 2, no. 4 (Winter 1996): 40–82.

29. Since September 11, lists of terrorist organizations have been the object of increasing attention within the U.S., the UN, the EU, and other regional organizations, including the OAS. Although some convergence has been evident, as in the past, differences are likely to emerge. For the EU's debate on the exclusion of Hezbollah from the list of terrorist organizations, see "La prisa del gobierno propició la difusión de una lista errónea de grupos terroristas," *El País*, December 29, 2001.

30. Clutterbuck, *Terrorism, Drugs and Crime in Europe After 1992*, 192.

31. Winer, "Combating Global Conflict."

32. See Stephen E. Flynn in "Report of the Workshop on Money Laundering of the Resource Committee on Transnational Crime of the International Scientific and Professional Advisory Council (ISPAC)," Courmayeur, Italy, March 23–24, 1992. In 1991, for example, the Clearing House Interbank Payment System handled some 37 billion transactions worth $222 trillion.

33. See Mónica Serrano and M. C. Toro, "From Drug-Trafficking to Transnational Organized Crime in Latin America," in Berdal and Serrano, eds., *Transnational Organized Crime and International Security*, 160.

34. Take the example of the sophisticated financial techniques employed by the FARC (Fuerzas Armadas Revolucionarias de Colombia) to "clone" government bank accounts to launder proceeds from drug-trafficking and kidnapping. At least, that is what the government said. According to another source, Leon Valencia, the insurgent movements in Colombia are inherently conservative in the management of financial resources and thus are unlikely to approach modern financial circuits. In addition to

being a widely esteemed analyst, Valencia also has the advantage of having been a guerrilla himself. "Las FARC blanquean dinero a través del gobierno," *El País,* August 30, 2002.

    35. See Naylor, *Wages of Crime,* 250–251.

    36. Roberts, "Terrorism and International Order," 20–21; and Vincent, "Concluding Observations," 104.

    37. Peter A. Hall, "This Is More Like 1914 Than 1941," *The Guardian,* September 28, 2001.

10

The Root Causes of Terrorism and Conflict Prevention

Rama Mani

Established in the bloody aftermath of the Second World War, the United Nations naturally included conflict prevention as a primary goal. The desire to prevent future generations from the scourge of war and to deliver to all peoples freedom from fear and want motivated the drafters of the Charter. Conflict prevention gained importance in the UN's fifth decade, as expressed in UN Secretary-General Kofi Annan's acceptance speech for the Nobel Peace Prize in 2001.[1] This followed the momentum stimulated in the 1990s by *An Agenda for Peace* and the independent work of commissions such as the Carnegie Commission on Preventing Deadly Conflict and the Commission on Global Governance.[2]

Since the events of September 2001, the desire to address the "root causes" of both terrorism and conflict has been reiterated vehemently throughout the UN system, implying some sort of organic link between the two. But is there a link? This chapter concludes that the current conflation in the UN of addressing the root causes of conflict and addressing the roots of terrorism is ineffective and potentially deleterious. First, however, the chapter addresses the debates around the nature and root causes of terrorism that have been stimulated within and outside the UN before and after September 11. Next, the chapter examines whether the world organization actually has addressed the root causes of terrorism. It raises the fundamental question of whether the UN's recent efforts at structural conflict prevention have contributed or could contribute to the attempt to address and eliminate such sources. In closing, the chapter considers some of the measures that might make a difference to the incidence and impact of both terrorism and violent conflict, though they might be unpalatable to the protagonists of the war on terror.

It should be noted at the outset that there is yet scant academic literature addressing the questions raised in this chapter. Bruce Jentleson observes, "Overall, international relations and political science as academic disciplines have limited answers to offer to the questions posed by September 11." His extensive survey of journals, books, Ph.D. dissertations, and conference papers on the two subject matters from 1998 to 2001 reveals the dearth of scholarly attention to terrorism. He writes, "The profession-based incentive structure that defines the culture of the discipline explains a lot. At every level it tilts against policy relevance."[3] Despite the proliferation of books and articles on terrorism since September 11, few publications have focused on its root causes or on the nexus between terrorism and conflict. This chapter draws substantially, therefore, on newspaper and Internet sources—where most academic and professional analysis and commentary has appeared—as well as on UN sources. This chapter presents its own analysis, typology, and terminology to contribute to filling this lacuna and stimulating debate, and it underlines the urgent need for more rigorous academic study in this neglected area.

Three Types of Terrorism

Following the tragic attacks of September 11, 2001, U.S. President George W. Bush launched a "war on terror" that was supported by a broad coalition of states drawn from all continents and endorsed by the UN. This appellation implied that such a war would address all fronts of terror.

September 11, however, focused the minds of world leaders on one particular form and expression of terrorism. This had two effects. First, it effaced from political and popular memory other forms of terrorism experienced in recent decades. Second, it made the definition of terrorism elusive, fluid, and arbitrary.

The UN's attention to terrorism and its root causes dates back three decades and is centered on the General Assembly, which has categorized several distinct kinds of terrorism according to agents, objectives, methods, or other factors. To illustrate this diversity, I identify here three types classified by agent or actor: non-state terrorism, state terrorism, and what I call "amphibolous" state–cum–non-state terrorism, each of which has subcategories according to objective or method.[4]

Non-State Terrorism

Although there were several acts preceding it, the event that put terrorism irrevocably on the UN's agenda was the taking of Israeli athletes as hostages by a Palestinian group at the 1972 Olympic Games at Munich. Secretary-General Kurt Waldheim called upon the General Assembly to undertake "[m]easures to prevent terrorism and other forms of violence which endanger or take innocent lives or jeopardize fundamental freedoms."[5] It is significant that an act of terrorism by a non-state actor was the first to merit a response to terrorism by the UN.

Non-state terrorism consists of two disparate types, however. The first is "self-determination terrorism," which encompasses a variety of claims for independence, autonomy, or cultural expression. This type of terrorism is associated primarily with independence movements against colonial rule and gained intensity and legitimacy with the establishment of the United Nations and its defense of the principle of self-determination. In the context of the repressive power of colonial armies and administrations, several independence movements, or factions within them, resorted to either guerrilla warfare or occasional acts of terrorism. This category also includes movements fighting for some measure of autonomy against a state authority that is perceived to be inimical to the group's well-being, identity, or survival and that undertake occasional or systematic acts of terrorism within their political struggle—for example, the Irish Republican Army (IRA), the Palestine Liberation Organization (PLO), and Liberation Tigers of Tamil Eelam (LTTE). They are manifestations of the General Assembly's observation that "colonialism, racism and situations involving mass and flagrant violations of human rights and fundamental freedoms and those involving alien occupation" may give rise to terrorism.[6]

Three features typically characterize the adoption of terrorism by self-determination movements: an opponent state possessing superior means and deploying overwhelming force against the movement and wider population; the state's lack of response to the movement's diplomatic, political, and conventional military means; and an urgent desire for international intervention to remedy a stalemated or worsening situation.[7] Terrorist tactics may serve to pressure governments to change course (e.g., the Moscow theater hostage-taking by Chechen rebels in late 2002) or to impel international action (e.g., the 1972 Olympics incident).

Often, terrorist acts are part of a wide spectrum of political, diplomatic, conventional military, and other strategies of a movement that may not be terrorist per se. An example is the African National Congress (ANC), which assumed governmental functions after democratic elections in South Africa 1994. Some, however, are primarily associated with terrorist operations, such as the Basque separatists Euskadi ta Askatasuna (ETA, or Basque Fatherland and Liberty) in Spain.

The second type is "hate terrorism." This includes ethnocentric, racist, fascist, or similar groups undertaking arson, assassination, lynching, and other violent acts against innocent members of a scapegoat group that is racially or culturally defined—for example, white extremist groups such as Afrikaner Weerstandsbeweging (AWB) in South Africa, neo-Nazi groups in Europe, and militant Hindu fundamentalist groups in India.

On a larger scale, armed rebel movements that systematically employ barbaric terror tactics en masse against civilians also qualify as hate terrorism—for example, the Union for the Total Independence of Angola (UNITA), the Revolutionary United Front (RUF) in Sierra Leone, and the Lord's Resistance Army (LRA) in northern Uganda. Hate terrorism is distinct from self-determination terrorism because it offers a less coherent political strategy and sometimes none at all. It is driven by the desire to humiliate, and in some cases destroy, a target group. Its victims, albeit more numerous than the victims of self-determination terrorism, are marginalized; hence such acts are rarely acknowledged as terrorism.[8]

State Terrorism

From 1972 onward, the General Assembly repeatedly condemned "the continuation of repressive and terrorist acts by colonial, racist and alien regimes in denying peoples their legitimate right to self-determination and independence and other human rights and fundamental freedoms."[9] It also declared the "[i]nadmissibility of the policy of state terrorism and any actions by states aimed at undermining the socio-political system in other sovereign States."[10]

Two types of state terrorism must be distinguished: "national" and "extranational." National state terrorism takes two forms. What we call "proactive terrorism" refers to state action that resorts to terrorist acts to oppress particular parts of the population for political, ideological, religious, cultural, racial, or other reasons or to act preemptively against suspected threats to authority—for example, Turkish and Iraqi treatment of Kurd minorities and Indonesian treatment of Acehnese and East Timorese. What we might call "reactive terrorism" refers to a state that responds to attacks by rebel movements or terrorist groups and acts to defend its citizens as well as its own authority from attack. When this represents a direct, proportionate, and legitimate response to non-state terrorism and respects state responsibility and international legal obligations, it could qualify as anti-terrorism (e.g., Spanish government action against the ETA). However, when states use disproportionate force to respond and violate state responsibility and legal obligations, it qualifies as terrorism (e.g., Guatemala, apartheid South Africa, and Israel).

Extranational state-sponsored terrorism is directed at noncitizens in foreign lands through support to either a non-state or state terrorist. The first includes cases where one state supports a non-state movement's terrorist actions partly with the aim of destabilizing or overthrowing the target government (e.g., South Africa's support of UNITA against the Movimento Popular para a Libertação de Angola [MPLA] government and the U.S. government's support of the contras against the Sandinista government in Nicaragua). In the second, one state provides political, military, or financial assistance to an allied state to enable it to conduct its proactive or reactive terrorism, as witnessed in the U.S. and former Soviet Union's competitive actions in South and Central America and Central Asia and Eastern Europe, respectively.

Amphibolous or State–cum–Non-State Terrorism

With the end of the Cold War, the UN's attention was called to "international terrorism" by an expansion of terrorist threats and attacks to Western countries. In tandem, the General Assembly ceded its place to the Security Council in addressing terrorism. A significant point of departure was the assembly's 1994 resolution 60, "Declaration on Measures to Eliminate International Terrorism." Member states declared that "[c]riminal acts intended or calculated to provoke a state of terror in the general public, a group of persons or particular persons for political purposes are in any circumstances unjustifiable, whatever the considerations of a political, philosophical, ideological, racial, ethnic, religious or any other nature that may be invoked to justify them." This ended the defense of non-state terrorism.

However, it was the attacks of September 2001 that launched the war on terror and seemed to redefine terrorism. The new amorphous terrorism typified by Al Qaeda is not typically non-state but rather a collusion between non-state and state actors with strong business, financial, and criminal connections. Based around the globe in countries ranging from highly industrialized to least developed, these groups use measures ranging from criminal activities to conventional and unconventional warfare or threats of such warfare with the nonspecific intention of weakening enemy institutions or governments by intimidating their citizens or disrupting their economies and societies. Exact motives are more often alluded to than specified, objectives may be diffuse as often as they are precise, and methods are versatile and varied. Consequently, targets and victims may be either the result of careful choice or chosen randomly with little symbolic or actual linkage to the "cause."

At the same time, tacit and covert state support to these movements can be significant, particularly regarding Islamic groups. At the national level, some post-independence governments encouraged Islamic movements to provide social services and support nets, as in Algeria and Egypt, little suspecting the eventual proportions and political aspirations of such movements. At the international level, at the height of the Cold War and particularly during the Soviet occupation of Afghanistan, the U.S. government trained and massively supported Islamic militant movements, little imagining that they would turn against their sponsors.

Consequently, they can be described as "amphibolous" terrorists, as they are an ambiguous and unclear mixture of various actors and methods, combining state and non-state terrorism with varying local, national, international, and transnational targets. As networks rather than organizations, they can encompass a seemingly infinite range of different composite parts. Al Qaeda is perhaps the only true prototype of this particular category.[11]

Which "Terrorism," Whose "Terrorism"?

The objective of examining these three types of terrorism is not to provide a comprehensive overview or prescribe a typology but to illustrate the varieties of terrorism that confronted the UN before attention narrowed to Al Qaeda–style terrorism in September 2001, when the amphibolous category became the obsession of anti-terrorist groups. Clearly the definition of terrorism itself is fluid and subject to the vagaries of the definers. One Asian commentator notes, "[T]he global community so far has not been able to reach a consensus on what constitutes terrorism. The fact that it is left undefined internationally implies that states have a wide margin of discretion to define it under national law."[12]

The nature of amphibolous terrorism has allowed governments around the world to categorize an endless and ever-changing gamut of activities as suspect, ranging from commonplace criminal activities such as money-laundering to traditional militaristic acts such as producing biological, chemical, or nuclear weapons. As one writer notes, "[T]he surreal combination of specificity and vagueness characterizing the terrorist alert has grown commonplace during this jittery and bewildering year."[13]

The switch of focus from the prototypical amphibolous terrorist, Osama bin Laden, to the prototypical state terrorist, Saddam Hussein, forced the protagonists of the war on terror to stretch their definition of terrorism yet again, this time somewhat awkwardly. The terrorist threat must now include states suspected of possessing or amassing weapons of mass destruction (WMD) as long as they are not currently allied with a major coalition member—thus excluding Israel, Pakistan, and even India but not entirely exculpating North Korea. This confusion about definitions that plagues the war on terror has inevitable repercussions for exploring terrorism's root causes.

The "Root Causes" Debate

The debate about root causes creates two misperceptions that grow from the preceding discussion. The first is the presumed existence of one definitive set of fundamental causes for terrorism, an implausible assumption given terrorism's myriad forms and various motivations. The second is that terrorism is a condition or malaise, which, once diagnosed, can be effectively treated and cured. Instead, "terrorism" is an umbrella term encompassing a range of situations in which different agents choose a particular set of means, targeting innocent civilians, in a sporadic or sustained way within their pursuit of a specific or nonspecific political objective. Terrorist acts are tactics rather than strategies; they are based more often on expediency than on any fundamental root causes. "Terrorism is not a philosophy or a movement. It is a method."[14] To state the obvious, the search for root causes is futile if the definition of terrorism itself is constantly shifting.

Nevertheless, and understandably, the dramatic nature of the September 11 attacks led to a frenzied search for its "root causes," the term used here, albeit with caution.[15] As Thomas Homer-Dixon argued, analyzing root causes was not a pretext to justify terrorism but rather was done to prevent its recurrence.[16] This discussion focuses primarily on the proposed root causes of the September 2001 attacks and the three arguments that have dominated the debate: poverty and despair, failed states, and the clash of civilizations, or Islamic extremism.

Poverty and Despair

This argument holds that poverty, ignorance, and despair breed terrorism and caused the September 2001 attacks. A variation sees not poverty per se but inequality deepened by economic globalization as the explanation. A poll conducted by International Herald Tribune and Pew Charitable Trusts in 2001 suggested that "much of the world views the attacks as a symptom of increasingly bitter polarization between the haves and have-nots."[17]

This argument is the most popular and frequently cited causal theory within the United Nations. In the 2001 General Assembly, delegates from countries as diverse as Costa Rica, Croatia, and the Netherlands concurred in drawing linkages between terrorism, poverty, inequality, and exclusion.[18] Most organizations of the UN system agree. For instance, UN Environment Programme (UNEP) Executive-Director Klaus Toepfer observed, "When people are denied access to clean water, soil and air to meet their basic human needs, we see the rise of poverty, ill-health and a sense of hopelessness. Desperate people can resort to desperate solutions."[19] World Bank President James Wolfensohn emphasized that September 11 was a wake-up call to the West about how urgently the poverty in the South and inequality between the two unequal halves of the world needed to be addressed.[20]

Political analysts, especially in the United States, counter vehemently that Osama bin Laden is a multimillionaire and that the perpetrators were "without exception scions of privilege" of the Arab world who were highly educated people "familiar with the ways of the West."[21] The obvious weakness of this critique is that it "assumes that people act only in response to their direct, personal experiences, which is absurd."[22]

Poverty and despair, moreover, offer an incomplete explanation. The proponents of this causal theory themselves admit that there is no "direct causal connection between deprivation and terrorism" but simply a heightened probability.[23] The economic globalization argument contains elements meriting further reflection, as noted below.

Failed States

The second argument holds that terrorism is a governance problem. In this theory, failed states or weak or simply "bad" (i.e., undemocratic) states violate human rights and create conditions for terrorism.[24] "Today's terrorist . . . seeks out a weak state that cannot impede a group's freedom of action but that has a veneer of state sovereignty that prevents other, stronger states from taking effective counter-measures."[25] The choice of Afghanistan as the base for Al Qaeda is cited as evidence. Somalia, Yemen, and other failed or weak states also share the criteria for terrorist recruits and bases.

This argument circulates almost as a truism, but it contains a contradiction. Proponents acknowledge that Al Qaeda–like terrorist networks rely on the highest level of technology and communications, as evidenced by the piloting skills and complex execution of the multiple plane crashes. Yet they claim that terrorist networks flourish in failed states, which lack the wherewithal essential for high-tech terrorism—namely, infrastructure, services, communication and technology, even roads and transport systems. Al Qaeda's previous safe haven in the Sudan is cited as another incontrovertible piece of evidence of terrorism's dependence on failed states. Despite its long-running war in the South, the Sudan is tightly ruled in the North by a militarized government with robust internal authority and international weight.[26]

Contrary to this theory, not only Al Qaeda–like networks but terrorist groups of all three forms discussed earlier have flourished in stable, strong, democratic, and industrialized states.[27] Such countries have long served as bases for financing, training, and recruiting militants, while their financial systems and offshore banking havens have provided additional benefits. Several organizations eventually classified as terrorist were based in Permanent Five (P-5) and Group of Eight (G-8) countries. Even in developing countries, the choice of base is governed as much or more by the host government's support of the cause as by the weakness of the state, as indicated by Al Qaeda's choice of the Sudan, LTTE's choice of Tamil Nadu state in India, or the PLO's earlier choice of Tunisia. Arguably, Al Qaeda–like networks would be unable to function solely in failed-state environments because they require access to Western financial systems, arms dealers, policymakers, industrialists, and specialized training institutes. The failed-state argument, therefore, provides only a partial explanation for one of several conducive environments for terrorist activities.

The democracy-deficient version of this argument holds that terrorists are motivated by "religious and political fanaticism bred in countries without democratic infrastructures."[28] According to its proponents, the "common enemy" shared by the Kurdistan Workers Party (PKK), the ETA, the LTTE, and the IRA is "the Western culture of democracy" and the associated Western values of capitalism and individualism.[29] This argument is linked to the Islamist clash of civilizations argument, discussed below, because it rests on the supposition that most Al Qaeda members hail from Islamic countries and that many or most Islamic countries are not democratically governed. Proponents argue that compared to Arab states, "[e]ven sub-Saharan Africa, with its searing poverty, offers its citizens more freedom and—not coincidentally—produces few terrorists."[30] One commentator goes so far as to suggest that "[p]erhaps most Muslim countries are undemocratic because they are Muslim."[31]

This argument ignores the numerous terrorist movements in democratic countries in North America and Europe.[32] It also overlooks political and religious fanaticism bred in countries *with* democratic infrastructures in both developing and industrialized countries. The ethnocentric following of extremist politicians in France, Austria, and the Netherlands as well as the religious followers of televangelists bear witness to their deadly toll of assassinations, arson, and hate crimes well before September 11.

The Clash of Civilizations or Islamic Extremism

In the aftermath of the Cold War, Samuel Huntington presaged both a clash between Muslim and Western civilizations and wars across fault lines in his controversial book *The Clash of Civilizations.* He also speculated that Islam might be intrinsically a violent and militaristic religion inimical to other faiths and civilizations, drawing on what he calls "overwhelming" evidence presented by other scholars.[33]

Proponents of this Islamic-extremism argument see Al Qaeda and September 2001 as the vindication of Huntington's argument because all the perpetrators were Muslims. Arab scholars counter that "terrorism has nothing to do with Islam and Arabism because these individuals cannot, by any stretch of the imagination, be considered representative of approximately one billion Muslims."[34] Yet this theory's proponents point out that Palestinians, Bosnian Muslims, Chechens, and even once secular Saddam Hussein are all Muslims, whether they practice the faith or not. This prevalent and hardy argument has encountered too little scrutiny.

Since the Iranian revolution, the rise of Islamic extremism at national (e.g., Iran and Algeria), regional (e.g., the Middle East), and, more recently, global levels has not abated. The reasons cannot be explored meaningfully here but are multiple and diverse and have complex linkages and distinctions from prior anticolonial, Muslim nationalist, and pan-Arabic movements. Nevertheless, wherever Islamic extremism rose or took control, it was challenged by a majority or a sizeable minority of Muslim moderates and reformers, as in Algeria and Iran.[35]

The rise of militant Islam with globally recruited youth ready and trained for jihad, or holy war, is only one of many manifestations of Islamic fundamentalism and was facilitated not only by rich Islamic nations such as Saudi Arabia but by massive U.S. support for highly trained Mujahideen.[36] A mix of financial, ideological, and other reasons besides religion attracted young recruits. Radical Islam is systematically portrayed as a threat to the West.[37] Yet, as longtime terrorist watcher Wilkinson notes, terrorist activities by Islamic groups in the 1980s and 1990s were overwhelmingly concentrated in their own countries. Ironically, writing as recently as 2000, he argued against the popular misperception that "such groups would initiate a campaign of wide-spread terrorist attacks internationally."[38]

After September 2001, the Palestinian situation was often cited as both the prime example and cause of Islamic fundamentalism.[39] However, the Palestinian cause is essentially political and not religious in origin. Since the creation of Israel in 1948, the PLO has fought against the displacement of Palestinians and for their right of return and self-determination, not for religious rights. The radicalization of Palestinians and the increase in both Muslim and secular support for their cause around the world cannot be attributed to Islamic fundamentalism, despite the fact that recent Israeli actions and international policies have fanned its flames.

It is erroneous to portray the trend toward radicalization as either a clash between Islamic and Judeo-Christian "civilizations" or as intrinsic violent characteristics of the former. Islam has a global history of creative cohabitation and artistic flourishing with other cultures and religions, whether Christian, Jewish, or Hindu. Islam has owed much of its spread historically not to the methods of conquest and empire but rather to its principles and practices of equality, justice, and charity that were distinct from more hierarchical and elitist religions. Islam offered the poor an escape from humiliation in deeply stratified and unequal societies. The carnage wrought by Western, ostensibly Christian, leaders over the last six decades—including a world war and a cold war, a Holocaust, two atomic bombs, repression of wars of independence, the fueling of proxy wars, nuclear brinksmanship, and the support of dictators and state and non-state terrorists—makes it spurious to view Islam as a more inherently violent religion or civilization.

Why Terrorism?

The three causal arguments offer insights into the nature, motivations, and facilitators of Al Qaeda or similar terrorists, but they share a common failing: the locus and motivation of terrorism is situated within and not outside the psyche and context of the terrorists. The arguments also cast terrorist acts, as Zbigniew Brzezinski puts it, "in a historical void."[40] The three arguments are more plausible and the acts of September 2001 more comprehensible when examined together and placed within a broader context.

Terrorism reflects a deliberate tactical relationship between the terrorist and the target. The victims who are instrumentalized to serve the terrorist's purpose may be randomly or deliberately chosen, but there is nothing accidental about the choice of the target government, institution, or actors put on notice through the terrorist act. Arguments that emphasize the nature of the terrorist and his or her background conditions miss this reality.

The reason that such arguments about terrorists' fanaticism or barbarism are so acceptable is that, as Homer-Dixon observes, "Such explanations aren't very threatening because they locate the cause in the nature of the perpetrators or the group." However, there is a reluctance to go farther for fear of finding answers "that might lie in the structure and functioning of the planet's economy, politics and society . . . because such factors could implicate us in the West."[41]

Brzezinski notes the historical void in which these terrorist acts are cast. "It is as if terrorism is suspended in outer space as an abstract phenomenon, with ruthless terrorists acting under some Satanic inspiration unrelated to any specific motivation." The public debate eschews "the simple fact that lurking behind every terrorist act is a specific political antecedent." Brzezinski correctly emphasizes the historical dimensions of current terrorism and its linkage to past policies and political actions. He also underlines the "emotional context of felt, observed or historically recounted political grievances."[42]

Homer-Dixon's emphasis on socioeconomic factors and Brzezinski's emphasis on historical and political factors bring us closer to an explanation, but a further piece of evidence is needed. The clue lies in the deliberate, carefully chosen targets of September 11: the symbols of financial, military, and political power in the world's most powerful country. This combined nexus of power concentrated in a few Western countries was put on notice by the ghastly attacks. The causes of September 11 and the more inexplicable public support in many quarters for it lie in an intricate mix of reality and perception that is based both on distant and recent history, policies, and events. The epicenter is growing resentment of the countries that share membership in the P-5 of the Security Council, the Group of Eight, and the North Atlantic Treaty Organization (NATO). They possess and consume a disproportionate share of world resources and are the decision makers on political, economic, and military matters that affect the livelihoods, security, and survival of humankind.

It is not the poverty or inequality caused by globalization alone that is resented but the perceived use of political and military power to enforce the rules of a global economy that is seen to benefit too few and harm too many. The tight embrace between politics and business and the nexus between weapons producers, the military, and policymakers deepen suspicions. In this climate, past and current policies perpetuate the perception of double standards and do little to reduce the suffering of a majority of the world's population or readjust the profound imbalance of power that created and perpetuates this situation. The collusion between Western leaders and certain despots across the developing world serves mainly to deify leaders who dare to be independent of the West—whether in rhetoric, like Mohamad Mahathir or Fidel Castro, or in action, like Muammar el-Qaddafi or Osama bin Laden.

The Islamic-extremism and failed-state arguments can be understood at more subtle levels in this light. The seemingly self-interested recent endeavors in nation-building in failed or post-conflict states are suspected by some as renewed exercises in empire and the imposition of Western values. The intense anger generated in the Middle East is directed not only at current regional and U.S. policies but also at the decisions of world leaders regarding the fate of the region throughout the twentieth century.

The spiraling rise of global media conglomerates that control information and communication, from book publishing to newspapers, film, music, and television, fuels fears of cultural hegemony among conservative Muslim, Hindu, or Jewish leaders just as it angers secular critics who value cultural plurality and free information.[43] From an Islamic perspective, the perception is of a world governed by a handful of global decision makers who are not simply non-Islamic in faith but anti-Islamic in their apparent disrespect for equality, charity, and humanity. Even the failed-state argument has greater explanatory power when the negative socioeconomic, political, and cultural impact of globalization experienced by many developing countries is placed alongside the beneficial cycle that G-8 countries experience.

Al Qaeda and similarly inspired terrorists, in violent and unscrupulous fashion, oppose this concentration of power and its consequences. This same confluence is also opposed in civic and primarily nonviolent fashion by growing numbers of ordinary citizens around the world, as witnessed in the vibrant groups that convened in Porto Alegre, Brazil, in 2003 for the third World Social Forum or that participated in the anti-war movement opposing the invasion of Iraq led by the U.S. and UK that same year. Whereas the resentment is widely shared by secular and religious, Western and non-Western critics, only a tiny, highly organized minority engages in globalized terrorism. What can the United Nations contribute?

The UN's Response to the
Roots of Terrorism

Two questions are asked here. First, has the UN directly addressed the so-called root causes or contextual factors underlying terrorism both before and especially since September 11? Second, has it done so indirectly via its recently renewed efforts in conflict prevention? And if so, to what effect?

The UN and "Root Causes"

What was the record of the UN's responses to the root causes of terrorism both before and after September 11? Between 1972 and 1991, the only consistent defender within the world organization of the need to grasp the context within which terrorism thrives, at least in rhetorical terms, was the General Assembly. As noted earlier, a number of delegates ensured that language was included in statements and resolutions that protected movements of self-determination from being labeled terrorists and that condemned state-sponsored terrorism. The General Assembly repeatedly urged the UN to find "just and peaceful solutions to the underlying causes which give rise to such acts of violence."[44] However, these references to roots dried up, and in 1989, resolution 29 was the last to contain a reference to measures to *prevent* international terrorism. After 1991, resolutions referred to "measures to *eliminate* international terrorism."

The Security Council remained largely silent except for a few resolutions on individual country cases until 1991.[45] Thereafter, however, it took over from the assembly and pursued a strategy of punitive responses to terrorism with no reference to underlying causes. The 1994 "Declaration on Measures to Eliminate International Terrorism" was adopted by the General Assembly and is indicative of this new tone.[46] It spelled out four practical steps designed to enhance international cooperation in anti-terrorism—and none addresses causes.

In legal terms, the Sixth Committee of the General Assembly was mandated to find measures to eliminate terrorism. It developed a raft of treaties and conventions between 1963 and 1999. However, all twelve conventions and protocols adopted by the UN concern the "suppression" of terrorist acts; none deals with their underlying causes or their prevention.

In institutional terms within the UN system, the UN Office for Drug Control and Crime Prevention (ODCCP) and later its Terrorism Prevention Branch (TPB) handled the portfolio. They treated the problem as a criminal activity, like trafficking in illicit drugs. Therefore, it required cooperation among law enforcement and intelligence agencies rather than political or economic ministries, and the ODCCP rather than the UN Department of Political Affairs (DPA) or the UN Development Programme (UNDP) was in the driver's seat.

Immediately after September 11, the Security Council again focused on punitive and aggressive responses, while the General Assembly returned to the underlying causes of the attacks.[47] The council's response is manifest in resolution 1368 of September 12, 2001, which urges punishment for the perpetrators, and in resolution 1373 of September 28, 2001, which spells out a range of mandatory universal counterterrorism measures and establishes the Counter-Terrorism Committee (CTC). That all council resolutions and actions eschew discussion of underlying causes may be explained by its mandate to respond to threats to international peace and security. In contrast, the 56th Session of the General Assembly, which opened one day late on September 12, 2001, dwelled on the underlying causes of the attacks alongside expressions of condemnation and sympathy.

Within the Secretariat, the secretary-general underlined the UN's central role and ability to respond to terrorism, and a range of UN agencies and departments rose to the challenge. While some made early observations about root causes, few institutional responses included programs designed to address or eliminate them. Rather, they stressed the impact and consequences of terrorism.

One set of responses to the terrorist attacks came from UN bodies whose mandates include responsibility for certain types of terrorism—including aviation, maritime, chemical, or nuclear attacks. The Terrorism Prevention

Branch serves as a clearinghouse for information, and after September 11 developed an extensive database. While ostensibly mandated to address causes as well as consequences, the reported activities of the ODCCP and its TPB indicate a focus on the latter. For its part, the International Civil Aviation Organization (ICAO) focused on evaluating and improving existing safety standards and measures to prevent air terrorism. The International Maritime Organization (IMO) developed twelve additional proposals to increase maritime security. The International Atomic Energy Agency (IAEA) accelerated efforts to secure nuclear facilities that could be used by terrorists. The Organisation for the Prohibition of Chemical Weapons (OPCW) mobilized experts and coordinated efforts to prevent and respond to chemical terrorist attacks. The Universal Postal Union (UPU) responded to the use of anthrax through the postal system as a means of terrorism and worked with the U.S. Postal Service to arrange for security presentations to postal services around the world.[48]

A second set of responses came after September 11 from UN organizations with social or economic mandates. The International Labour Organization (ILO) addressed the employment effects, especially the downturn in the tourism and aviation industries. The World Health Organization (WHO) responded to the anthrax attacks by trying to raise the vigilance and capacity of health systems to respond to such infections and by disseminating guidelines to combat bioterrorism. The office of the UN High Commissioner for Human Rights (UNHCHR) has been particularly vocal in focusing attention on the impact of terrorism on human rights. Since 1995, the Commission on Human Rights (CHR) has addressed the impact of terrorism and human rights repeatedly. The UN High Commissioner for Refugees (UNHCR) has raised concerns about violation of the rights of refugees under the 1951 Geneva refugee convention. The World Bank swiftly highlighted the estimated impact and consequences of the economic downturn on poverty and child mortality.

Such prompt and sustained responses across the UN system demonstrate the importance the world organization attributed to the gravity of the September 2001 terrorist attacks. However, they may also testify to the pressure on the UN system to demonstrate that it could respond seriously and concretely to the terrorist threat and its consequences and not waste its resources on tackling more abstruse causes.

Speaking on the first anniversary of the establishment of the CTC, the secretary-general proposed a three-pronged counterterrorism plan—dissuasion, denial, and cooperation—that summarizes the future direction of the UN's response to terrorism. The plan endorses the recommendations submitted by the Policy Working Group on the United Nations and Terrorism, which includes UN agencies and departments as well as independent experts. Dissuasion might suggest prevention in the sense of addressing and eliminating underlying factors that might provoke terrorist acts. However, according to the secretary-general, "Would-be perpetrators must be dissuaded from terror by setting effective norms and implementing relevant legal instruments; by an active public information campaign; and by rallying an international consensus behind the fight against terrorism." In closing, however, he noted, "Just as terrorism must never be excused, so must genuine grievances never be ignored simply because terrorism is committed in their name. It does not take away from the justice of a cause that a few wicked men or women commit murder in its name. It only makes it more urgent that the cause is addressed, the grievances heard, and the wrong put right."[49] Clearly, therefore, the UN acknowledges but does not elevate to top priority the prevention of terrorism by addressing root causes.

UN Initiatives to Prevent Conflict

Has the UN nevertheless managed to address the factors underlying the attacks and the terrorist threat indirectly via its attention to conflict prevention? If so, what effect have these activities had and what is the potential of such activities to prevent conflict?

In recent years, the secretary-general raised conflict prevention to the top of his agenda and "pledged to move the United Nations from a culture of reaction to a culture of prevention."[50] Conflict prevention was the theme of his acceptance speech on behalf of the UN organization for the Nobel Peace Prize in 2001. In June 2001, he presented his report called *Prevention of Armed Conflict* to the General Assembly and the Security Council as the basis for an organization-wide plan.[51] This report looked at length at the root causes of conflict and proposed several system-wide conflict-reduction measures and approaches. It noted that "one of the principal aims of preventive action should be to address the deep-rooted socio-economic, cultural, environmental, institutional and other structural causes that often underlie the immediate political symptoms of conflicts."[52]

In August, the council's resolution 1366 responded to the report, noting "the importance of a comprehensive strategy comprising operational and structural measures for prevention of armed conflict." It also underlined the "overriding political, humanitarian and moral imperatives as well as the economic advantages of preventing the outbreak and escalation of conflicts."

The report was on the agenda for the 56th session of the General Assembly. So too was the annual (since 1984) report from the secretary-general on *Measures to Eliminate International Terrorism,* which did not address root causes.

The assembly was scheduled to begin on Tuesday, September 11, and the attacks naturally colored the discussion of both conflict prevention and terrorism.[53] The conflation of conflict prevention and terrorism prevention perhaps originated here; subsequent debates addressed root causes of conflict and terrorism as if the two were equivalent. The representative of the Netherlands, for example, noted that the UN had been active in eliminating the root causes of conflict, which were breeding grounds for terrorism. The representative of Slovakia noted that the world organization had been born out of war and that the face of war since then had become uglier—its latest, ugliest form bearing the name of "terrorism."[54] A system-wide response to conflict prevention appears to have been shaped by this conflation of conflict and terrorism.

What have been the consequences, if any, of lumping together the discrete task of tackling terrorism and its roots with that of addressing conflict and its roots?[55] On the surface, it might appear that a possible consequence is the likelihood, emanating from the debate, that financial and technical assistance for conflict prevention specifically and for development more generally might increase as a way to stem terrorism that is supposed to be bred by conflict and poverty. Notwithstanding President George W. Bush's announced increase of U.S. official development assistance (ODA) in the name of reducing poverty to fight terrorism at the UN Conference on Financing for Development in Monterey in March 2002, real increases in ODA fall far short of requirements to meet Millennium Development Goals.

While this potential benefit has not yet materialized, a host of detrimental effects and risks have become obvious that result from the correlation between conflict and terrorism prevention. The first set relates to conflict prevention and has three components. First, it presupposes that terrorism is related to conflict and stems from unresolved and festering wars. While this was true in several older cases of non-state and state terrorism, it is not a truism and is not applicable to amphibolous terrorism such as Al Qaeda's. This confusion runs the risk that the search for potential terrorists will be skewed and that genuine terrorist threats may be overlooked when they do not originate in conflict zones. Second, all participants in conflicts are suspect as combatants who may adopt terror tactics at any time. Ignoring genuine grievances is an inevitable consequence, and conflict resolution and serious attention to the legitimate claims of opposing parties may be overlooked in the eagerness to suppress potential terrorism. Finally, the current fluid definition of terrorism results in a preoccupation with various targets in the West, and there will be pressure on the UN and other donor-funded organizations to focus their structural prevention only on certain countries deemed to be risks for the West rather than where the need is objectively most pressing.

The second set of potential negative consequences includes the effects of this conflation of attitudes and approaches to poverty and development more broadly. Long before September 2001, mainstream development thinking had shifted toward a view of poverty, inequality, and illiteracy as factors conducive to conflict.[56] The simplified public attitude in the North was that poverty breeds conflict; hence, conflict was primarily a developing-country phenomenon. Now, poverty and illiteracy are seen as causes for terrorism as well. Terrorism, however, is no longer safely confined to distant countries but is global and unpredictable. Government policies toward immigration and asylum have become more rigid and restrictive in Europe and North America as ostensible counterterrorism measures. Xenophobia results from media portrayals of the developing world generally and poor parts of the Muslim world particularly as hotbeds for terrorists. In tandem, sympathy for the distant poor and consequent public support for development assistance or potentially beneficial trade policies for the South are likely to dwindle further, as indicated by the lackluster response of donors at the Financing for Development Conference in March 2002.

Before September 11, there already was a disconcerting tendency in the donor community to treat ODA as a tool for conflict prevention.[57] Now major donors no longer see conflict prevention as one possible corollary benefit of effective ODA but as its direct objective. Bilateral donors such as the UK's Department of International Development (DfID), multilateral agencies such as the UNDP and the World Bank, and numerous NGOs have conflict-prevention advisors or units within their development programs. Conflict prevention and peacebuilding programs compete for limited donor funding, and development—social justice and a decent, sustainable livelihood for all—no longer represents an end in itself. Development assistance increasingly is a means to an end defined by the donor community, namely, conflict prevention and, more pressingly, terrorism prevention. As a result, it is difficult to stem the tendency to direct aid where politically shaped goals of preventing conflict and terrorism can be served rather than where need is greatest.[58]

Conclusion

This discussion suggests that the UN has not addressed the underlying causes and motivations of the September 2001 attacks and that it does not intend to do so within its planned response to terrorism. In addition to the risks and possible negative impacts resulting from conceptual confusion, neither the UN's structural conflict-prevention nor development programs will be effective in preventing what I call amphibolous terrorism because the underlying causes of this type of terrorism lie in the global system. To be fair, these causes lie beyond the reach of the UN system, which cannot address the real global grievances underlying the phenomenon.

Effective prevention that will reduce the terrorist threat will require more than effective domestic and international police and military measures, improved information-sharing, and other such collaboration. Effective prevention will necessitate structural changes within the global system. In terms of attitude, it will require an honest avowal by the most powerful countries that they are responsible for the perpetuation of a global system that endangers the lives and impoverishes the livelihoods of the vast majority of humanity. In terms of power, it will require the extension of political, economic, and military decision-making to countries from all regions of the world. Within the Security Council, the G-8, and NATO, such changes would help to ensure other requisite developments. They would include gradual but real improvements in policies of global investment, finance, trade, migration, and environment. They would include even-handed global disarmament of nuclear as well as conventional and small arms and a rejection of militarism. As noted by Robert Hinde, "The root causes of terrorism will never be addressed as long as national governments are motivated solely by self-interest or guided by the self-righteous belief that their way is the right way and must be imposed on others."[59]

Seasoned statesmen have called for similar far-reaching changes in global governance since the end of the Cold War to little avail. Is anything likely to change now? A possible silver lining to the September 11 cloud is the realization that terrorism of ever-newer and more inscrutable and dangerous forms will besiege the planet unless serious measures are taken to construct a "global order with a human face," a phrase that has often been quoted but rarely seen.

Notes

1. UN Press Release SG/SM/8073, December 11, 2001.

2. See Boutros Boutros-Ghali, *An Agenda For Peace* (New York: United Nations, 1992); Carnegie Commission on Preventing Deadly Conflict, *Preventing Deadly Conflict* (New York: Carnegie Corporation, 1997); and Commission on Global Governance, *Our Global Neighbourhood* (Oxford: Oxford University Press, 1995).

3. Bruce Jentleson, "The Need for Praxis: Bringing Policy Relevance Back In," *International Security* 26, no. 4 (2002): 178.

4. The typology and terminology used here are entirely my own and are intended to be illustrative rather than prescriptive or comprehensive. For an academic typology, see, for example, Paul Wilkinson, *Terrorism versus Democracy: The Liberal State Response* (London: Frank Cass, 2000), 18–21. Wilkinson distinguishes between state and

factional terrorism and describes my broader "self-determination terrorism" more narrowly as nationalist terrorists, but his typology combines motivations and agents.

5. "Terrorism, Corruption & Human Trafficking," UN Terrorism Prevention Branch, UN Office for Drug Control and Crime Prevention, Vienna. Available online at http://www.undcp.org.

6. "Measures to Prevent International Terrorism Which Endangers or Takes Innocent Human Lives or Jeopardizes Fundamental Freedoms, and Study of the Underlying Causes of Those Forms of Terrorism and Acts of Violence Which Lie in Misery, Frustration, Grievance and Despair and Which Cause Some People to Sacrifice Human Lives, Including Their Own, in an Attempt to Effect Radical Changes," General Assembly resolution A/RES/40/61, December 9, 1985, point 9.

7. This observation is my own. However, also see Wilkinson's explanations, which differ; *Terrorism versus Democracy,* 21–22, 30.

8. British writer George Monbiot notes that international terrorism focuses only on "violence directed at US citizens, US commercial interests, or white citizens of other nations. Non-whites are perpetrators of terror, but not its victims." See his "War on the Third World," *The Guardian,* March 5, 2002.

9. "Measure to Prevent International Terrorism," General Assembly resolution A/RES/3034 (XXVII), December 18, 1972. Repeated in "Measures to Prevent International Terrorism Which Endangers or Takes Innocent Human Lives or Jeopardizes Fundamental Freedoms, and Study of the Underlying Causes of Those Forms of Terrorism and Acts of Violence Which Lie in Misery, Frustration, Grievance and Despair and Which Cause Some People to Sacrifice Human Lives, Including Their Own, in an Attempt to Effect Radical Changes," General Assembly resolution A/RES/34/145, December 17, 1979.

10. "Inadmissibility of the Policy of State Terrorism and Any Actions by States Aimed at Undermining the Socio-Political System in Other Sovereign States," General Assembly resolution A/RES/39/159, December 17, 1984.

11. A host of books describing this new terrorism have appeared. See, for example, Strobe Talbott and Nayan Chand, eds., *An Age of Terror: America and the World After September 11* (New York: Basic Books, 2001); and François Heisbourg, ed., *Hyper-terrorisme: La Nouvelle Guerre* (Paris: Odile Jacob, 2001). However, the description of terrorism as amphibolous is entirely my own.

12. Vitit Muntarbhorn, "Terror Doesn't Stop with Violence," *Bangkok Post,* September 25, 2002.

13. Oliver Burkeman, "US: Hyper-Alert, But for What?" *The Guardian,* January 1, 2002.

14. Wilkinson, *Terrorism versus Democracy,* 13.

15. A Google search on the Internet of "root causes of terrorism" conducted in mid-August 2002, eleven months after September 11, found 46,700 hits in the first few seconds. My search, though not exhaustive, indicates the magnitude and range of global soul-searching.

16. Thomas Homer-Dixon, "Why Root Causes Are Important," *Toronto Globe and Mail,* September 23, 2001.

17. Andrew Johnston, "Disparities of Wealth Are Seen as Fuel for Terrorism," *International Herald Tribune,* December 20, 2001.

18. These observations are drawn from an analysis of press releases and verbatim reports of the 56th session of the General Assembly, especially between September 12 and mid-November 2001. See especially Press Releases GA/9919 and GA/9921 of October 1, 2001; GA/9927 of October 4, 2001; GA/9928 of October 5, 2001; GA/9959 of November 11, 2001; and GA/9964 of November 13, 2001.

19. "UN Environment Chief: Fight Root Causes of Terrorism," September 21, 2001, *Environment News Service.*

20. James Wolfensohn, "Fight Terrorism and Poverty," *Development Outreach,* World Bank Institute, Fall 2001. Available online at http://www1.worldbank.org/devoutreach/fall01/special.asp.

21. Michael Radu, "E-Notes: The Futile Search for 'Root Causes' of Terrorism," Foreign Policy Research Institute, Philadelphia, Pennsylvania, April 23, 2002. Available online at http://www.fpri.org/enotes/americawar.20020423.radu.futilesearchforrootcauses.html.

22. Homer-Dixon, "Why Root Causes Are Important." Nonetheless, his own list of what he sees as the complex, varied, and interlinked root causes is a disappointing one of mainly local and regional factors including demography, environment, agricultural failure, and bad governance alongside the international political economy.

23. Johnston, "Disparities of Wealth."

24. Nicholas Kristof, "What Does and Does Not Fuel Terrorism," *International Herald Tribune,* May 8, 2002.

25. Ray Takeyh and Nikolas Gvosdev, "Do Terrorist Networks Need a Home?" *Washington Quarterly* 25, no. 3 (2002): 98.

26. The Sudanese government dictates where international humanitarian supply planes may fly within its territory. In a decision that was controversial, the Sudan was able to win the African seat on the UN Human Rights Commission. During my visits to Khartoum and Juba in 2000–2001 while working for an NGO, I witnessed the government's tight control and supervision over all its territory; what I saw was far from the failed-state scenario that some claim for the Sudan.

27. See, for example, Michael Radu, "E-Notes: The Problem of 'Londonistan': Europe, Human Rights, and Terrorists." Available online at http://www.fpri.org/enotes/americawar.20020412.radu.londonistan.html.

28. Jane Eisner, "Terrorism's Tenuous Link to Poverty," *Philadelphia Inquirer,* 2 July 2002. Available online at http://www.philly.com/mld/inquirer/news/special_packages/sunday_review/3616464.htm.

29. Radu, "E-Notes: The Futile Search for 'Root Causes.'"

30. Eisner, "Terrorism's Tenuous Link to Poverty."

31. Radu, "E-Notes: The Futile Search for 'Root Causes.'"

32. For a historical account, see, for example, Wilkinson, *Terrorism versus Democracy,* 23–36.

33. Samuel Huntington, *The Clash of Civilizations and the Remaking of World Order* (New York: Touchstone, 1996), 256. He cites "overwhelming" evidence produced by other analysts (256–257).

34. Cairo University scholar Mustafa Al Sayyid, "Mixed Message: The Arab and Muslim Response to 'Terrorism,'" *Washington Quarterly* 25, no. 2 (2002): 179.

35. See, for instance, Shahram Chubin, *Whither Iran? Reform, Domestic Politics, and National Security* (Oxford: Oxford University Press, 2002); and Khalida Massaoudi, *Unbowed: An Algerian Woman Confronts Muslim Fundamentalism—Interview with Elisabeth Schemle* (Philadelphia: University of Pennsylvania Press, 1998).

36. Two insider accounts from both U.S. and Saudi perspectives of their support are provided in: Interview with Zbigniew Brzezinski, "How Jimmy Carter and I Started the Mujahideen," *Nouvel Observateur,* January 15–21, 2002, 76; Interview with Prince Turki Al-Faisal, former Saudi intelligence chief, by Arab News, reported by Syed Rashid Hussain, "US Made Deal to Buy Back Weapons from Mujahideen," *Dawn,* Riyadh, November 10, 2001.

37. The titles themselves are often suggestive, as in Anthony Dennis, *The Rise of the Islamic Empire and the Threat to the West* (Lima, Ohio: Wyndham Hall Press, 1996).

38. Wilkinson, *Terrorism versus Democracy,* 36.

39. See frequent statements at the 51st session of the General Assembly by government delegates. See also Yossef Bodansky, *The High Cost of Peace: How Washington's Middle East Policy Left America Vulnerable to Terrorism* (Roseville, Calif.: Prima Publishing, 2002).

40. Zbigniew Brzezinski, "Focus on the Political Roots of September 11," *New York Times,* September 4, 2002.

41. Homer-Dixon, "Why Root Causes Are Important."

42. Brzezinski, "Focus on the Political Roots."

43. On media conglomerates, see, for example, Robert McChesney, *Rich Media, Poor Democracy* (New York: New York Press, 2000).

44. General Assembly resolution A/RES/40/61, December 9, 1985, point 9.

45. See list of actions by Security Council at http://www.un.org/terrorism/sc.htm.

46. "Measures to Eliminate International Terrorism," General Assembly resolution A/RES/49/60, December 9, 1994, point 3.

47. Further discussed in Rama Mani, "In Pursuit of an Antidote: 9.11 and The Rule of Law," *Conflict, Security and Development* 3, no. 1 (April 2003), 97–108.

48. As early as 1989, the UPU had set up a Postal Security Action Group, which has since identified ways to eliminate the use of the postal system for drug-trafficking, money-laundering, fraud, and child pornography.

49. UN Press Release SG/SM/8417SC/7523, October 4, 2002.

50. Opening line of executive summary of United Nations, *Prevention of Armed Conflict: Report of the Secretary General* (A/55/985-S/2001/574), June 7, 2001. See also Fen Osler Hampson and David M. Malone, eds., *From Reaction to Conflict Prevention: Opportunities for the UN System* (Boulder: Lynne Rienner, 2002).

51. *Prevention of Armed Conflict.*

52. *Prevention of Armed Conflict,* 2.

53. *Measures to Eliminate International Terrorism: Report of the Secretary-General* (A/56/160), July 3, 2001.

54. UN Press Release GA/9916, September 25, 2001.

55. Space constraints do not permit an examination of the various theories of conflict causation. For an analysis and review of the literature, see Rama Mani, *Beyond Retribution: Seeking Justice in the Shadows of War* (Cambridge: Polity, 2002), 127–133.

56. Organisation for Economic Co-operation and Development (OECD), *Conflict Peace and Development Cooperation on the Threshold of the 21st Century* (Paris: OECD, 1998), Development Cooperation Guidelines Series.

57. See for example Mark Duffield, *Global Governance and the New Wars: The Merging of Development and Security* (London: Zed, 2001).

58. This could actually encourage rather than deter terrorist acts that seek to attract international attention or assistance.

59. Robert Hinde, "Root Causes of Terrorism," *Pugwash Online,* January 30, 2002. Available online at www.pugwash.org.

About the Contributors

Jane Boulden is Canadian Research Chair in International Relations and Security Studies at the Royal Military College of Canada. She is a former MacArthur Research Fellow at the Centre for International Studies, University of Oxford. Her most recent work includes her edited volume *Dealing with Conflict in Africa: The United Nations and Regional Organizations* (2003).

Chantal de Jonge Oudraat is Adjunct Professor at the Edmund A. Walsh School of Foreign Service, Georgetown University, and vice-president and member of the Executive Board of Women in International Security. She formerly was co-director of the Managing Global Issues project at the Carnegie Endowment for International Peace; senior research associate at the United Nations Institute for Disarmament Research; and researcher at the Belfer Center for Science and International Affairs, Kennedy School, Harvard University. She is the co-editor of *Managing Global Issues: Lessons Learned* (2001) and the author of articles in journals such as *Survival, Current History,* and the *European Journal of International Law.*

Edward C. Luck is Director of the Center on International Organization and Professor of Practice in International and Public Affairs at Columbia University. Since 2001, he has served as a member of the UN Secretary-General's Policy Working Group on the United Nations and Terrorism. A past president of the United Nations Association of the U.S.A. and a specialist in Washington's policies toward the world organization, he is the author of *Mixed Messages: American Politics and International Organization, 1919–1999.*

S. Neil MacFarlane is Lester B. Pearson Professor of International Relations and Director of the Centre for International Studies at the University of Oxford and also a faculty member of the Geneva Centre for Security Policy. A specialist on the Soviet Union and its successor states as well as international security more generally, he is the author, most recently, of *Intervention in Contemporary World Politics* (2002) and *Humanitarian Action: The Conflict Connection* (2001). He is currently completing a volume for the UN Intellectual History Project, titled *Human Security and the UN: A Critical History.*

Rama Mani is a Visiting Fellow at the Geneva Centre for Security Policy and a founder of Justice Unlimited. She is the author of *Beyond Retribution: Pursuing Justice in the Shadows of War* (2002) and articles on conflict and peacebuilding. Previously, she served as the Senior Strategy Advisor to the Centre for Humanitarian Dialogue; the Africa Strategy Manager and Regional Policy Coordinator for Oxfam Great Britain while based in Uganda and Ethiopia; and Senior External Relations Officer for the Commission on Global Governance.

M. J. Peterson is Professor of Political Science at the University of Massachusetts, Amherst. She is the author of *The General Assembly in World Politics* (1986) and articles on international environmental cooperation, international fisheries management, and the development of outer space law. She is currently pursuing research on changing patterns of relations between the UN system and non-state actors.

Nico Schrijver is Professor of International Law, Vrije Universiteit, Amsterdam. He is the author of "Responding to International Terrorism: Moving the Frontiers of International Law for 'Enduring Freedom'?" in *Netherlands International Law Review* (2001); "The Changing Nature of State Sovereignty" in *British Year Book of International Law* (1999); and *Sovereignty over Natural Resources: Balancing Rights and Duties* (1997). He is a member of the Advisory Council on International Affairs of the Dutch government, president of the Netherlands Society of International Law, and Past Chair of the Academic Council on the United Nations System.

Mónica Serrano is Professor of Politics at the Colegio de México and Research Associate at the Centre for International Studies at the University of Oxford. She is the editor of *Transnational Organized Crime and International Security: Business as Usual?* (2002). She is currently completing research for a book on *The Privatization of Violence in Latin America*.

Thierry Tardy is a faculty member at the Geneva Centre for Security Policy. Previously he was a researcher at the Foundation for Strategic Research and Lecturer at the Institut d'Etudes Politiques and at the Inter Services Defense College. He is the author of *La France et la gestion des conflits yougoslaves, 1991–1995* (2000) and *Enjeux et leçons d'une opération de maintien de la paix de l'ONU* (1999), and the editor of *Peace Operations in World Politics after 11 September 2001* (2003).

Karin von Hippel is a Senior Research Fellow at the Centre for Defence Studies, King's College London, where she has been directing a project on European counterterrorist reforms that is funded by the MacArthur Foundation. She has also advised the OECD on what development cooperation can do to address the root causes of terrorism. Previously, she worked for the United Nations and the European Union in Somalia and in Kosovo. Her publications include *Democracy by Force* (2000), which was shortlisted for the Westminster Medal in Military History.

Thomas G. Weiss is Presidential Professor at The CUNY Graduate Center and Director of the Ralph Bunche Institute for International Studies, where he is co-director of the United Nations Intellectual History Project and editor of *Global Governance*. He also was Research Professor at Brown University's Watson Institute for International Studies, Executive Director of the Academic Council on the UN System and of the International Peace Academy, a member of the UN secretariat, and a consultant to several public and private agencies. He has written or edited some 30 books about multilateral approaches to international peace and security, humanitarian action, and sustainable development.

Index

Note: Page numbers in **bold** indicate chapter entries. Page numbers in *italics* indicate charts and illustrations.